OXFORD CANADIAN HISTORY

CLOSE-UP CANADA

J. BRADLEY CRUXTON

W. DOUGLAS WILSON

ROBERT J. WALKER

OXFORD
UNIVERSITY PRESS

OXFORD
UNIVERSITY PRESS

70 Wynford Drive, Don Mills, Ontario M3C 1J9
www.oup.com/ca

Oxford University Press is a department of the University of
Oxford. It furthers the University's objective of excellence in
research, scholarship, and education by publishing worldwide in

Oxford New York

Auckland Bangkok Buenos Aires Cape Town Chennai
Dar es Salaam Delhi Hong Kong Istanbul Karachi Kolkata
Kuala Lumpur Madrid Melbourne Mexico City Mumbai
Nairobi São Paulo Shanghai Taipei Tokyo Toronto

Oxford is a registered trade mark of Oxford University Press in
the UK and in certain other countries

Published in Canada
by Oxford University Press

Canadian Cataloguing in Publication Data

Cruxton, J. Bradley
    Close-up Canada

For use in grade 7.
Includes index.
ISBN 0-19-541544-2

1. Canada – History – To 1763 (New France) – Juvenile
literature. 2. Canada – History – 1763-1867 – Juvenile literature.
I. Wilson, W. Douglas. II. Walker, Robert J. (Robert John), 1941-
. III. Title.

FC161.C775 2000   971   C99-932600-7   F1032.C789 2000

    6 7 8 9   04 05 06 07

This book is printed on permanent (acid-free) paper. ∞

Printed and bound in Canada

Project Development, Editing, Page Layout and Production:
First Folio Resource Group, Inc.
    Fran Cohen
    Tom Dart
    Matthew Gourlay
    Cathy Oh
    Debbie Smith
    Evelyn Steinberg
    Amanda Stewart

Cover and Interior Design: Brett Miller

Photo Research: Robyn Craig

Acknowledgements

The authors express their thanks to Susan Froud,
Managing Director International Division; Joanna
Gertler, President Oxford Canada; MaryLynne Meschino,
Education Director; Loralee Case, Editorial Manager; and
Tiina Randoja, Education Editor. In particular, we
express gratitude to Fran Cohen and the First Folio
team for creative advice, editorial support, and tireless
effort.

J. Bradley Cruxton   W. Douglas Wilson   Robert J. Walker

Close-Up Canada Cover credits
front cover, clockwise from top left: Cincinnati Art
Museum/Subscription Ford Purchase/Webber/1927.26;
NAC/C-073717(S); NAC/C-002774; Artist Claude
Picard/originals displayed at Grand Pré National Historic Site;
back cover, (top) C.W. Jefferys/NAC/C-10687/Courtesy of
the C.W. Jefferys Estate, Toronto; (centre) Hudson's Bay
Company Archives, Provincial Archives of Manitoba;
(bottom) National Gallery of Canada, Ottawa

Cartography pages 3, 4, 6, 15, 27, 64, 110, 124, 125, 133,
144, 148, 281 Paul Sneath; pages 77, 115, 177, 207, 256, 296
Dave McKay; page 304 Linda Mackey

Illustrations pages 159, 253, 280 Valentino Sanna; pages 120-
123 Nicolas Debon

Page 12 Lyrics - Arnold Sampson/Cyril MacPhee/Wayne
Touesnard http://www.spydar.com/brakin

Contents

New France

he archaeologists were excited. It was 1941. Stories of mysterious piles of bricks had brought them from the Royal Ontario Museum in Toronto to a site near Midland. After clearing the site and digging all through the summer, they could now see a line where the remains of two stone walls joined three crumbling bastions, or stone towers. They realized that this was the exact spot where the French mission known as "Sainte-Marie-among-the-Hurons" had once stood.

Sainte-Marie had been built in the lands of the Huron in 1639 by French missionaries (Jesuits). A mere 10 years later, the Iroquois attacked Huron villages and missions. Thousands were killed and Sainte-Marie was burned to the ground.

In 1941, archaeologists found a multitude of artifacts at the site which provided clues about life at Sainte-Marie. These included hammers, axes, hand-forged nails, and foundations showing where stone buildings once stood. Forks, fish hooks, and bones of cows, pigs, and chickens suggested something about their eating habits and diet.

The mission has been restored to look as it did more than 350 years ago. Sainte-Marie today gives us a picture of the society called New France. It describes a time when little forts like Sainte-Marie laid claim to the wilderness of North America in the name of New France.

Timeline

10 000 BCE –	Aboriginal peoples are well established in North America
1492 –	Columbus arrives in the Americas
1497 –	Cabot sails to Newfoundland
1534 –	Cartier claims New France for the king of France
1604 –	Attempts are made to build a settlement in Acadia
1608 –	Founding of Quebec
1665 –	First filles du roi arrive
1670 –	Hudson's Bay Company is created
1756 – 1763	Seven Years' War
1760 –	End of French rule in North America

Focusing In!

After studying this unit, you will be able to answer the following questions:

1. What were the main reasons for the exploration and settlement of North America?
2. How did merchants, missionaries, religious women, and coureurs de bois help to develop New France?
3. Why were the Aboriginal people important in the development of the fur trade?
4. What impact did their first contact with Europeans have on the Aboriginal people?
5. What role did the king, governor, intendant, and bishop play in the organization of government in New France?
6. What was it like to live on a seigneury in New France? In a town?
7. Why were the French and English rivals in North America?
8. Who were the Acadians and what happened to them?
9. What were the causes and results of the Seven Years' War in North America? Who were the key personalities?
10. What happened to New France after it fell into British control?

The Age of Discovery

It's Worth the Trip to Asia

In the Middle Ages, the people of Europe went to great efforts to obtain silks, spices, and other luxury items from Asia. Overland journeys were long, hard, and dangerous. Asian merchants carried their goods by camel across mountains and deserts to the ports of the eastern Mediterranean Sea. There, the goods were put onto ships and taken to Venice or Genoa by European merchants. The goods were then taken by mule train or riverboats to the marketplaces of Europe. Since every country that was passed through charged a tax, it is no wonder that only the rich could afford goods from Asia. The journey from China to Europe and back again took three years.

Many people living in Europe at this time hoped to find a shortcut to Asia across the western sea. What they found instead was a land they didn't even know existed.

Reflecting/Predicting

1. Use an atlas to compare the climates of Canada, China, and India. How might the differences in climate help explain why Asian silks and spices were not to be found in Canada?
2. Beaver pelts from North America were to become highly prized by Europeans. Yet Europe was also a home to the beaver. What reasons can you think of for why North American beaver pelts became so valuable?
3. How do you think the Aboriginal peoples living in what later became Canada would view these new arrivals (the Europeans) and their activities?

Explorers from Europe travelled west looking for a shortcut to the spice and silk routes.

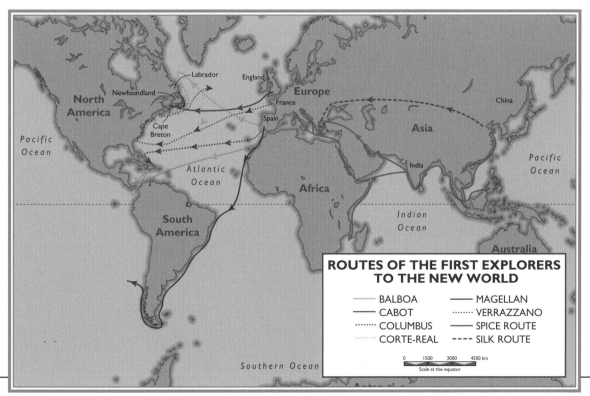

ROUTES OF THE FIRST EXPLORERS TO THE NEW WORLD

——— BALBOA ——— MAGELLAN
——— CABOT ········ VERRAZZANO
········ COLUMBUS ——— SPICE ROUTE
········ CORTE-REAL - - - - SILK ROUTE

0   1500   3000   4500 km
Scale at the equator

Aboriginal Cultural Areas

The Aboriginal peoples were the first Canadians. By the time the Europeans arrived, Aboriginal peoples had lived for more than 10 000 years in what today is called Canada. There were many different Aboriginal groups. In each part of Canada, Aboriginal peoples developed their own way of life based on the land and the resources they found there.

The Arctic

The Arctic people adapted to their environment by building houses from blocks of snow for winter living. In the summer, they lived in cone-shaped tents made of caribou skins. Seals and other sea mammals were hunted for their meat. People used the animals' oil for fuel and their skins for clothing.

The Eastern Woodlands and the Plains

Groups who lived in the Eastern Woodlands and on the Plains lived migratory lives. They moved around within their specific territory, following the seasons and taking advantage of the abundant wildlife. They hunted wild game, trapped small fur-bearing animals, and camped where fish were plentiful. They lived in semi-permanent homes made of wooden frames covered with birchbark or animal skins. These dwellings could be easily packed up and moved to new hunting grounds. On the Plains, the people migrated with the buffalo. The people of the Plains relied on these huge animals for food. They also used their hides and bones to make clothing, shelter, and tools.

Before the arrival of the Europeans, the Aboriginal peoples of Canada were roughly divided into seven cultural areas.

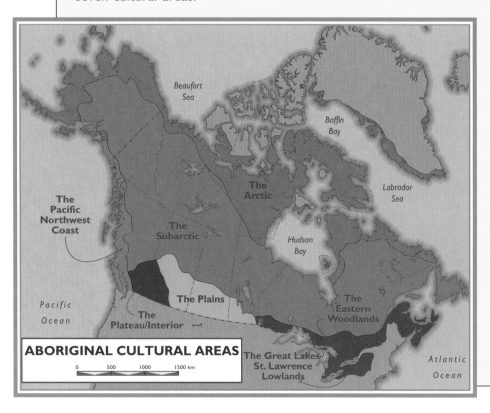

ABORIGINAL CULTURAL AREAS

0   500   1000   1500 km

Today, many Aboriginal peoples, such as the Inuit, are returning to their traditional names rather than those given by European explorers. Inuit means "the people" in Inuktitut, the Inuit language.

The Aboriginal people of the Subarctic travelled throughout the year to secure a supply of food. They were nomadic, meaning that they did not have permanent villages. They hunted together in small groups consisting of one or two families. Often, they used snares made of rawhide for trapping. Rawhide traps were so strong that not even caribou or moose could break through them.

Canada 8

Indians of the Subarctic   Les Indiens du Nord

A Siksika (Blackfoot) family on the Plains with a travois made by tying two poles together. Webbing was stretched between the poles. A family could load all their household goods onto these "moving vans."

The Great Lakes–St. Lawrence Lowlands

Aboriginal groups who lived in the area now called Ontario and Quebec tended to move around less. Soil in the Great Lakes–St. Lawrence Lowlands was rich and the climate was suitable for agriculture. People took advantage of good farming conditions to grow crops. They built large longhouses made of wood and bark and settled in permanent villages. Every 10 to 20 years, they moved their villages when the soil became less productive because of continual farming. They also hunted both large and small animals for food and for their skins.

In this painting, "Birth of the Earth," Onondaga artist Arnold Jacobs tells an Iroquois story of creation. A woman falls from the sky. On the back of a turtle, with the help of the animals, she creates the earth. "Turtle Island" is the Ojibwa name for North America.

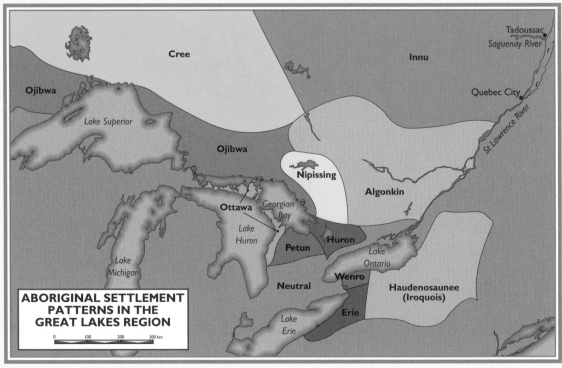

ABORIGINAL SETTLEMENT PATTERNS IN THE GREAT LAKES REGION

0   100   200   300 km

The Haida of the Pacific Northwest coast carved tall totem poles and placed them at the entrance to their houses. The poles were fashioned from the trunks of cedar trees. They were carved with figures of animals, humans, and supernatural figures that told the history of the family living in the house. Most of the old totem poles still standing or found in museums were made after 1800. Earlier poles have rotted away in the rain forests of the Pacific Northwest coast.

The Pacific Northwest Coast

On the Pacific Northwest coast, the Aboriginal peoples also adapted well to their environment. The milder climate meant that it was possible to get food from the sea year-round. There were so many fish that there was no need to travel great distances in search of food. People could remain in the same location. The forest provided wood for large dugout canoes, plank houses, and huge totem poles.

The environment was harsher in the interior than on the coast of British Columbia. That meant that the people on the Plateau needed to spend more effort finding food. They travelled in small family hunting groups during the spring,

On the Pacific Northwest coast, the Aboriginal peoples lived in settled villages such as this one. Large homes were made from cedar planks and decorated with the crests and totems of the clans.

summer, and fall to find food. In winter, larger groups gathered together in settled villages.

Aboriginal Cultures

The Aboriginal peoples developed their own distinct cultures in each part of Canada. **Culture** is the way of life of a group of people. It includes everything about the way people live—their homes, clothing, art, tools, daily routines, and seasonal activities. Ideas and beliefs are also a part of culture.

A Ktunaxa community on the Plateau

Fast Forward

Aboriginal Languages

About 50 to 60 different languages were being spoken by the Aboriginal peoples when the Europeans first arrived. In the past century, eight of these languages have disappeared and most of the others are in danger of being lost. Some of the languages continue to be used in daily life in both spoken and written form. But most are used only by adults and have not been passed down to younger generations. Experts fear that only four—

Cree, Inuktitut, Ojibwa, and Dakota—will survive. Today, Aboriginal peoples are trying to preserve their languages. Many Aboriginal communities offer language classes in their child-care centres and schools. Some newspapers and magazines are published in Aboriginal languages. Radio and television programs are also available in Aboriginal languages such as Inuktitut and Oji-Cree.

Teacher Annie Boulanger gives a language lesson to a student.

The land and the available resources largely influenced the culture of each group of Canada's Aboriginal peoples. Each group learned to use the resources around it and adapted to its own environment. The Mi'kmaq on the east coast, for example, developed a culture very distinct from the Haida on the Pacific Northwest coast or the Assiniboine on the Prairies.

Aboriginals and Europeans Meet

Many Aboriginal groups traded regularly with one another. Sometimes, they even formed political alliances such as the Iroquois Confederacy. They had their own governments, laws, and social structures. They educated their children in their own ways and traditions and practised Aboriginal sacred rituals. Then one day, strangers from Europe appeared in their lands.

There are no written records describing how the Aboriginal peoples felt about the new arrivals. However, their oral traditions tell us that different groups had different reactions. Some were curious; some were cautious; others were friendly; and still others were suspicious. The Europeans, on the other hand, viewed the Aboriginal peoples as backward and uncivilized. This impression lasted for centuries.

The various groups of Europeans brought their own cultures and ways of living to North America, which they called the "New World." Contact between the two groups would lead to profound changes for both the Aboriginal peoples and the

A pair of Mi'kmaq moccasins. These soft leather shoes were decorated with colourful ribbons and beads.

A splint basket made by the Mi'kmaq. These baskets were made of shaved wood strips woven into intricate patterns.

Quilled boxes. Dyed porcupine quills were sewn by the Mi'kmaq through birchbark to produce decorative patterns.

Europeans. As more Europeans settled in North America, the pressure on the Aboriginal peoples would increase. This pressure would threaten their traditional ways of life. Eventually, it would threaten the very existence of the Aboriginal people and their cultures.

1. In what ways did the Aboriginal groups live in harmony with their environment?
2. How has Aboriginal life changed since the early days? What caused those changes? Do you think the changes have been an improvement? Explain.
3. Find information about one aspect of Aboriginal lives in the present, for example, arts, government, family life, the role of elders, land claims, city life, or literature. Prepare a brief report for your class.

Europe Looks West

By the 1400s, Europeans had begun to look for a way to bring goods from the East by sea, hoping it would be faster and easier than overland. Explorers prepared to sail westward in the hope of discovering a route to Asia.

Explorers from Spain

In 1492, Christopher Columbus made this promise to the king and queen of Spain: "Let others take the long route to Asia through Africa. I will find a direct route which will take but a few days." So began Columbus's great voyage. Instead of a few days, however, it took him two months to reach land. When Columbus finally sighted land, he was convinced that he had arrived in India. To his dying day, Columbus believed that he had sailed to India and that the people he had seen were "Indians." Instead of Asia, Columbus had arrived in Central and South America. He returned to Spain, not with silks and spices, but with ships filled with silver and gold that had belonged to the Aboriginal peoples.

Other Spanish explorers followed in search of gold and other goods. In 1513, Vasco Balboa crossed a narrow strip of land in Panama and discovered the Pacific Ocean. This was an astonishing discovery. It showed that the world was much bigger than people had thought. They would have to cross land that was new to them and then sail across another ocean before reaching Asia.

In 1519, Ferdinand Magellan sailed along the coast of South America. He discovered a passageway into the Pacific Ocean that he named the Strait of Magellan. Now the Spanish had a southwest passage to the Far East.

Tech Link Aids to Navigation

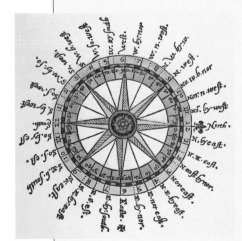

The Compass

For thousands of years, sailors could only use the sun and the stars to steer their ships. It was a fine method when the sun and stars could be seen—but it was of no use in cloudy, overcast conditions. What sailors needed was a more certain guide to direction.

Nature provided this guide in the form of iron oxide, also called "lodestone," which has magnetic properties. If you stroke an iron needle with lodestone and then float the needle, it will always point north. This discovery was the basis for the **compass**.

Early explorers used a compass card such as this one to set their direction. The card moved freely on a pin inside a waterproof case. Underneath the north point was a lodestone which, because of its magnetic properties, made the pin always point in a northerly direction. The north point was commonly marked with a fancy fleur-de-lys, seen pointing right.

When the centre line on the astrolabe was level with the horizon, the sighting rule ("hand") was adjusted to line up with the sun or North Star. The number that the sighting rule pointed to on the circumference gave the sailor the angle. The number of the angle was subtracted from 90° to provide the approximate latitude.

The Astrolabe

While a compass showed sailors which direction was north, an **astrolabe** showed them about how far north or south of the equator they were positioned. In other words, it showed the sailors' latitude. It did this by measuring the angle between the sun or North Star and the horizon. The astrolabe was suspended so that the centre line of the instrument was level with the horizon. A sighting rule, like a hand on a clock, was turned so that the sun or star could be sighted along it.

The astrolabe looked like a clock with one hand. The numbers around the circumference helped determine latitude.

1. What challenges would sailors have faced before the compass and astrolabe were invented? In what ways would these inventions have changed sea travel?

2. Find out about more recent inventions that have improved long distance voyages.

Netsurfer

Learn more about how an astrolabe works by visiting the Canadian Museum of Civilization website at www.civilization.ca/ membrs/treasure/222eng.html

Explorers from England

Columbus believed that he had reached Asia by travelling west, and the news soon reached England that he had done so. King Henry VII of England sponsored his own voyage of discovery. He hired an Italian navigator known as John Cabot. Cabot set sail aboard the *Matthew*, heading west across the Atlantic. On 24 June 1497, he reached land in the north Atlantic. There, he planted the flags of England and Venice. Evidence suggests that Cabot had arrived in Newfoundland and perhaps Cape Breton. Like Columbus, Cabot believed he had reached the Far East. Cabot found no silver or gold as the Spaniards had done. However, he did discover rich fishing grounds off the coast of Newfoundland.

Fast Forward

Matthew's Voyage

In July 1997, Canadians marked the 500th anniversary of the voyage of the *Matthew*. A replica of Cabot's ship, with a crew of 19, crossed the Atlantic from Bristol, England to Newfoundland. To celebrate the event, Cyril MacPhee, lead singer of the band Brakin' Tradition, co-wrote a song about Cabot's ship, the *Matthew*, called "*Matthew*'s Voyage." It was chosen as an official song of the 500th John Cabot anniversary. What does this song tell you about the purpose of the *Matthew*'s voyage and the experiences of those who sailed on it?

My name is the *Matthew* with the wind away I'll sail
I'll beat to the westward on a northerly gale
In search of the spices and silks of the West
With my master Cabot and eighteen young sailors
Held close to my breast

King Henry did charge me Columbus to best
The riches awaiting my hold for to dress
And so the adventure through swell and through gale
It brought us to land in the fog on the strand
A new world away

Chorus:
So raise up the cross of St. George my good lads
For England and God this rock will now stand
Our cannon and cutlass will be our command
For a new generation hold the world in their hands

In Bristol a dandy I was proud to be
This hellish long voyage this rock in the sea
It chills to my mainmast to be so alone
But claiming this country for Cabot and King
Gives me the strength to go home

Chorus

So the wealth they imagined they found here that day
Not silks not spices but the fish in the bay
And the furs in the forest would many more bring
And the wealth of our country this new land of ours
Would cause us to sing

So sing out for Canada stands here today
Sing out a song for our homes by the bay
Sing of John Cabot who ventured this way
My name it is *Matthew*; sing with me today

Explorers from Portugal

In 1500 and 1501, Portugal sent out Gaspar Corte-Real and his brother Miguel. They reached Newfoundland and explored the coast of Labrador. In 1520, the Portuguese explorer Fagundes established a small colony on modern Cape Breton Island. This was probably the first European settlement in eastern North America since the time of the Vikings.

France Joins In

France was the last European nation to join in the voyages of discovery. The French had been so busy with wars that they had made no effort to explore for new lands and wealth. However, in 1523 and again in 1524, France sent Giovanni de Verrazzano to try to find a route to Asia. He explored almost 3000 km of the coastline of eastern North America. He was looking for a passage to the Pacific Ocean. Verrazzano finally realized he was travelling northward along the coast of a large land mass. The way to Asia was blocked by the North American continent!

Francis I, the king of France, was jealous of Spanish and English successes. France's rivals, Spain and England, must be beaten! France must be the first nation to find a direct way to Asia! In 1534, he chose Jacques Cartier of St. Malo for the task. He ordered Cartier "to discover lands where it is said there must be great quantities of gold and other riches."

This replica of Cabot's ship, the *Matthew*, is typical of ships of the 15th century. What problems would you face crossing the ocean in a ship like this?

Skill Building: Using an Outline Organizer

Making notes is a lot of work. Have you ever asked, "Why bother?"

In everyday life, there are a lot of practical reasons for taking notes. Good notes can help you do something complicated. You might want to have notes on how to prepare one of your grandmother's special recipes, program a VCR, or find your way in an unfamiliar neighbourhood.

In school, notes are organizers that help you remember what you read and learned. Often, just the act of writing down information helps you to remember it later. Outline notes are a simple and effective way of recording information.

Making Notes

1. What should be in an outline note? Notes should record only the important information, such as the main idea and supporting details.

The **main idea** is the key topic. It tells what the rest of the paragraphs are about. The main idea is usually placed in the first few sentences.

Supporting details tell something more about or prove the main idea. They make the main idea clearer.

2. What should an outline note look like? Outline notes should be in your own words and be easy to read. An outline note can follow this form:

1. main idea _____
   a) supporting detail _____
   b) supporting detail _____
   c) supporting detail _____

For example, an outline note for the section entitled "France Joins In" might look like this:

1. France finally begins exploration
   a) had not explored before because of wars
   b) 1523-4: Verrazzano searches for passage to the Pacific Ocean/Asia, but fails
   c) king of France determined to be first to find direct way to Asia, obtain gold and riches
   d) 1534: Cartier is chosen for new expedition

Challenge Yourself!

Use what you learned to make outline notes on the following groups. When preparing your notes, look for the main idea and supporting details.

1. the Spanish explorers
2. the English explorers
3. the Portuguese explorers

Fast Forward
Jacques Cartier Slept Here

The explorer Jacques Cartier lived in this manor house. It is on the outskirts of St. Malo in the French province of Brittany. The picture shows what it looked like in the mid-19th century. In 1974, some Canadians purchased the house. Their plan was to restore it and turn it into a museum. In 1984, their work was finished and the museum was opened as part of the 450th anniversary celebrations to honour Jacques Cartier's arrival in Canada.

Cartier Explores the Coast

Cartier set out with two little ships on 20 April 1534. After a trip lasting 20 days, his crew reached Newfoundland. They skirted the shores of Newfoundland, surveying the coastline. His first contact with Aboriginal people was probably with the Montagnais, also known as the Innu, on the Labrador coast.

Cartier then turned west and began to search for the passage to Asia. He explored many straits and inlets. On 3 July 1534, the ships entered Chaleur Bay. The expedition landed at Gaspé. From there, the ships sailed north and east around the eastern end of Anticosti Island. Twice,

Cartier missed the entrance to the St. Lawrence River because he thought the inlet led to a land mass. He thought that Anticosti Island was a peninsula. This great river would have taken him into the interior of North America. However, since winter was coming, the two little ships had to return to France.

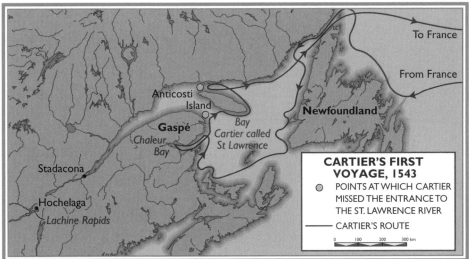

CARTIER'S FIRST VOYAGE, 1543
○ POINTS AT WHICH CARTIER MISSED THE ENTRANCE TO THE ST. LAWRENCE RIVER
— CARTIER'S ROUTE

Cartier and the Mi'kmaq

At Chaleur Bay, Cartier recorded the first exchange of furs between Europeans and Aboriginal people. The description in his journal reads:

> The next day some of the Indians came in nine canoes to the point where we lay anchored with our ships ... As soon as they saw us, they began making signs that they had come to barter and held up some furs of small value with which they clothed themselves ... We sent two men on shore to offer them some knives and other iron goods and a red cap to their chief ... They bartered all that they had to the extent they all went back naked without anything on them.

Cartier and the Haudenosaunee

When he landed at Gaspé, Cartier met a group from the Haudenosaunee (or Iroquois) Confederacy. The word "Iroquois" is French. With their chief, Donnacona, the Iroquois had come from the interior to fish and hunt for seal.

The Six Nations

In Cartier's time, the Iroquois were a confederacy of five nations: the Mohawk, Oneida, Onondaga, Cayuga, and Seneca. In 1715, the Tuscarora joined the confederacy, which from then on has also been known as the "Six Nations."

At Gaspé, Cartier and his crew set up a huge wooden cross. This was a sign that Cartier was claiming the land in the name of France. On the top of the cross were the words *Vive le Roi de France*. The Aboriginal spectators gestured that they did not like the cross. Cartier told them it was only a marker for his ships.

Fast Forward

The Importance of Names

The names used to refer to the first inhabitants of Canada have changed over time. For centuries, they were known as "Indians" and, in the north, as "Eskimos." But these are names given by Europeans and are no longer the preferred terms. We now use the term "Aboriginal peoples" to refer generally to the wide variety of groups that make up Canada's indigenous (native) population. More specifically, we distinguish between "First Nation," "Inuit," and "Métis" peoples, the three broad Aboriginal groups.

Aboriginal nations are groups living in a particular area and sharing a common national identity. Their names have changed too. Many nations were given European names, which were used for hundreds of years. Now, many Aboriginal nations are again known by their traditional names. For example, the traditional name "Siksika" is used instead of "Blackfoot." Since these names come from languages that are very different from English, you will often see them spelled in different ways.

Cartier captured two of Donnacona's sons to take them back to France. He wanted to use the young men as interpreters on his next trip. Cartier promised Donnacona that he would return one day with his sons.

Cartier's Second Visit

On his first voyage, Cartier did not find a route to the East. He did not return to France with treasures. But he was the first to explore beyond Newfoundland. He was also the first to take possession of land for France. He recorded the first exchange of furs with the people who lived there. He took back Donnacona's sons who knew a great deal about the land in the interior. The king of France was impressed. He sent Cartier out again with three ships and more than a 100 sailors.

In the spring of 1535, Cartier's ships again arrived on the river that he named the St. Lawrence. This time, he had Donnacona's sons as his guides. They sailed up the river as far as Stadacona, near modern-day Quebec City. Cartier wanted to explore more of this mighty river. He travelled in his smallest ship as far as Hochelaga (Montreal), another Iroquois settlement. Rapids blocked his way. Later, these rapids were called the Lachine Rapids. "La Chine" means China. The French still dreamed of finding a passage to the East. Cartier turned back to Stadacona where he decided to spend the winter. This would be his first experience with a North American winter.

They Call it Canada

When Cartier's ships sailed into the Gulf of St. Lawrence, Donnacona's sons became very excited. They recognized the way to their village. They started to use the word "Canada," meaning the area where they lived around Stadacona. Within 15 years, "Canada" was appearing on maps to denote the whole area along the banks of the St. Lawrence River.

A Difficult Winter

Cartier and his crew were totally unprepared for winter in Canada. Their ships were trapped in ice four metres thick. The inside walls of the ships were coated with a layer of ice. The small log fort they had built on the shore provided little warmth and comfort. They were freezing in their European clothing. Many of the crew began to get sick. One by one, Cartier's crew died and were buried in the snowdrifts. By the middle of February, only one in ten of the crew was healthy.

Cartier Explores North America

When spring came, Cartier and his crew were anxious to return to France. This time, he took Donnacona and some of his people back to France. On the way, Cartier discovered the strait that separates Newfoundland from Cape Breton. Earlier, Cartier had sailed around the north of Newfoundland. The southern passage he followed on this voyage showed him that Newfoundland was an island.

This voyage was important for other reasons, too. Cartier had explored the river that leads into the heart of the North American continent. He had passed many other rivers that could be used as highways for a future French empire. He had also spent a winter in Canada and managed to survive.

The king was impressed when Donnacona told him about a land rich in gold that lay beyond Hochelaga. But Donnacona and some of the others died in France.

Cartier's Third Visit

In 1541, the king of France appointed an important noble, Sieur de Roberval, to lead an expedition to New France. Cartier was to serve only as a guide. Most of the crew were criminals who had been let out of prison when they agreed to sail for Canada. Cartier set out ahead of Roberval. When he arrived, he found the Iroquois to be unfriendly because Donnacona had not returned with him. They did not believe him when he said that Donnacona had married and stayed in France.

Cartier built two forts upriver from Stadacona. He wanted to travel up the St. Lawrence River as far as he could, but was stopped by the Lachine Rapids. As would be expected, the now hostile Iroquois would not help Cartier get past this obstacle.

Cartier and his crew spent another terrible winter near Stadacona. The only bright spot was finding large quantities of what they believed to be gold and diamonds. They returned to France with 10 barrels of "gold" and a large quantity of "diamonds." Unfortunately, the gold turned out to be nothing more than iron pyrite, or fool's gold. The diamonds were equally worthless quartz crystals.

Roberval's Settlement

Roberval followed Cartier to Canada. He established a settlement at the fort Cartier had built, renaming it "France-Roy." The first French colony in North America had a population of about 200, most of whom were ex-convicts.

The colony lasted only two years. In 1543, discouraged by sickness and the harsh climate, everyone boarded ship and returned to France.

The first attempt to build a French colony in Canada had failed. The French were now discouraged. They had not discovered a short route to Asia. They had found no gold. Cartier had, however, found and mapped a great river that one day would lead the French into the riches of North America. But 60 years passed before France again considered trying to build a colony in New France.

Fishing on the East Coast

For a long time after Cartier's last voyage, the French returned to North America only to fish. Every spring, fishing boats arrived at the Grand Banks, rich fishing areas off Canada's east coast. There were unlimited quantities of cod for the catching. In Europe, there was a huge demand for fish, especially on the part of Roman Catholics, who were not allowed to eat red meat on Fridays and feast days.

From the Iroquois of Stadacona, Cartier learned about a secret medicine that could cure **scurvy**. Scurvy is caused by a lack of vitamin C from fresh fruit and vegetables. The Iroquois crushed and boiled the bark and leaves of the white cedar tree. This mixture had a high content of vitamin C. When the crew members drank this medicine, they very soon began to regain their health. The Aboriginal people of Canada had discovered this cure long before the civilizations of Europe.

The fresh fish had to be preserved. This drawing shows a cod fishing boat anchored off the Grand Banks. The fishermen are using the **wet method**. The fish are cleaned on board and packed in thick layers of salt. People sometimes complained that so much salt made the fish unpleasant to eat.

This drawing shows the **dry method** of processing fish. Crews came on shore. (Note that one of the workers is a child.) They cleaned the fish and salted them lightly. They left them to dry in the sun on racks called flakes. In four or five days, the fish were hard and light. Three times more fish could be taken home using this method. The dried fish tasted better and was less salty. When it was soaked in water, the fish filled out like a sponge.

Fast Forward

The Fate of the Cod Fishery

In about 1500, John Cabot told the English that the seas off the coasts of Newfoundland were "swarming with fish." The cod were so plentiful that they could be caught in baskets weighted down with a stone. In 1992, the Canadian government shut down the cod fishery. The stocks had become almost extinct from overfishing. Thousands of people were put out of work in the fishing and fish-processing industries. In 1999, fishing was reopened with a limited quota. It was thought that the cod stocks were being restored. Some scientists argued, however, that it was too early to tell whether the cod had returned. They suggested that the cod fishery remain closed for the time being.

The French shared the fishing grounds with boats from other countries such as England, Spain, and Portugal. They set up temporary camps along the coast where they lived and worked during the fishing season. After a summer of fishing, the boats returned to Europe for the winter months.

The Beothuk were the Aboriginal people of Newfoundland. They did not adapt well to contact with the European fishermen and settlers, and died out completely in the 19th century.

The Fur Trade

The fishing crews soon came in contact with the local Aboriginal people, who were especially interested in the sharp metal knives and iron kettles that they saw the Europeans using. **Bartering**, or trading, began. The Aboriginal people traded furs in exchange for European items. The fishing crews soon realized that, back home in Europe, furs were more valuable than fish.

The beaver was nearing extinction in Europe and the price of furs rose there. But beaver were plentiful in North America. The French saw a chance to make a lot of money. They realized that they could obtain a plentiful supply of beaver pelts from Aboriginal trappers in Canada. The fur trade soon became the main reason for Europeans to cross the Atlantic to North America. Those who arrived first in the spring got the best furs from the winter hunt.

Then, some traders decided that it would be better to stay in New France all winter. That way, they would always be close to the supply of furs. Settling permanently in New France would also confirm France's claim to the land. This was important because other nations, such as England and Holland, were beginning to build colonies in the New World.

France's king did not want France to be left out of the competition to claim the New World. On the other hand, he also did not want to pay the huge cost of building settlements. So, he offered rich fur merchants a deal. In exchange for taking settlers to New France, the king would grant each merchant a monopoly. The merchant would pay all the costs, but he was the only one allowed to trade in the territory.

Pierre de Gua, Sieur de Monts, was one of the first traders to receive a monopoly. In 1604, de Monts and his map maker, Samuel de Champlain, attempted to build a settlement in Acadia, in the Atlantic region of New France. They chose the small island of Ste. Croix in the Bay of Fundy. It was an unfortunate choice, as a harsh winter proved to them. They moved their little settlement to a new site on the mainland. They called the new site Port Royal.

Netsurfer

To find out more about Port Royal, visit the Canada Hall exhibit of the Museum of Civilization. Click on #5 for early Acadia. Here, you will find information on this early French farming settlement.
www.cmcc.muse.digital.ca/cmc/cmceng/canpleng.html

Mathieu Da Costa

Two people of African heritage were involved with the establishment of Port Royal. One, whose name is not known, died of scurvy soon after arriving. The other was a freeman, Mathieu Da Costa, who served as a translator between the Mi'kmaq and the French. It is possible that he made earlier trips with Champlain. In 1996, the Mathieu Da Costa Awards program was established by the federal government in recognition of the many Canadians of African origin who have contributed to the building of Canada.

At Port Royal, the settlers built a weatherproof building around a closed courtyard. This photograph shows a reconstruction of the original building. It was a two-storey structure protected by a gun platform that was armed with four cannon. Nearby were forests that provided firewood and building materials. The settlers planted wheat and large vegetable gardens near the fort. They had learned from their hard winter experience at Ste. Croix.

Skill Building: Brainstorming

Brainstorming is a way to think of solutions to a problem. For example, suppose you are planning a class trip to Quebec City for Carnaval. The class will have to raise some money to help pay for the trip. What is your first step? As a class, you will have to come up with some good ideas for raising money. Someone suggests holding bake sales. Somebody else suggests asking local businesses to help you put together a coupon book that you can sell. Another person recommends holding a raffle for a donated prize. What are other ways you could raise money?

It is best to brainstorm in groups. That way you have more people using their brain power to try to solve the problem.

Guidelines to Follow

1. Record all the ideas on a chalkboard or chart paper where everyone can see them.

2. Brainstorm as many ideas as possible. A large quantity of ideas will help to produce excellent ideas.

3. Ideas may range from serious to far out and even wacky.

4. Don't allow any criticism of the ideas as they are offered. This is important. All ideas are acceptable and there must be no putting down of anyone's idea at this point.

5. Get everyone in the group involved.

6. Combine or improve upon ideas. This is called "piggy-backing" on another person's idea. One person's idea may trigger a similar, but better, idea in someone else's mind.

7. Don't give up when the group first seems to run out of ideas. Keep going. There is usually a break between the obvious ideas and the less obvious ones.

8. When the group finishes brainstorming, it is time to analyze and evaluate each of the solutions suggested. Don't discard any idea too quickly. Instead, sort out all the ideas. Which one, or ones, best solve the problem?

Try It!

Brainstorm as many answers as you can to the following questions.

1. Why would people leave their homeland in the early 1600s and set out for Canada?

2. What kind of preparations would you have to make before a journey to Canada in the early 1600s?

3. Why do people move to Canada from other countries today?

Order of Good Cheer

To keep up the settlers' spirits in winter, Champlain organized a club. He called it *L'Ordre de Bon Temps*, or "The Order of Good Cheer." Every two weeks, one settler acted as host for a special evening. His responsibility was to put on a big supper for the community. This meant hours of planning and preparation. It also meant going out to hunt game and catch fish. Each person tried to provide a better feast than the others did. There were roasts of moose, venison, duck, goose, rabbit, bear, or porcupine. Beaver tail was considered a great delicacy. Fish, caught through the ice, were also served. There were huge loaves of freshly baked bread and often some kind of dessert.

The host was also responsible for providing entertainment. Usually, there was music and singing, and sometimes even short plays. In 1606, Marc Lescarbot wrote a playlet called *The Theatre of Neptune*. It was the first play performed in Canada. The Order of Good Cheer worked wonders and helped the settlers survive the winter in Acadia.

"The ruler of the feast ... having had everything prepared by the cook, marched in, napkin on shoulder, wand of office in hand, and around his neck the collar of the Order... after him all the members of the Order carrying each a dish."

Acadia

Bad news reached Port Royal in 1607. The French king cancelled de Monts' fur trading monopoly. Without the profits of the fur trade, de Monts could no longer support the colony. The settlers packed up and returned to France.

Further attempts to build a French settlement in Acadia ran into difficulties. Small groups of French settlers tried to start again in Acadia. However, there were frequent conflicts with the English colonists to the south and little support from France. Gradually, a small French farming community did grow up along the Bay of Fundy. Acadian farmers made a success of farming the marshlands along the bay. They built dikes to keep the sea water out. In this way, they claimed the fertile meadow lands for agriculture and pasture. They survived many hardships. The Acadian population that still exists in Nova Scotia, New Brunswick, and Prince Edward Island are the descendants of this small energetic group of settlers.

Membertou and the Mi'kmaq

The Mi'kmaq were probably the first Aboriginal group to have contact with the French in Acadia. The Mi'kmaq were skilled hunters and gatherers. They travelled between summer fishing villages near the coast and inland locations for winter hunting.

Netsurfer

View Mi'kmaq arts and crafts and learn more about the rich Mi'kmaq heritage at http://sae.ca/abt/micmac/index.html

The success of the fur trade depended on the willingness of the Aboriginal peoples to trade. The Mi'kmaq welcomed European traders and made alliances with them. In time, some Mi'kmaq intermarried with the Europeans.

Membertou, a Mi'kmaq chief, was especially friendly with the French settlers. In return, the French greatly respected Membertou and often invited him to their feasts of The Order of Good Cheer. Membertou was the first Aboriginal person to be baptized as a Christian in New France.

The settlers were able to survive at Port Royal because of the kindness and advice offered by Membertou and the local Mi'kmaq. When the French abandoned Port Royal in 1607, it was Membertou who looked after the fort until the French returned.

Fast Forward

The Mi'kmaq Today

Contact with the Europeans and the fur trade changed the Mi'kmaq way of life considerably. Their lifestyle and diet were affected. They were highly susceptible to European diseases. They got into conflicts with the Europeans. With the expansion of European settlements, the Mi'kmaq were forced to wander over wider areas to find food. By 1850, sickness, hunger, and warfare had reduced their numbers dramatically.

Today, most Mi'kmaq live in the Maritime provinces. Some live on reserves where the older people practise some of the old ways. Some councils on reserves have set up their own businesses, for example, an oyster farm and a sawmill. Others earn a living fishing and lobster trapping. Since unemployment is a problem on many reserves, some Mi'kmaq have moved to cities to find work. Although the Mi'kmaq have faced many challenges over several centuries, they have been able to maintain their distinctive culture.

Mi'kmaq trapper Mike Martin peels spruce root to use as thread for sewing a wigwam cover.

Quebec

In 1608, Champlain returned to New France. This time, he was planning to build a settlement along the St. Lawrence. The French had discovered that Acadia was too far from the centre of the fur trade. They needed to be located along Cartier's great river in the heart of the fur trade country. Champlain chose the same site near Stadacona that Cartier had occupied in 1535. This is a place where the river narrows and there is an excellent harbour. Since Cartier's visit, the Iroquois of Stadacona and Hochelaga had mysteriously disappeared.

Assassination Attempt

On 3 July 1608, Samuel de Champlain barely escaped a plot to kill him. Some of his settlers were grumbling about the hard work and the mosquitoes. They were afraid they would die far from France. They planned to kill Champlain and to turn the fort over to Spanish traders who were down the river. When Champlain heard of the mutiny, he took swift action. Duval, the ringleader, was hanged. The others were sent back to France in chains.

Champlain's sketch of the Habitation at Quebec 1608. Check the key to the drawing. Find each part of the building on the sketch. What was the purpose of each part?

Key to Drawing:
B: Pigeon house
C: Building for arms and for workers to live
D: More lodgings for workers

E: Sundial
F: Forge and workers' lodgings
G: Galleries all the way around
H: Lodging for Champlain

I: Gate with drawbridge
M: Moat all the way around
N: Platforms for the cannons
O: Gardens

An unpopulated area lay between two opposing groups: the Iroquois of present-day New York and the Algonkin of the Ottawa River valley, along with their allies the Huron. Here, Champlain started to build the first permanent settlement along the St. Lawrence. He called the place *Kebec* (Quebec), which means "where the river narrows" in Algonkian.

Champlain set his workers clearing a spot for the fort. It was close to the river, with a high cliff behind it so it was easy to defend. The fort contained three main buildings of three storeys. All the way around was a gallery with a platform for cannons. It was surrounded by wooden fences. There was even a moat and a drawbridge. Champlain called it the "Habitation." It would be a fort, a warehouse, a home, and a trading post for the French.

Many times during the next few years, Champlain travelled back to France. He urged the king to send settlers to Quebec. But the fur merchants in France were afraid that settlers would ruin their business because they would clear the land and drive out the beaver. So, in spite of all Champlain's efforts, in 1627, the population of Quebec numbered only 65 settlers.

Other European Settlements in North America

While the French were busy trying to establish settlements in Acadia and along the St. Lawrence, other Europeans were settling other parts of North America.

Spanish Settlements

Spanish explorers had been bringing settlers to the southern portion of North America for many years. By the end of the 16th century, the Spanish had claimed Mexico, Florida, and the southern United States west of the Mississippi River. In 1565, the settlement of St. Augustine in Florida was founded. Its main function was as a military post, to protect Spanish fleets from the French and the English. Other posts stretched from Tampa Bay to Port Royal, South Carolina. The settlement of Santa Fe, in present-day New Mexico, was founded in 1609. The Spanish did not make friends with the Aboriginal peoples in the areas they settled. The hostility of the Aboriginal peoples forced settlers to leave and many settlements failed.

In the 1770s, Spanish sailors sailed from Spain, around the bottom of Africa, and across the Pacific Ocean. They arrived at the coast of British Columbia. The Spanish explorer Perez recorded that he met the Haida in 1774, 160 years after the French had met the Huron in eastern Canada.

English and Dutch Colonies

In the 17th century, English and Dutch colonies began to flourish along the Atlantic seaboard. The Dutch wanted to compete with the Spanish. Their settlements came first, following the exploration of the Hudson River in 1609. "New Netherland" was founded in 1624 in the territory surrounding the Hudson River (including present-day New York City, some of

---

The Town of Quebec

Pierre Boucher was one of the first Canadian writers. In 1664, he published a book in France in which he described the town of Quebec. His writing shows us how much the town of Quebec grew in less than 40 years.

> Quebec is therefore the principal habitation where the Governor General of the whole country resides. There is a fine fortress and a fine garrison. There is also a beautiful church which serves the parish and which is the cathedral for the whole country ... There is a Jesuit college and an Ursuline convent that teaches all the young girls.
>
> Sometimes the ships come right up to there because that is as far as they can sail.

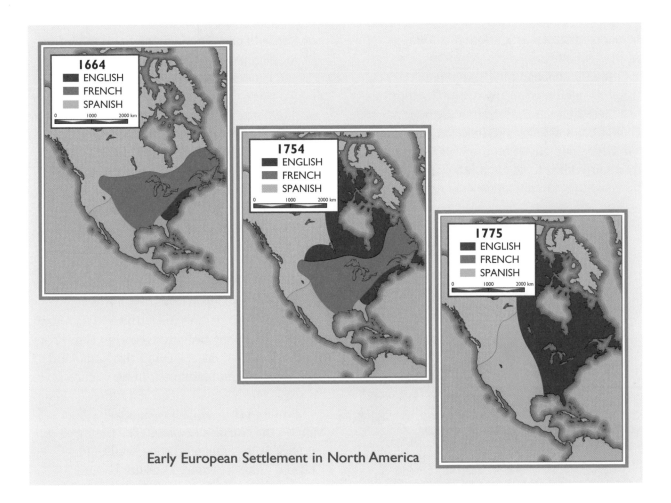

Early European Settlement in North America

Connecticut, some of New Jersey, and parts of Long Island). It contained valuable farming land and became an important trading centre. The Dutch had contact with the New France fur traders, and a handful of Dutch settlers chose to move north into Canada.

In 1664, the English seized the territory and divided it into three colonies, named New York, New Jersey, and Delaware. These and several other English territories came to be known as the Thirteen Colonies. The other 10 colonies were: New Hampshire, Massachusetts, Rhode Island, Connecticut, Pennsylvania, Maryland, Virginia, North Carolina, South Carolina, and Georgia.

Champlain and the Huron

Champlain wanted to form partnerships with his Aboriginal neighbours. He knew his little community was greatly outnumbered.

Aboriginal warriors could, if they wished, attack and destroy it at any moment. It was important they remain friendly. Aboriginal hunters were also absolutely essential for the fur trade. They knew how to trap beaver and prepare beaver pelts. As expert canoeists, they could use the rivers as highways to bring furs to Quebec.

Of the many Aboriginal peoples in New France, the Huron became Champlain's chief allies. The Huron were also bitter enemies of the Haudenosaunee (Iroquois).

Iroquois Relations

In 1609, Champlain's Aboriginal friends requested his help. The Algonkin, a few Huron, and the Montagnais asked him to join them in an attack on their enemies, the Iroquois. They were testing Champlain's friendship. Champlain and two French settlers paddled south into

Iroquois territory with about 60 of his Aboriginal allies.

Near Lake Champlain, they met 200 Iroquois paddling toward them. The Iroquois beached their canoes and quickly built a fort. Champlain's side lashed their canoes together for safety, but stayed on the water. All night, they hurled insults at each other. The next morning, the French allies went ashore and

the battle began. That day was a great victory for the Algonkin, the Montagnais, and their French friends. The following year, Champlain helped them to defeat another group of Iroquois near the mouth of the Richelieu River. After that, the Iroquois made friends with the English who had settled to the south.

By joining in battle against the Iroquois, the French won the friendship of the Algonkin, the Huron, and the Montagnais. But of course this placed the French in bitter conflict with the Iroquois, making them enemies for almost 100 years.

In 1615, Champlain set out on a long canoe trip to visit his Huron allies. With Algonkin guides, he travelled up the Ottawa River, along the French River, and into Georgian Bay. From there, he turned into Huronia, the homeland of the Huron. Champlain drew maps of the areas he explored.

While in Huronia, he was asked to join a raid on the Huron's enemies. The plan was to attack the Iroquois who were south of Lake Ontario near Syracuse. The Huron were confident that with the help of Champlain and his guns, called **arquebuses**, they would win. The attack was a dismal failure. Even with European guns, the Huron could not destroy the fortified Iroquois village. Many of the attackers were killed. Champlain was wounded in the leg by an arrow and had to be carried back to the canoes. The Huron refused to transport Champlain back to Quebec. Perhaps they were thinking that they wouldn't have the protection of his guns on their return trip. Champlain was forced to spend the whole winter among the Huron. During this time, he continued exploring and learning a great deal about the Huron. In 1613, he wrote about his adventures in a book called *Voyages*. Champlain did not return to Quebec until June 1616.

Champlain making a portage on his expedition to Huronia. His life was devoted to making the settlement at Quebec a success. He died in Quebec on Christmas Day 1635.

Samuel de Champlain
c. 1567–1635

Samuel de Champlain, the "father of New France," was born around 1567 in the town of Brouage, a seaport on France's west coast. A sailor, he also came to be respected as a talented navigator and mapmaker.

After Champlain helped found the French settlement in Acadia, the French authorities put him in charge of founding a French settlement on the St. Lawrence. This new settlement, called Quebec, gave the French a better location from which to participate in the fur trade.

In the early fur-trading society of New France, Champlain was known for his courage, strength of character, persistence, and determination. Despite many hardships and setbacks, he was confident that New France would become a thriving settlement. Besides working to develop the young colony, Champlain also made lasting alliances with a number of Aboriginal nations in the region such as the Montagnais and the Huron.

At the age of 43, on a return to France, Champlain married a 12-year-old girl, Hélène Boullé. Their marriage was not a happy one, and they spent long periods of time apart. She was with him in Canada only between 1620 and 1624.

When the French regained control of Quebec from the British in 1633, Champlain worked hard to turn that settlement into a self-sufficient farming community rather than just a fur-trading post. He had a vision of New France as a full-fledged colony that would grow and prosper. Champlain died on Christmas Day 1635, living only long enough to see the beginnings of this development. However, by then he had already seen the colony through its most difficult early days. Thanks in large part to his confidence and devotion, it would become the important and prosperous settlement he had imagined. Centuries later, we still look to Champlain as a Canadian hero and one of our country's founders.

1. What kinds of things might Champlain have told his wife when he returned from his travels?

2. Based on what you know about Champlain, make a list of words that would describe what kind of person he was. Then, write a short character sketch that describes him.

Activities

Understanding Concepts

1. Start a personal dictionary of key words. Add new words as you encounter them.
   a) Divide a page of your notebook into two columns. Make the column on the left narrower than the column on the right. Title the column on the left "Word" and the column on the right "Meaning."
   b) In the left column, write the key word. In the right column, write the meaning of the word or draw a sketch of it. Try to write the definition in your own words.

   Start your dictionary with the following words.

compass	astrolabe	main idea
brainstorming	barter	culture
scurvy	arquebus	supporting detail
wet method	dry method	

2. Using the maps on pages 4 and 6, describe the settlement patterns of
   a) the Mi'kmaq
   b) the Haudenosaunee (Iroquois)
   c) the Huron
   d) the Algonkin
   e) the Montagnais (Innu)
   f) the French
   g) the English and the Dutch

3. Identify these places and locate them on a map of Canada.
   a) the bay where Cartier made the first exchange of furs with Aboriginal people
   b) the place where the French set up a huge cross
   c) the Aboriginal village near Quebec City
   d) the Aboriginal village near Montreal
   e) the second site of de Monts' settlement

4. Why were the Europeans looking for a shorter route from Europe to Asia? What were the advantages of finding this route?

5. List the reasons why each of Jacques Cartier's voyages was important.

6. Explain how European fishing trips to the east coast eventually led to the development of the fur trade.

Digging Deeper

7. **MAP STUDY** On a blank map, trace the major voyages of discovery of the Spanish, English, Portuguese, and French explorers in North America between 1492 and 1541.

8. **THINK/DISCUSS** What were the advantages and the disadvantages of the French alliances with the Algonkin, Montagnais, and Huron?

9. **RESEARCH/ROLE-PLAY** Imagine you are an early settler at Quebec or Port Royal. List the challenges and problems you might face. Research how these challenges were met. Role-play the experience of a settler trying to solve the problems.

10. **CREATE** Make a model of Champlain's Habitation at Quebec. Explain to your classmates the purpose and function of all the parts.

Making New Connections

11. **COMPARE** Conduct research to find out what the first American astronauts did when they landed on the moon in 1969. Compare their actions to what Cartier did when he landed in Gaspé.

12. **WRITE/ROLE-PLAY**
    a) Imagine that you are one of Donnacona's sons. Cartier has brought you back to France. Describe how you feel and what you will do.
    b) Imagine you are the king of France. Make a list of questions you would ask Donnacona's sons. With a partner, role-play the first meeting between the king and Donnacona's sons.

13. **RESEARCH** Research the reasons for the decline of cod fishing off the coast of Newfoundland in the 1990s. Report to the class what action governments and scientists are taking to solve the problem and how successful they have been to date.

Chapter 2

Fur Traders and Missionaries

The Beaver

The United States has the eagle as its emblem. England has the bulldog. Russia has the bear. Canada has the beaver.

Without the beaver, there would have been no fur trade. Long before the Europeans arrived, the Aboriginal peoples were trapping beaver for their own use. During the winter months, they kept warm by wrapping themselves in their beaver robes, made of six or eight beaver pelts sewn together. A beaver robe was worn with the coarse side of the fur on the outside and the smooth, downy under-fur against the skin. The coarse outer fur soon wore off, while the inside became somewhat greasy with sweat. These beaver pelts were known as **castor gras** (greasy). They were especially valuable to the French. Since the outer hairs had worn off and the under-fur was already matted, the pelts were ready to be made into items such as hats.

The other type of beaver pelt was called **castor sec** (dry). It was trapped and traded without having been worn for a few seasons. It was not as valuable to the French because it was not ready to be used. The fine under-fur had to be scraped off and then wet and crushed until it was matted together to make a material like thick, wet cardboard. Only after all this work was done could the pelts be dried and shaped into hats.

The beaver is an emblem of Canada. It appears on the nickel.

Predicting
1. Why is the beaver recognized as an emblem of Canada?
2. Why was the beaver so important in Canada's early history?
3. How did the quest for beaver help to open up this country?

Skilled Hunters

The Aboriginal peoples were expert hunters. They knew how to use the plentiful resources of the environment. They hunted deer, moose, bear, muskrat, wolf, fox, otter, marten, seal, and of course the beaver. The beaver became the most valuable fur to trade with the French.

A traveller to New France described the different ways the Aboriginals killed beaver:

- Some hunters built a simple trap with a heavy log balanced at the end of a stick. The traps were baited with food. When the animal began to eat, the movement brought the log crashing down on its head.
- Other hunters trapped beaver by breaking open their dams and draining their ponds. The animals were killed with bows and arrows as they tried to flee.
- In winter, nets were placed near beaver lodges in holes chopped in the ice. When the hunter broke into the top of the lodge, the escaping animal swam into the nets. It was killed swiftly with a blow to the head. The hunter had to act quickly because the beaver could gnaw through the net in seconds. It could also bite right through a hunter's arm with its sharp teeth.

The Aboriginal peoples considered beaver meat very good to eat and they prized its thick warm pelt. The pelts could be fashioned into robes for the winter or made into blankets. The four large teeth of the beaver were useful for woodworking. They made excellent tools for
scraping and shaping wooden bowls.

The Aboriginal Peoples and the Fur Trade

The Aboriginals played an essential role in the fur trade. The Huron were especially important since they acted as middle traders between the French and other Aboriginal groups. They were well situated to do this since they lived in the region of the Great Lakes west of the St. Lawrence River. In their birchbark canoes, the Huron travelled north and west on the lakes and rivers. They visited distant Aboriginal nations, such as the Cree, who lived far away from the French settlements along the St. Lawrence. In exchange for European knives and blankets, the Huron brought back furs for the French.

A brigade of birchbark fur trade canoes glides through the fog on the way to Fort William. Examine the picture carefully to look for ways that these canoes differ from modern canoes.

Birchbark Canoes

Long before the Europeans arrived, the Aboriginals used logs, animal skins, and tree bark to make boats. In eastern Canada, they built birchbark canoes for transportation. The word "canoe" actually comes from the Spanish and Haitian word *canoa*. The word was carried throughout North America by Europeans who used it to describe Aboriginal boats, both birchbark and dugout. Each Aboriginal group had its own name for these boats. For example, the Cree called the boat a *cîmân*.

The Aboriginal peoples were experts at paddling and handling canoes, even through dangerous rapids. They travelled the waterways in canoes to fish, hunt, and trade. The birchbark canoe was especially useful because it was

- large enough to transport big game or the personal belongings of people on the move
- seaworthy in the rough waters of the Great Lakes
- easy to handle in the swirling waters of the Ottawa River
- light enough to be carried when necessary

Birchbark canoes played an important part in the fur trade that developed with the French. Precious cargoes of furs were delivered in

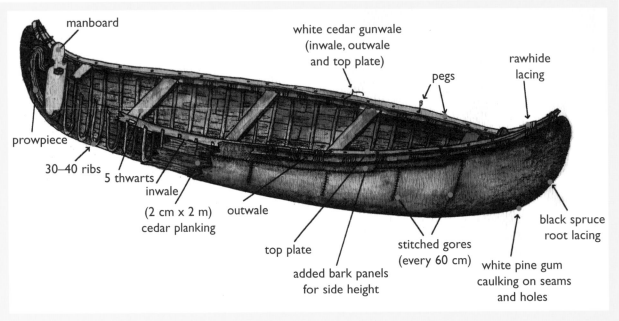

The northeastern Native-American birchbark canoe was just over 3.5 m long. It was made from the *Betula papyrifera* tree, which had a circumference of about 2 m.

Did You Know…?

- One person could carry a small canoe upside down on his or her shoulders on a portage.
- A canoe placed on its side at night could be used as a shelter.
- Aboriginal people always carried a supply of spruce gum to repair any damage to canoes caused by rocks or sunken logs.
- The French adapted the Aboriginal technology to carry freight for the fur trade and for military purposes. They built canoes up to 11 m long.
- A freight canoe loaded with cargo could cover 140 km a day with the current.
- Freight canoes could carry a crew of six to twelve.
- The French established a canoe factory at Trois-Rivières.

canoes to the trading posts along the St. Lawrence River. Later on, Europeans adopted this Aboriginal method of transportation. The French learned to handle the birchbark canoe on the rivers of North America. Birchbark canoes took French fur traders deep into the heart of the continent.

Merchants of the Fur Trade

There was a large market in Europe for furs. By the end of the 16th century, the wide-brimmed beaver fur hat had come into fashion. The rich liked coats, hats, and trims made from fur. This fashion trend increased the demand for beaver pelts. European countries competed to supply the growing market. It was not long before fur traders flooded into North America.

French merchants began to organize fur-trading companies. They built trading posts and warehouses in Quebec and Ville-Marie (later Montreal). These towns were ideally located along the St. Lawrence River, the major highway of the fur trade. The intense competition for the furs reduced their profits. The supply of furs became more available and rivals strove to undercut each other. The French king supported the French companies by granting them fur trade **monopolies**. This meant that a company received exclusive rights to the fur trade in a given area. In exchange, the company was expected to secure land for the French and participate in missionary work.

The most famous company was known as The Company of One Hundred Associates. It was given the fur trade monopoly for all of New France from 1627 to 1663. In return, the merchants were supposed to bring in settlers and build up the colony. However, the merchants were only interested in trading and making a profit. They did little to encourage settlement. By 1663, the actual population of New France was only 2500.

The merchants imported shiploads of clothes, tools, blankets, guns, gunpowder, and brandy to trade for furs. Guns were a popular

Netsurfer

You can view pictures of how to build a canoe at
http://collections.ic.gc.ca/canoe/vtour/a.htm
Click on the pictures to make them larger.
See what Champlain had to say about the birchbark canoe at
www.mvnf.muse.digital.ca/expos/champlain/expl3_en.html

trade item with the Aboriginal peoples. Guns made hunting easier and this meant there were more furs to trade the next year. Brandy caused serious problems. The Aboriginals were not used to European alcohol and its effects. The Church in New France urged the traders to stop providing the Aboriginals with brandy. However, the merchants were afraid of losing their customers. They feared that without brandy, the Aboriginal peoples might decide to trade their furs with the English and Dutch further south. The French decided to continue selling brandy to the Aboriginals.

The merchants were among the wealthiest and most powerful people in New France. They took risks, but they were usually paid back with enormous profits from selling the furs at much higher prices back in France.

Table of Exchange in New France

12 beaver pelts buy 1 gun.
4 beaver pelts buy 4.5 L of brandy.
2 beaver pelts buy 10 fishhooks.
1 beaver pelt buys 0.25 kg of glass beads.
8 muskrat equal 1 beaver pelt.
1 bearskin equals 2 beaver pelts.

Tech Link

Building a Birchbark Canoe

The materials needed to build a birchbark canoe were all close at hand in the eastern woodlands—birchbark, white cedar, spruce roots, and spruce gum.

Step 1 A huge piece of birchbark is peeled and stripped from a tree.

Step 2 Cedar poles are used to make the canoe gunwales (the upper edges of the sides of the vessel). The inwales are lashed together at the ends with babiche (animal sinew). A notched stick spreads the inwales.

Step 3 The inwales are centred on the bark. The bark is bent up around the inwales inside a frame of poles. The frame helps to bend the bark and shape the canoe.

Step 4 Tucks are made in the bow and the stern. With a sharpened bone, holes are bored for laces. The tucks are secured with babiche and the gunwales are sewn into place with split spruce roots.

Step 5 Young branches are bent and used as ribs for the craft. They are secured between the gunwales. Thwarts (seats) are cut and lashed together with babiche. Thin slats of cedar are laid on the birchbark for the floor.

Step 6 The ends of the canoe are clamped closed and sewn with babiche. Spruce gum is boiled. Then, all seams and lacing holes are painted with the gum to make the canoe watertight.

1. Why was the canoe an important invention for the Aboriginals? For the Europeans?
2. The canoe is often seen as an important Canadian symbol. Explain why.
3. Which Aboriginal groups used dugout canoes? How were they made?

Large sheets of birchbark are laid inside a frame of poles.

Impact of the Fur Trade on Aboriginal Peoples

Aboriginal peoples such as the Mi'kmaq and the Montagnais lived close to the trading posts at Tadoussac and Quebec. These groups became so involved with the fur trade business that they no longer had time to make their own tools and weapons or produce enough food to survive. For them, European technology soon replaced tradition. As they came to rely more and more on European goods, they gave up many of their cultural traditions.

In the early years of the fur trade, the Huron were very self-sufficient. They did not become dependent on the French for some time. The Huron population was large and they lived far away from the French trading posts. They could not carry large quantities of European goods back to their villages. So, they made use of some European technology but continued to produce traditional tools and weapons.

As the fur trade expanded, competition for the pelts increased. Because of overtrapping, the animals became scarcer. This led to war between rival Aboriginal groups. By 1649, the Iroquois in New York were completely dependent on their trade with the Dutch. They desperately needed a new source of furs and hoped to gain access to the Huron trapping areas. The Iroquois attacked Huron trading parties and villages, killing many Huron.

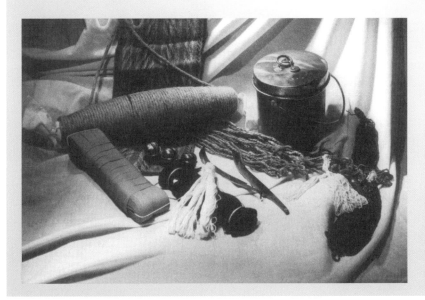

Furs were exchanged for a variety of European goods such as copper kettles, skeins of beads, curved metal knives, black and white linen thread, tobacco, and trade sashes. Aboriginal traders were knowledgeable and would not accept inferior goods.

The Coureurs de Bois

After the Iroquois attacks of 1649, the Huron were no longer able to fill the role of intermediary between the French and Aboriginal peoples. Some of the French decided to go west and north themselves to collect furs from the Aboriginal peoples in the interior. Many young men jumped at the chance for adventure. They were called **coureurs de bois,** which means "runners of the woods." They made friends with the Aboriginal peoples. They learned hunting and canoeing skills from the men, and bought their furs. The Aboriginal women also worked with the traders. On trading trips, they were responsible for making the food, setting up camp, carrying goods around the rapids, and mending clothes and canoes. Often, the coureurs de bois lived with the Aboriginals for months at a time, building up trust. Sometimes, they married Aboriginal women and became part of their communities, learning to speak Aboriginal languages. When the Iroquois threat discouraged

Aboriginal peoples from bringing in their furs, the coureurs de bois took charge. These daring men transported cargo to and from the interior.

Life for the coureurs de bois was often lonely and risky and sometimes violent. As a rule, they travelled in threes, hunting for their food along the way. There are stories of starving coureurs de bois having to boil and eat their own moccasins when game was scarce!

There were 600 coureurs de bois in New France by 1678. They played a vital role in the fur trade. Many of them were independent entrepreneurs who became skilled at business. They acted as interpreters for both Aboriginal peoples and merchants. They made friendly contact with the Aboriginals and were trusted by them. This contact guaranteed a steady supply of furs for French trading posts. Always on the lookout for more furs, the coureurs de bois explored and opened up the interior of New France.

Eventually, the government and the Church decided that the coureurs de bois should stay at home and develop the settlements. So, the governor passed a new law. All traders would have to have permits, but only a limited number of permits were given out. Those traders who had trading permits were called **voyageurs**. However, the coureurs de bois continued to operate, even without permits. They knew that if the Aboriginals could not trade their furs with the French, they would go to the English instead.

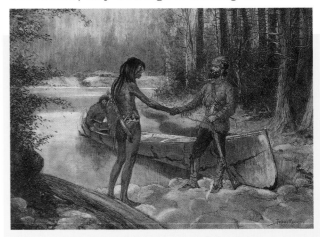

Coureurs de bois were some of the first Europeans to meet Aboriginal peoples.

Fast Forward

Economics of the Fur Trade

In 1670, the British founded the Hudson's Bay Company. The new rival company threatened the French fur trade operating out of Montreal. The Aboriginal peoples could now choose who to trade with—the French or the English. They could compare **market values**, or the price the buyer was willing to pay. Sometimes, by threatening to sell to the rival traders, the Aboriginal peoples could obtain better terms. At times, the Crown would interfere with the law of **supply and demand** by controlling the quantity of furs available and fixing prices for certain furs at a set rate. However, New France was able to hold its position in the fur trade in spite of the competition. It remained the leading supplier of furs to Europe.

By the start of the 18th century, too many furs were reaching Europe. This created a massive **surplus**. The supply was much greater than the demand. As a result, prices for furs fell rapidly. The French government temporarily shut down the fur trade. The colonists were shocked by this action and resisted the government's decision. The two sides reached a compromise—fur trading was allowed to continue, but at a much slower rate. In time, the fur trade expanded again and grew larger than ever.

Later on, after the British conquest of New France, the North West Company and the Hudson's Bay Company competed for furs in the West. Hundreds of new trading posts were built. But the high rate of growth was not sustainable. In 1821, the two companies entered a **merger**, combining their operations.

Profile

Etienne Brûlé
c. 1592–1633

Etienne Brûlé travelled to many places Europeans had never been before. His adventurous spirit remains legendary to this day.

Etienne Brûlé was one of the first coureurs de bois in New France. In 1610, when he was only 17 years old, he begged Samuel de Champlain to allow him to go and live with the Aboriginals. Champlain agreed and Brûlé went to live among the Huron. In exchange, a Huron boy went on a trip to France with Champlain. Brûlé was asked to find out more about the Aboriginals: the areas where they lived, their language, and their customs. Any information he could learn would be vitally important to the French.

Brûlé was a trailblazer. He was the first European to travel up the Ottawa River and portage overland to Georgian Bay. Later, he acted as an interpreter and a guide when Champlain visited Huronia. Without Brûlé, Champlain would have had difficulty charting and mapping the interior of New France. Sometimes, Brûlé worked for the fur merchants of New France. They paid him to make sure that the Aboriginals brought their furs to the French traders.

Brûlé broke with Champlain in 1629 when England and France were at war. Brûlé was accused of siding with the British and helping them capture Quebec for a short time.

Brûlé faced danger and death many times. Once, he was captured by some Seneca, who were enemies of the Huron. He avoided death by persuading them that an approaching thunderstorm was a sign that his life should be spared. He managed to find his way to safety, through hundreds of kilometres of wilderness, to the territory of the Huron.

Eventually, the Huron turned against Brûlé. No one knows why. Perhaps he insulted them or betrayed them in some way. In the summer of 1633, he was killed by the people he had lived with for years.

---

1. What characteristics and traits made Brûlé a trailblazer?
2. What would other people in the colony, for example, fur merchants, the habitants, Champlain, the king of France, and the Huron, have thought about Brûlé?

The Missionaries in New France

On the north shore of the St. Lawrence River, you can still see the oldest church in Canada. The tiny chapel is found at Tadoussac. Jesuit priests built it for the fur traders and the Aboriginal peoples.

Religion was always a strong force in New France. One of the most important groups of settlers was the Roman Catholic priests and nuns who came as missionaries.

Duties of the Priest

Priests played an important role in the settlements of New France. The colonists needed priests to tend to their spiritual needs. The priests baptized babies, prayed for the sick, conducted Mass, and buried the dead. Priests also looked after more practical matters. Often, a priest was the most educated person in the community. Settlers who could not read or write asked him to draw up wills and record business dealings. The priest was also in charge of registering all births and deaths.

The first **missionaries** arrived from France in 1625. They were **Jesuits**—members of a religious community known as the Society of Jesus. The missionaries believed it was their duty to convert the Aboriginal peoples to Christianity. Most of the people in France at that time were Catholic. The Jesuits were sent to New France under the command of the king. They played a very important role in helping to found the settlements of New France.

In 1635, the Jesuits established the only college in New France where the sons of settlers could be educated. The next year, there were 20 boys studying there. The Jesuits encouraged two orders of nuns to come to Quebec in 1639. The nuns opened a school for girls and a hospital.

Some of the first missionaries travelled on foot or by canoe into the wilderness of Huronia. Being a priest in New France was neither easy nor comfortable. A priest's life was filled with personal danger and many hardships. The priests worked and lived among the Huron. In each village, they built a church and held services. The Huron referred to the Jesuits as the "Black Robes" because of the long, black priests' robes. The missionaries taught, preached, and visited the Huron longhouses.

Jesuit priests arrive at Quebec in 1625.

Huron Religion

Some Aboriginal groups had special individuals who would perform religious ceremonies for the entire community, in a role similar to that of a Roman Catholic priest. However, the Huron had no one in such a role, nor did they build special altars or buildings for religious use. Rather, religion was part of all their activities. They practised a wide range of ceremonies and rituals. For example, during the hunt, they would not give the bones of their kill to their dogs or let any of the fat from the dead animal drip into the fire. They believed this would appease the soul of the dead animal. The Huron believed that their dreams contained messages. If those messages were correctly interpreted, they could help the individual make good choices in life and avoid negative situations.

Jesuit Relations

Some of the most valuable sources of information about New France are the Jesuit *Relations*. Every year, the Jesuits sent a report back to France. These reports are primary-source material about New France. They contain first-hand accounts of the Jesuit work in the Huron villages and of some of the hardships facing the missionaries. The *Relations* also describe the fur trade in detail. The accounts in *Relations* encouraged people to leave France and seek new lives in Canada.

They tried to learn the Huron language and to win the friendship of the Huron with kindness. But progress was slow, and, initially, very few Huron became Christians.

Conflicts with Aboriginal Culture

Although some missionaries respected the Aboriginals' culture, many tried to change Aboriginal traditions and religious practices. Before contact with Europeans, ceremonies and rituals were an everyday part of many Aboriginals' lives. The missionaries wanted to convert the Aboriginal peoples to Christianity. To many, this meant convincing them to give up these traditional rituals. They wanted to assimilate and convert the Aboriginal peoples to European ways.

The conversion of some Aboriginal people created conflict within Aboriginal communities. Some Christian converts wanted to move away from traditional behaviours, while others wanted to preserve their culture.

What Direction for New France?

In the early years, the fur trade was the most important activity in the colony of New France. Fur traders made money from fur trading, and also added territory to the French empire through their explorations into the wilderness.

Fast Forward

Aboriginal Religion Today

The division between Aboriginals who want to move away from traditional behaviours and those who want to retain their traditions and beliefs persists to this day. Some Aboriginal people see Christian outreach work as an unwelcome interference in their lives, while others are devout Christians.

Today, Aboriginal peoples are again practising their rituals and ceremonies openly. It is seen as a way to revitalize their culture and retain a link with their history. Traditional rituals have been adapted to address their present needs and concerns, and some Aboriginals incorporate both Christian and Aboriginal religious practices into their worship.

Although the fur trade expanded rapidly, the population grew very slowly. Even a hundred years after Cartier, there were no more than 500 people living in all of New France. The fur-trading companies were supposed to bring in shiploads of new settlers and help them get established. But the companies really were not interested in settlement. Perhaps they worried that settlers would clear the wilderness and damage the habitat of the fur-bearing animals. Settlement would mean less profits.

The colonists who did arrive complained that the companies did nothing to protect them from Iroquois attacks. In France, stories about the hardships of settling in New France discouraged others from moving there. To many people, it seemed better to face poverty at home than to risk their lives in the wilderness.

The French government would soon have to make a decision. What direction should the new colony take? Who should be in charge—the fur traders or the settlers?

Profiles

Marie de l'Incarnation
1599–1672

Marie de l'Incarnation was one of the first Ursuline nuns to arrive in New France. She spoke out strongly about the wrongs she observed in New France, especially trading brandy for furs.

Marie de l'Incarnation was the daughter of a baker in Tours, France. When she was 19 years old, her husband died and she was left to raise her baby son on her own. While her son was growing up, she managed her brother-in-law's transportation business. She decided to enter a convent after she read about the missionary work taking place in New France.

In 1639, Marie de l'Incarnation travelled to New France and founded two convents for the education of French and Aboriginal girls. She taught them reading, writing, housekeeping, and Christianity. Throughout her life, she wrote thousands of letters to people in France to inform them about Aboriginal customs and the Catholic missions. Her letters generated a lot of interest in the settlements and convinced many French people to move to the colony. They have also taught us a great deal about life in New France at that time.

Marie de l'Incarnation played an important diplomatic role in the colony. It was customary for Aboriginal peoples to exchange children as tokens of goodwill and friendship. By taking Aboriginal girls into her schools, Marie de l'Incarnation was viewed as participating in this tradition. As a result, she was able to establish ties with the girls' kinship groups. She also wrote dictionaries in Huron and Algonkian. These dictionaries helped to improve communications between the French and Aboriginal peoples.

Jeanne Mance
1606–1673

Jeanne Mance was a capable and devoted woman. Born in 1606, she came to feel that she was called by God to serve in Canada. Although she had no money of her own, she persuaded some wealthy women in France to support her.

Two years after the Ursuline nuns came to Quebec, Jeanne

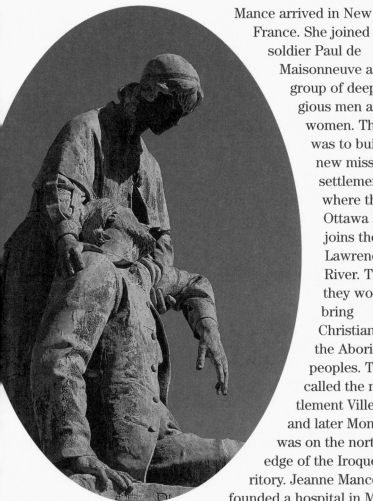

Jeanne Mance returned to France several times to raise money for her hospital. She also encouraged settlers to come and live in Montreal. Over the years, she watched with pride as the town she helped to found grew steadily.

Mance arrived in New France. She joined the soldier Paul de Maisonneuve and a group of deeply religious men and women. Their goal was to build a new missionary settlement where the Ottawa River joins the St. Lawrence River. There, they would bring Christianity to the Aboriginal peoples. They called the new settlement Ville-Marie, and later Montreal. It was on the northern edge of the Iroquois territory. Jeanne Mance also founded a hospital in Montreal with the money that the wealthy women in France had given her. The hospital, the Hôtel-Dieu, opened on 8 October 1642.

At first, the Iroquois were opposed to the building of a settlement in their territory. They continually attacked supply boats travelling between Montreal and Quebec. At times, it was not safe to leave the **palisades** of Montreal to work in the fields. The palisades were fences made of strong, pointed wooden stakes. While some colonists tended the gardens, others had to stand by with guns for protection. During the first attack in 1643, several colonists were wounded and some were killed. Almost as soon as the Hôtel-Dieu was built, there were wounded patients for Jeanne Mance to care for. In the years that followed, Jeanne Mance continued to look after the sick, tending to both French and Aboriginal people.

At the time of her death, Montreal had a population of 1500. It would soon become an important fur trade centre in New France.

Netsurfer

This website shows a reconstructed convent hospital. It also explains the role of nuns in providing medical care.
www.cmcc.muse.digital.ca/cmc/cmceng/canpleng.html
Click on #11.

Marguerite Bourgeoys
1620–1700

The Congregation de Notre-Dame, founded by Marguerite Bourgeoys, still exists in Montreal.

In 1653, a young nun named Marguerite Bourgeoys arrived in Montreal. She had heard about the needs of the people of New France and thought she could help. For the next 47 years, she worked tirelessly to educate both Aboriginal and French girls in the colony.

Her first school at Montreal had a humble beginning. Classes were held in a stable loaned to her by Paul de Maisonneuve. Here, she taught girls cooking, sewing, needlework, and a little reading and writing. These were very useful skills since women in New France had to be able to make almost everything they needed. At night, her pupils slept in the loft of the stable.

Marguerite Bourgeoys founded a group of nuns called the Congregation de Notre-Dame. These nuns were not **cloistered**. That is, they were not required to stay inside their convent as most nuns were at that time. They went out into the community to help others. They travelled along the St. Lawrence by foot, horseback, and canoe to visit the colonists.

Marguerite Bourgeoys and her nuns looked after orphan girls who arrived in New France. She helped them to find husbands and get established in the colony. She also encouraged other women from the colony and from France to join in her work. Marguerite Bourgeoys died at the age of 80, but the order of nuns she founded still exists today.

1. What personality characteristics did these three women have in common?
2. How did they influence the development of the fledgling colony? How might life have been different had they not arrived in New France?
3. What do you think each of these women would most like to be remembered for? Explain your answer.

Culture Link

Picture Gallery
Sainte-Marie-Among-the-Hurons

The work of Jesuit missionaries in Huronia began in 1626. They went to live among the Huron, staying in their villages. The villages were scattered around Sainte-Marie, which was the headquarters of French missionary activity. Sainte-Marie consisted of 20 buildings surrounded by stone walls and a palisade.

From the Aboriginals, the priests learned how to grow corn, beans, and squash. They learned which wild berries and fruits were edible. Cattle and pigs were brought to the fort by canoe all the way from Quebec. Fish and game added variety to their diet. In a small garden, they grew leaf and root vegetables from seeds imported from France.

The priests at Sainte-Marie were assisted by **donnés**. These were men who helped the Jesuits with their work. They dedicated their lives to working for the mission. In exchange, they were given food, clothing, shelter, and protection, although no wages.

The community included a blacksmith, carpenter, tailor, surgeon, and cook. The inhabitants had to make or grow almost everything needed to keep the community alive. They also fed the Aboriginal people who converted to Christianity and joined the mission.

Netsurfer

Two sites with information about Sainte-Marie-Among-the-Hurons are
www.sfo.com/~denglish/
wynaks/wn_stmar.htm
and
www.saintemarieamong
thehurons.on.ca
These sites will help you find out more about Sainte-Marie and plan a possible field trip to Huronia.

Mass is celebrated in the reconstructed church at Saint-Marie-Among-the-Hurons. At dawn on the morning of 16 March 1649, a thousand Iroquois attacked the mission village of Saint-Ignace. Saint-Louis, 5 km away, was captured a few hours later. Two Jesuit priests, Jean de Brébeuf and Gabriel Lalemant, were put to death. Thousands of Huron were killed and their villages destroyed. Sainte-Marie, the main mission station, was not destroyed by the Iroquois. The Jesuits themselves burned it down before they fled with their Huron allies to nearby Christian Island in Georgian Bay.

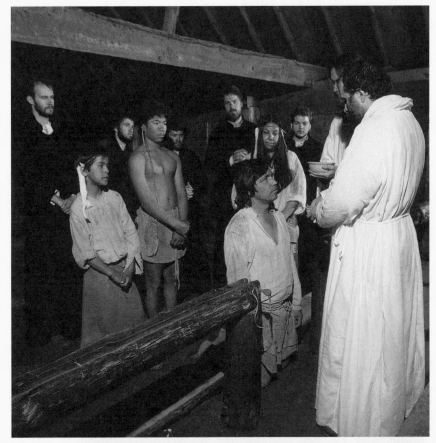

Attached to the mission was a compound for Huron who had become Christians. They lived in Huron longhouses. Sainte-Marie's hospital was also in this area, so the Aboriginal peoples had easy access to it. A 4 m palisade separated the Christian Huron from the non-Christian Huron. Huron visitors used Sainte-Marie like a hotel. Many came for a few days to observe the French and to take religious instruction, and then moved on.

1. Why was this famous fortress-mission important to the development of New France even though it existed for only nine years?
2. How did interaction between the Jesuits and the Huron change both groups?

Profile

St. Jean de Brébeuf 1593–1649

Of all the Jesuit priests in Huronia, Father Jean de Brébeuf was the most popular. He was a strong man who stood 200 cm tall. He spent 23 years in Huronia and founded five missions. He loved the Huron and was totally devoted to them.

Jean de Brébeuf was born in Normandy, France in 1593. As a young Jesuit in New France, he travelled 1290 km by canoe to work with the Huron at Saint-Ignace. It was six years before he gained his first adult convert to Christianity.

Brébeuf learned the Huron language. He wrote a Huron dictionary and a grammar book to help other missionaries with the language. He also wrote a Christmas hymn in the Huron language.

When European diseases killed thousands of Aboriginal people, the Jesuits were blamed. In 1637, Brébeuf watched the Huron tear down his crosses and kill fellow Jesuits. But he endured it all and eventually won back their respect.

In 1649, the Iroquois attacked the Huron at Saint-Ignace. Jean de Brébeuf, along with Gabriel Lalemant, was tied to a stake and put to death.

In 1954, an archaeologist excavated a section of the church floor at Sainte-Marie. He discovered the gravesite of Jean de Brébeuf. A pattern of nails formed the shape of a very large coffin. There was a small iron plaque bearing this inscription:

P. Jean de Brébeuf
Bruslé par les Iroquois
le 17 de mars l'an
1649

It seems likely that the bodies of Brébeuf and Lalemant were retrieved from Saint-Ignace and buried at Sainte-Marie. The plaque is now on display in the Sainte-Marie museum.

1. What were Brébeuf's greatest challenges and how did he deal with them?
2. Why is Brébeuf a memorable figure in Canadian history?

Skill Building: Using a Historical Document

Imagine detectives trying to solve a murder. They have to examine the crime scene and look for clues or evidence. One of the best sources of evidence would be an eyewitness—somebody who saw exactly what happened. An eyewitness can give a first-hand account.

Historians call first-hand evidence, such as an eyewitness report, a **primary source**. Examples of primary sources for the historian are items such as maps or diaries prepared by people who were alive at the time of the event. Old newspapers, sketches, census records, and letters are other examples of primary sources. Primary sources help historians to determine what a real person in history was thinking or feeling.

Detectives also consider information that is gathered from people who heard about the event from an eyewitness. These people were not present themselves at the scene of the crime, but they have some information about it. This is called second-hand information or a **secondary source**.

Historians also use secondary sources. Biographies or history books written about the past are secondary sources. A book written today about the early explorers of North America is a secondary source. Many history books, like this textbook, use secondary information from other books to tell their stories.

Sorting It All Out

Imagine you are a historian studying the fur trade in New France. To get an accurate picture of what happened, you have to study both primary and secondary sources.

Test Yourself!

In your notebook, make two columns. Label one "Primary Sources" and the other "Secondary Sources." Place the items in the following list under the correct headings:
a) *The Fur Trade in New France*—a television special
b) a diary account by a Jesuit priest, dated 1526
c) a newspaper article written 100 years ago
d) a voyageur's song about the fur trade
e) a Huron legend passed down from generation to generation
f) a painting of a hunting camp by Champlain
g) Chapter 2 of this book
h) a word-of-mouth description by a descendant of a fur trader about the fur trade in New France

Key Steps

Here are some steps to follow when you examine a historical document.

1. Read the document carefully.

2. Decide what event in history the author is talking about.

3. Think about whether you are reading a primary or secondary source. How do you know?

4. Find the author's name. Was the author present at the event? How soon after the event was it recorded? Is the author reliable? How do you know?

5. Look up the meaning of any words you do not understand.

6. Decide what information this source can give you. What questions does it answer?

7. Consider why this source is an important piece of information for the historian.

A Closer Examination

Now you are ready for a greater challenge. Read the following passage and then discuss the questions with your group.

Two merchant ships from France arrived in the St. Lawrence in June 1626. Charles Lalemant, a French priest, was present. He described what happened next at the fur fair.

These two ships bring all the merchandise which these Gentlemen use in trading with the Indians; that is to say, cloaks, blankets, nightcaps, hats, shirts, sheets, hatchets, iron arrow-heads, bodkins, swords, picks to break the ice in Winter, kettles, prunes, raisins, corn, peas, crackers or sea biscuits, and tobacco. In exchange for these the ships will carry back the hides of the moose, lynx, fox, otter, badgers, and muskrats; but they deal principally in beavers in which they find the greatest profit. I was told that one year they carried back as many as 22 000. The usual number for one year is 15 000.

The day of their arrival they erect their huts and the Indians arrive in their canoes. The second day the Indians hold a council and present their gifts. Gifts are always given when people visit each other. The French give presents then to the Indians. The third and fourth day the Indians trade and barter their furs for blankets, hatchets, kettles, capes, little glass beads, and many similar things. It is a pleasure to watch them during this trading. When it is over they take one more day for the feast and the dance. Early the next morning the Indians disappear like a flock of birds.

From Jesuit Relations

1. What was Charles Lalemant describing?

2. Do you think this is a reliable source of information? Why?

3. Describe the ceremonies that took place.

4. What goods were traded to the Aboriginals? List these under three headings: "Tools," "Clothing," and "Food."

5. What important piece of information about the beaver does this source provide?

6. Do you think the Aboriginal peoples were treated fairly in the trading situation? Explain your answer.

Activities

Understanding Concepts

1. Define the following terms and enter them in your personal dictionary.

coureur de bois	missionary	primary source
supply and demand	market value	castor gras
monopoly	surplus	secondary source
castor sec	voyageur	Jesuits
merger	cloistered	donné
palisade		

2. Explain the difference between *castor gras* and *castor sec*. Which was better and why?

3. Why were priests such important individuals in the lives of the settlers of New France?

4. What services did women of religious orders provide in New France?

Digging Deeper

5. **CREATE AND PRESENT** Divide the class into six groups. Create a bulletin board display of pictures and text to describe the importance to the fur trade of each of the following: the beaver, the Aboriginal peoples, fashions in Europe, the birchbark canoe, the coureurs de bois, and the merchants.

6. **WRITE** Imagine you are a coureur de bois living among the Huron. Describe
   • why you like this lifestyle
   • how you earn a living
   • some of your adventures in the wilderness
   • why some people object to the coureurs de bois
   • what you think is the contribution made by the coureurs de bois to New France

7. **RESEARCH/WRITE** Many of the French missionaries were killed doing their work. The church called these men "martyrs" because they were killed for holding on to their faith and their beliefs. Jean de Lande, Isaac Jogues, René Goupil, Antoine Daniel, Noel Chabanel, Charles Garnier, and Gabriel Lalemant were all martyr-saints. Conduct some research and write a profile of one of these men.

8. **WRITE** Imagine you are a Jesuit missionary living in Sainte-Marie-Among-the-Hurons. Write a letter to your family in France describing your experiences.

9. **ROLE-PLAY** Who should control New France—the fur traders or the settlers? Why? Imagine you are one of the following people in New France. Role-play an answer to this question.
   • a farmer
   • a fur merchant
   • a coureur de bois
   • an Ursuline nun
   • a Huron trader
   • a Jesuit priest

10. **WRITE** Write a newspaper article about a fur fair.

Making New Connections

11. **RESEARCH** At the end of the fur trade era, the beaver almost became extinct because of over-trapping. Find out what rules apply to the trapping of beaver today. What animals are presently on the endangered species list in Canada?

12. **RESEARCH** In 1649, most of the Huron villages were destroyed by the Iroquois. A few Huron escaped to Christian Island in Georgian Bay. In 1650, the Jesuits moved the group to a location near Quebec City called Lorette. Lorette is the only remaining Huron community in Canada. Conduct some research to find out how many Huron descendants live at Lorette. What are they doing to revive their language and culture?

13. **THINK/DISCUSS** Why were some young French settlers attracted to the Aboriginal way of life? Would you also find the way of life of a coureur de bois attractive? Explain.

14. **INVESTIGATE/FIELD TRIP** Plan and carry out a field trip to a historical site from the early French period in Canada. Sainte-Marie-Among-the-Hurons and Fort Frontenac are excellent examples of places you could visit.

The Crown Takes Charge

The Sun King

The diary of Louis XIV, King of France, might have contained the following entry:

Versailles, 1663

It is time to take control of that bothersome situation in New France. After all, I am the Sun King, ruler of France and all she possesses, and the centre of the universe. It is my royal right to take charge of everything that belongs to France—all my colonies, even tiny New France.

I am tired of hearing nothing but problems from that troublesome place. My agents tell me that it isn't growing fast enough—only 24 new settlers a year. That will never do! At that rate, it will take forever for the colony to be profitable for me. I have heard that the settlers are afraid of the Iroquois. Perhaps that is why so few want to settle there. Not only that, the Iroquois take the furs that are rightly mine!

Then there are the fur traders. They don't want farmers to settle the land since that would reduce the amount of trapping land. The traders cause all sorts of trouble with the few settlers who do go there. On top of it all, there are those greedy fur-trading merchants who only want to fill their own purses. They don't want any more settlers in New France either.

This problem will not go away by itself. New France is on its last legs. The colony is dying. I must do something and do it soon. I have already invested so much money; I am not prepared to give the place up. I want to build a great empire in New France, one that is worthy of me, the King of France.

During his 72-year-long reign, Louis XIV of France was an absolute monarch, which means that he held all political authority. He is said to have boasted "*L'état c'est moi*" ("I am the State") and associated himself with the sun, calling himself the Sun King.

Predicting
1. What options does the king have for improving the situation in New France?
2. What strategies would you recommend to the king for dealing with the problems in New France?
3. What might happen to New France if the problems don't get resolved?

Problems in New France

Jean-Baptiste Colbert has a problem. He is a powerful minister in the government of France. He controls the country's finances and is an advisor to the king on colonial matters. One day in 1663, he is called to King Louis XIV's palace at Versailles. The king is not happy. He has heard of the many problems in New France. Why are more French not moving to New France and taking advantage of the opportunities there? The king wants answers and he gives Colbert a task: Find a way to get New France under control and settled with people.

Skill Building: Solving Problems

Colbert now needs to find a solution to his problem. **Problem solving** may be defined as "what to do when you don't know what to do." Here is one problem-solving model that Colbert could follow. In Chapter 13, you will see how this process can be applied to making decisions.

1. Understand
What is the problem? What is known? What is not known?

2. Plan
Brainstorm a list of as many solutions as possible. For each solution, think about the advantages and disadvantages. What are the risks involved? What are the possible effects? Then, choose the best solution.

3. Act
Carry out the chosen plan.

4. Think Back
Was the solution reasonable? Was this the only solution?

Colbert and his officials begin to look for a solution. First, they need to understand the problem. This is what they know.
- Between 1608 and 1661, New France grew by an average of only 24 people each year.
- The fur-trading merchants are a problem. They are only interested in making money.
- There are very few farmers in New France because the merchants discourage farming.
- The colonists fear attack by the Iroquois.
- The fur trade is losing money. The number of furs has been reduced to a trickle because the Iroquois are intercepting cargo along the rivers.
- Officials in New France seem to be powerless to do anything.
- New France is on its last legs.

This is what is not known.
- Will the king agree to any plan Colbert comes up with?
- Can people be persuaded to go and settle in New France?

Colbert and his officials consider their options. They think about the advantages and disadvantages of various plans. Then, they make their recommendations to the king.
- The king should end the rule of The Company of One Hundred Associates.
- New France should be a royal colony.
- The colony should be governed by the king and his ministers.
- The king should provide money and settlers for New France.

The Royal Government in New France

King Louis XIV liked Colbert's plan. He decided to act. The Company of One Hundred Associates was now out and a new government was formed for New France.

There were three officials who acted on the king's behalf in New France—the governor, the bishop, and the intendant. The **governor** was responsible for the security of the colony. The **bishop's** job was to oversee churches, missions, hospitals, and schools. The **intendant** had the most important job. He had to look after the day-to-day operation of the colony. He was responsible for law and order, trade, industry, and transportation. The Sovereign Council assisted the three officials in their work. The members of the Council were appointed for five years. Lesser officials included local governors appointed from Montreal and Trois-Rivières.

There were also **seigneurs**, or landowners, who carried out the instructions of the king and the government. The king or governor granted large tracts of land to certain wealthy and important citizens. These land grants were called **seigneuries**. The seigneur parcelled out sections of the land to settlers known as **habitants**. This land-holding system was modelled on the system used in France. You will learn more about it in Chapter 4.

Jean Talon: The Great Intendant

The first intendant in New France was Jean Talon. He was one of the most remarkable officials ever sent out from France. He wasted no time in setting about his work.

Talon liked to see things for himself. When he first arrived at Quebec, he found a message waiting for him from the nuns. They wrote that they hoped he would protect them.

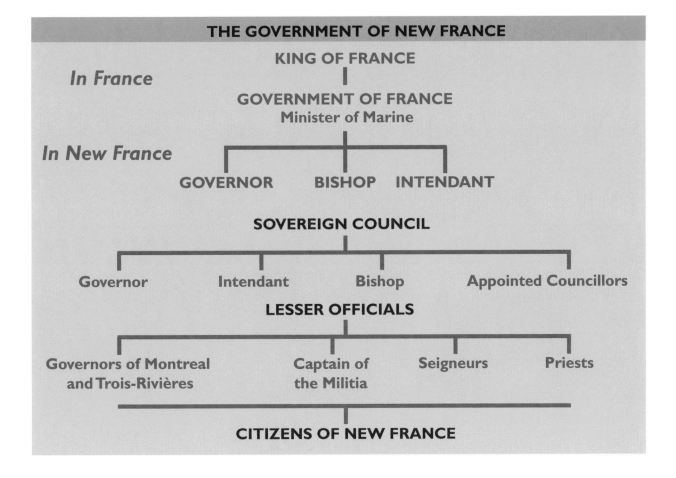

THE GOVERNMENT OF NEW FRANCE

In France

KING OF FRANCE

GOVERNMENT OF FRANCE
Minister of Marine

In New France

GOVERNOR   BISHOP   INTENDANT

SOVEREIGN COUNCIL

Governor   Intendant   Bishop   Appointed Councillors

LESSER OFFICIALS

Governors of Montreal and Trois-Rivières   Captain of the Militia   Seigneurs   Priests

CITIZENS OF NEW FRANCE

The Sovereign Council of New France met every Monday morning at the intendant's residence in Quebec. The Council included the three most powerful men in New France—the governor, the intendant, and the bishop. There were also five appointed councillors. They set the rules for the colony, passing a number of regulations. They also acted as a court.

Jean Talon visited settlers at home. What information would he learn from such visits?

That same day, a man called at the convent and introduced himself as the intendant's valet. He said he wanted to know what the nuns needed in the way of protection. The sisters quickly realized that their visitor was Talon himself. He often disguised himself and went from door to door asking questions and learning about living conditions in this manner. Likely, he did this so that the people wouldn't fear him and would be open with him. He wanted to find out why New France was not prospering.

Everywhere, Talon heard the same complaints. People were concerned about their safety. They lived with the constant fear of attack by the British and their Aboriginal allies, the Iroquois. They never knew if it was safe to go hunting or fishing, or even out into their fields. Talon listened to their concerns. He immediately wrote to the king requesting soldiers.

Barbe Duclos was an early hero of New France. In 1661, the Iroquois attacked and killed some settlers collecting firewood outside the settlement of Montreal. The French had forgotten to bring their weapons. Barbe Duclos quickly gathered the forgotten muskets and raced through the snow with them. Her courage allowed the remaining men to defend themselves.

A junior officer of the Carignan-Salières Regiment, which arrived from France. The regiment's uniform was a chestnut brown coat, brown breeches, and a black felt hat. The shoes could be worn on either foot.

Solving the Safety Problem

In 1665, Sieur de Tracy arrived from France. He brought about 1500 experienced soldiers of the Carignan-Salières Regiment with him. It was a happy day for the colonists when they saw soldiers arriving to protect them.

De Tracy constructed a chain of forts from the St. Lawrence River to Lake Champlain that would block the Iroquois' route into New France. Then in 1666, he marched with over 1000 armed soldiers into Iroquois territory. As they advanced on the Iroquois villages, they found them deserted. The Iroquois had fled. De Tracy ordered the villages and the surrounding crops burned. Since he had destroyed their food supplies, many Iroquois died that winter. But no fighting took place and no one on either side died in battle.

The following summer, in 1667, the Iroquois realized that the French forces in the colony could overpower them. They agreed to make peace with the French. However, it would be only a temporary peace.

De Tracy returned to France with some of his soldiers. But more than 400 professional soldiers decided to stay in New France. They were each given a grant of land. This encouraged the other colonists because now there were experienced soldiers living among them on farms along the St. Lawrence River.

Earthquake Hits New France

Marie de l'Incarnation described an earthquake that rocked the St. Lawrence River valley in 1663.

The day was calm and still when we heard a fearful rumbling as if hundreds of carts were rattling wildly over the cobbles. A horrifying sound as of rushing waters assailed our ears from under our feet, from over our heads, and all around us. In the granaries and in our rooms, a sound like a shower of stones on the roofs. Clouds of dust swirled through the air. Doors banged open and shut. Church bells and clocks rang of themselves. Bell towers and houses swayed like trees in a storm, and inside confusion reigned as chairs and tables toppled over, the walls cracked open and stones fell out of them, floors split, and the animals ran howling in and out of the house.

Modern scientists suggest that this 1663 earthquake probably measured 7.0 on the Richter scale. It was at least as powerful as the earthquake that rocked San Francisco in 1906. It was located in the Charlevois-Kamouraska region of Quebec. It caused extensive landslides in the area, and for days after, the rivers ran muddy.

Fast Forward

More Earthquakes in Quebec

The first recorded earthquake in Quebec was in 1663. The same region had large earthquakes in 1791, 1860, and 1925 as well as many smaller ones up to the present. An earthquake that struck Montreal in 1732 damaged 300 houses. It probably measured 5.8 on the Richter scale. In 1988, an earthquake measuring 6.0 struck the Saguenay region in a wilderness area south of Chicoutimi, Quebec.

Les Filles du Roi

One of the first things that Talon did was conduct a census. A **census** is an official count of the population. The census showed a short-age of women. In fact, men outnumbered women two to one. So, Talon's next task was to encourage more young, single, healthy women to emigrate to the colony from France. They could marry the single men of New France. The women were called **filles du roi**, or "king's daughters." Many were orphans from the city, but some were poor country girls from large families. They were looking for a better life. Each girl was given a dowry by the king to help her start her new life—an ox, a cow, two barrels of salt beef, and a purse of money.

Between 1665 and 1673, about 900 young women arrived as filles du roi. When they first arrived, they were housed in convents. But within a few days, they were introduced to the bachelors and marriages were arranged. There didn't seem to be much chance for romance. Talon even threatened that he would not let the single men go hunting or trading until all the women were married! The plan worked. Within 14 years, the population of New France increased from 3215 to 9400.

Talon had other plans for increasing the population of the colony. A special allowance was granted to families who had more than 10 children. Men who married before the age of 20 and women who married before the age of 16 were given a gift of money on their wedding day.

Women from France were sent to New France to marry the men there and help increase the population of the colony.

Civics & Society

The Census of 1666

Here are the results of the census that Jean Talon conducted in 1666. Farmers and members of the clergy, nobility, and government were not included in Talon's list of occupations and trades.

	2034
Males	1181
Females	3215
Total population	1250
Colonists under age 16	4
Colonists over age 81	63
Seigneurs	36
Carpenters	32
Stonemasons	20
Shoemakers	30
Tailors	3
Teachers	18
Storekeepers	8
Coopers	4
Armourers	7
Gunsmiths	7
Hatters	27
Joiners	9
Millers	6
Ropemakers	401
Servants	22
Ship captains	1
Slaters	16
Weavers	

1. Compare the number of females with the number of males in the colony.
2. What age were the majority of the colonists?
3. Look up the meaning of any occupation you are not familiar with. Explain what that occupation involves.
4. Why do you think there were so many carpenters and stonemasons and so few teachers?
5. Suggest some reasons why there were so many servants.
6. Why did the census figures cause the French government to worry about New France?

An habitant woman. The census showed that there were few women in New France in comparison to the number of men.

Talon's Plans for Agriculture

As Talon visited in the colony, he met many habitants living on the farms along the St. Lawrence River. Talon discovered that they were spending a lot of time hunting and trapping. Many were ignoring their farms because trapping was more profitable. Talon encouraged the habitants to spend more time clearing and cultivating their land. Most of the habitants at this time lacked experience in farming since many of them had been business people or soldiers before they moved to New France.

On his own farm, Talon tried out new strains of grain and seed. He wanted to discover which crops would grow best in New France. Cattle and pigs were imported into the colony. Ten horses arrived in 1665. Talon's goal was to make sure that the colony could always produce enough food for its people.

Talon's Plans for Industry

Talon wanted to develop various industries in New France. With financial help from France, he started a shipbuilding yard in 1664. He also set up a small iron foundry. High-quality iron ore had been discovered near Trois-Rivières. The foundry produced cannons, cannon balls, pots, hammers, and stoves for the local market. Talon also expanded the fisheries and opened a shoe factory and a brewery. The brewery produced an average of 40 000 barrels of beer a year. Half of this was exported. He encouraged spinning so that wool from sheep could be made into fine yarn and woven into clothing. In a letter to King Louis XIV, he boasted that he was clothed from head to toe with goods made in New France.

Talon dreamed of developing New France into a "great and powerful state" with its own industries. Unfortunately, Louis XIV did not agree. The policies of France restricted industry

Talon had dreams of starting a strong shipbuilding industry in New France. There was a plentiful supply of timber for the ships. But the industry grew slowly because of a lack of skilled workers. It probably reached its peak from 1740 to 1750, when 12 warships were built.

in New France. French colonies were expected to supply raw materials for the manufacturers of France, who made the raw materials into goods. These manufactured goods were then shipped back to the colony to be sold at higher prices. New France was expected to buy these manufactured goods from France. Nothing could be made in the colonies that would compete with the manufactured goods of France. New France was only allowed to produce things for its own immediate use.

Unfortunately, Talon did not remain in New France for long. He returned to France in 1672 and became a personal secretary and advisor to the king. Without his presence and enthusiasm, many of his good ideas for the colony were soon forgotten.

François de Laval: A Powerful Church Leader

Religion had always been important in New France. Almost all the people of New France were Roman Catholic and attended church regularly. They looked to the Church for guidance. It had a very strong influence on their behaviour, values, and daily lives. The bishop was the head of the Church in New France. He was in charge of all the priests, nuns, and missionaries. He also supervised the schools and hospitals that the Church managed. He was responsible for the spiritual welfare of all Roman Catholics in the colony.

The first bishop of Quebec was François de Laval. He was appointed bishop in 1674. As a member of the Sovereign Council, he played an important role as one of the "big three" in government. Locate the bishop in the painting of the Sovereign Council on page 56.

Here are some of the things that Bishop Laval did. He
- organized New France into religious districts called parishes
- appointed priests for the parishes to conduct religious services, including weddings and burials

- established a school to train priests so that the colony would not need to import priests from France
- encouraged the founding of primary schools for girls and boys
- set up a trade school for cabinet makers
- encouraged carvers, painters, and other artisans whose work decorated the interiors of churches
- supported more advanced education at the Jesuit college
- strongly encouraged family life
- insisted on proper behaviour, frowning on dancing, drunkenness, and pretty clothes
- strongly opposed the brandy trade with the Aboriginal peoples and threatened that anyone who took part in it would not be allowed to attend church
- demanded that the Church be allowed to collect a tax called a **tithe** from all people in order to build and maintain churches and support the priests

Bishop Laval was a controversial figure. He quarrelled bitterly with a number of governors. However, under his leadership, the Church in New France grew and flourished.

Count Frontenac: The Most Important Governor

Count Frontenac was a colourful character. He was a soldier experienced in battle when he arrived in Quebec in 1672 to begin his first term as governor. Shortly after his arrival, he travelled up the St. Lawrence River with about 400 soldiers. They arrived in a long procession of canoes at Cataraqui, now called Kingston, Ontario. Frontenac had invited the Iroquois to meet him there.

For four days, he entertained the Iroquois with feasts and presents. Meanwhile, his soldiers were building an armed fort that they called Fort Frontenac. The fort was completed in a very short time. The Iroquois could see that Frontenac was a determined man, a quality they esteemed in their own people.

Frontenac held discussions with Iroquois chiefs. He invited the Iroquois to start coming to Fort Frontenac to sell their furs and get supplies. He suggested that doing this would be to their advantage. He promised that goods at the French fort would be cheap. Also, the Iroquois could save themselves the long trip to the south to sell their furs to the English at Fort Albany. During the time that Frontenac was governor, there were no Iroquois raids on French settlements.

This statue of Governor Frontenac pointing at a cannon stands in Quebec City. In 1690, Frontenac was governor of New France when some English soldiers tried to capture Quebec. They sent a messenger to demand that Frontenac surrender the town. He answered by saying, "I will not write an answer to your master on paper. Tell him the mouths of my cannons will deliver my reply." What does this event tell you about Count Frontenac?

The Iroquois and Governor Frontenac meet at Cataraqui.

Frontenac and the Fur Trade

Frontenac made expansion of the fur trade his main concern. He frequently used his military excursions as excuses to pursue trading opportunities. Fort Frontenac, founded in 1673, was the first in a line of French forts to the south and to the west.

That same year, Louis Jolliet and Father Jacques Marquette explored the Mississippi River as far south as the Arkansas River. The colonial government sanctioned these voyages because it recognized their importance in expanding the sphere of the French fur trade. Between 1676 and 1682, Frontenac supported the explorer Robert de la Salle. La Salle established a series of fur-trading posts beyond Lake Ontario and into the Ohio River valley. Frontenac was anxious to prevent the English from moving into this area. La Salle was killed in 1687 by members of his own crew when he tried to set up a French colony at the mouth of the Mississippi River.

Frontenac Returns to France

Governor Frontenac held strong beliefs. Many found him bossy and conceited. He seemed to upset just about everybody at one time or another. He wanted to extend the fur trade into the Ohio valley, but Talon preferred that the settlers stay on the farms. Frontenac angered the fur traders of Montreal when he built Fort Frontenac. Many furs that would normally have ended up in their hands would be traded at Fort Frontenac instead. Frontenac's disagreements with settlers and fur traders led to arguments and squabbling. Finally, King Louis XIV grew weary of the problems in New France and ordered Frontenac back to France.

Iroquois Attacks

In Europe, Britain and France were at war. They were enemies who had been in conflict for centuries. France had Europe's finest army and Britain claimed the most powerful navy. Battles in Europe affected the colonies. The

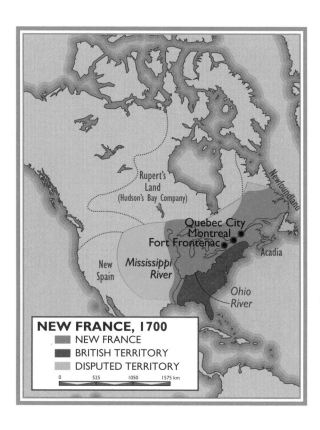

NEW FRANCE, 1700
- NEW FRANCE
- BRITISH TERRITORY
- DISPUTED TERRITORY

0   525   1050   1575 km

two countries competed for territory in North America. The newly settled land was often used for bargaining in European peace treaties. There were British North American colonies located along the east coast of North America, south of New France. The British encouraged the Iroquois to attack the French settlements. New France faced its gravest danger since the days of Champlain.

With Frontenac gone from the colony, the Iroquois were once again drawn into the conflict between Britain and France. The Iroquois were encouraged by their trading partner, Britain, to attack the tiny French settlement of Lachine. Lachine was close to Montreal, a final target for the British. On 25 August 1689, 1500 Iroquois attacked Lachine. They burned 50 of the 80 houses. Twenty-four settlers were killed. Almost 90 people were dragged away as prisoners. The losses to the Iroquois were not recorded. For weeks, the Iroquois maintained their assault against communities around Montreal, on behalf of the British.

King Louis XIV once again turned to Frontenac. He said, "You are a proven commander who has experience with the military abilities of the Iroquois. I am sending you back to Canada where I expect you will serve me as well as you did before." Soon, Frontenac was back as governor of New France.

In the meantime, French settlers along the St. Lawrence River had to be on guard constantly. At a moment's notice, they might have to defend their settlements from Iroquois raids.

Profile

Marie-Madeleine Jarret de Verchères 1678–1747

One of the heroes of New France was Madeleine de Verchères. She was the daughter of an officer of the Carignan-Salières Regiment. She lived on a seigneury on the south shore of the St. Lawrence River. On 22 October 1692, at about 8 a.m., the habitants of Verchères were bringing in their harvest from the fields. Suddenly, they were surprised by an Iroquois attack. The Iroquois captured about 20 prisoners. Fourteen-year-old Madeleine de Verchères managed to rush back into the palisade and close the gate behind her. Since her parents were away, she fired a cannon to call for help and to warn her neighbours. She summoned her younger brothers and a few other terrified defenders and rallied them with her courage. This small group held the fort for a night and a day until help arrived from Montreal. Madeleine de Verchères became a proud native-born hero for French Canadians. She represented their struggle to establish and protect their farms in New France.

Madeleine de Verchères leads the defence of her family farm against the Iroquois.

1. If you had been in Madeleine de Verchères' position, how might you have reacted?
2. What might she have said to her parents when they returned to the seigneury? How might they have replied?

French-Iroquois Peace Treaty

When Governor Frontenac arrived back in New France, he organized a series of raids against the Iroquois. He headed south of Lake Ontario, into the territory of the Onondaga and Oneida. He took 2000 French soldiers and Aboriginal allies. In Iroquois territory, they found nothing but deserted villages. Nevertheless, as de Tracy had done in 1666, Frontenac ordered the crops burned and the storehouses destroyed. Although the Iroquois experienced hunger that winter, most survived. Eventually, in 1701, the French and the Iroquois signed a peace treaty. The Iroquois agreed to stay out of any war between the French and the English. Frontenac was not present to see the treaty signed. He had died in Quebec City in 1698.

Netsurfer

www.axess.com/mohawk
This is the Mohawk-Iroquois home page. Go to the main menu and click on The Iroquois Confederacy. Scroll down to Iroquois Stories. "The Boy Who Lived With Bears" and "Dogs Who Saved Their Master" are just two of the many interesting Aboriginal stories you can read.

Women in New France

Although males and females were not considered to be equal under the law, life in New France did offer some advantages for women. Education was not restricted to the wealthy. Habitant parents could afford to send their daughters to schools so that they got a good education at a low cost. Women could own property. When her husband died, a woman automatically inherited half of his estate. She was also responsible for managing the other half until her children were old enough to handle it themselves. The fact that there were so few women in New France compared to the number of men improved their position in the colony.

The wives of noblemen, who held the most important positions in the colony, attended political functions in support of their husbands. They did not participate in bringing up their children. Nursemaids and nannies took care of them as infants. As soon as the children were old enough, they were sent to boarding school.

Some of the women gained more power and responsibility than women in France. Their husbands were often away from the colony for long periods of time to wage war or conduct business. A woman in New France might make important decisions and oversee some of her husband's responsibilities while he was away. If she was a widow, a woman could take over her husband's business. Women were involved in a variety of businesses—construction, timber, saw milling, clothing manufacturing, and the fur trade.

Women were not allowed to hold political office. But some women did have influence. One such woman was Elisabeth Joybert de Soulanges, marquisse de Vaudreuil, the wife of the governor. In 1709, she began to worry that her husband was losing respect and influence in the colony. She travelled to France to secure his position. She discussed the matter with the minister in charge of colonial administration. He was impressed with her intelligence and understanding of politics.

Skill Building: Making a Simple Timeline

You have just read about the first 40 years of the Royal Government in New France. Can you recall all the jumbled events of that time? So much was happening quickly that it is not easy to sort out all the events. A **timeline** is an excellent way to record the most important events in **chronological** order, that is, the order in which they happened.

Previously, you may have constructed a timeline of your own life. You divided the timeline into years and recorded the most important events for each year. Timelines may be divided into shorter or longer periods. They can be in hours, days, or weeks, or longer periods such as months, years, 10-year periods called **decades**, or even 100-year periods called **centuries**.

Historians sometimes talk about historical periods. You live in the **Technological Age**, a period that has seen many advances in technology such as computers, the Internet, biotechnology, and specialized space inventions. An example of a historical period from the 20th century is the Age of the Automobile.

You could make a timeline mural of a historical period.

1.   Decide what you want your mural to show. For example, it could show the first four decades of the Royal Government in New France.

2.   Divide the class into four groups. On a long strip of mural paper, draw four equal columns from top to bottom. Each column represents one decade. Each group is responsible for one decade. Label the four decades at the tops of the columns.

3.   Give the timeline a title that clearly describes its content.

4.   Select the most important events of each decade. Record them in the order that they happened. For this example, a timeline has been started for you below.

5.   Add sketches to your timeline to illustrate some of the events.

6.   Clearly label each picture and event. Write a a brief explanation for each event. Do you have the events in the correct chronological order? If you are in doubt, double-check by rereading the text.

7.   Each group should present its part of the timeline to the class, using the pictures and captions to describe each decade. Discuss with the class why a timeline is a useful tool for history students.

Timeline of the First Four Decades of Royal Government in New France

1663–1672	1673–1682	1683–1692	1693–1702
1663 – Royal Government is established for New France. 1663 – An earthquake rocks the St. Lawrence River valley. 1665 – Sieur de Tracy arrives from France with soldiers.			

Culture Link

Cultural Exchanges Between the Europeans and the Aboriginal Peoples

As you have read in this and earlier chapters, contact between the French and the Aboriginals had both positive and negative results for each of their cultures.

- The French adopted many practices from the Aboriginals. They experienced food they had never tasted before, such as corn, which was the staple food for the Aboriginal peoples. It was boiled with fish or dried and ground into cornmeal. Pumpkins and blueberries were also new to the French. Berries were eaten raw or they were dried and added to cornmeal, soups, and cakes. Meats such as moose, bear, wild geese, and beaver were new to the French as well.

- The Aboriginal peoples taught the French a number of agricultural techniques, for example, forced germination. The Aboriginal women would soak pumpkin seeds in water, plant them in a bark box, and then store them in a warm place. In a few days, the seeds would sprout. The seedlings would then be removed from the box and planted in the fields.

- The Aboriginal peoples helped the French cope with the challenges of transportation in the winter. They taught them how to make snowshoes that kept them from sinking into the deep snow. They also showed the French how to use toboggans made from large planks of wood. These toboggans could be used to move supplies and goods during the snowy winter months.

- Some of the French participated in Aboriginal sweating rituals. Hot stones were laid in a low, round tent. In the tent, men would sit in a circle, drinking lots of water to enable them to sweat a lot. Afterwards, they would throw themselves in the river or wash themselves in very cold water. This ritual had religious significance for the Aboriginal peoples. For the French, it would have been like sitting in a sauna to clean and refresh their bodies.

- The Huron received metal objects from the French. They named the French people *Agnonha*, which means "iron people." The Huron traded goods for knives, awls, and axes. The cutting edge of these metal tools was much sharper than their traditional tools, which were made from stones and bones.

- In the early years, trade with the French fostered the development of the Huron culture. The Huron used the metal tools they obtained through trade to create more intricate and elaborate designs on the items they made. For example, decorations on pottery became more complex. In addition, with iron knives, they could carve materials such as bone and wood with greater precision and detail.

- The French introduced the Aboriginal peoples to European goods and customs. The Aboriginals adopted French foods such as beans, peas, prunes, figs, biscuits, and bread. In addition, the French introduced alcohol to the Aboriginals, whose bodies had a great deal of difficulty tolerating it.

- The Aboriginals became fond of European hats and began to use them as a symbol of social status.

- Traditionally, Aboriginals did not say "goodbye" when they were leaving someone. But they began to imitate the French in this fashion.

---

1. In your opinion, did Aboriginal groups or the French benefit most from contact with one another? Who benefited least? Explain your answer.

2. Find out about other ways in which the Aboriginals and the Europeans affected each other's lifestyles.

The French quickly adopted snowshoes from the Aboriginals, which enabled them to hunt in deep snow.

Activities

Understanding Concepts

1. Define the following words and enter them in your personal dictionary.

governor	seigneur	tithe
census	filles du roi	seigneury
bishop	intendant	habitant
timeline	chronological	decades
centuries	The Technological Age	problem solving

2. What problems led King Louis XIV to establish a new government for Canada?

3. How would an increase in population help the colony to become stronger?

4. Decide which official in New France would deal with each of the following situations.
   a) The colony is desperately short of settlers.
   b) An epidemic of smallpox has broken out at Trois-Rivières and there is a need for nurses.
   c) The king has asked for a census to be taken.
   d) Word has just reached Quebec that a band of Iroquois has attacked the seigneury at Verchères.
   e) Citizens and priests complain that the coureurs de bois are providing many kegs of brandy to the Aboriginals.
   f) Two habitants are squabbling about fishing rights on the river.

5. Why did King Louis XIV decide to send the Carignan-Salières Regiment to New France? Was this an important turning point for the colony? Explain.

6. Explain how the Iroquois were pulled into a conflict between Britain and France. Do you think the French handled the situation effectively? Explain your answer.

Digging Deeper

7. **Discuss** Outline the problems revealed in the census of 1666. What actions did Talon take to try to correct these problems? Was he successful?

8. **WRITE** Imagine you are young women arriving in New France as filles du roi. How would you feel being picked as a wife for someone you had never seen before? Or imagine you are an unmarried man in New France. Talon is pressuring you to marry. How would you feel about marrying someone you just met for the first time? Write about your feelings and experiences.

9. **THINK/DISCUSS** Talon is often described as "the great intendant." Does he deserve this title? Why?

10. **WRITE** Imagine you are one of the Carignan-Salières soldiers who came to New France with de Tracy. Write a letter to a friend back in France describing your experiences fighting the Iroquois.

11. **THINK/DISCUSS** What heroism did Madeleine de Verchères display? Do many people have the chance to be heroes today? Explain.

Making New Connections

12. **RESEARCH** Find out more about the Iroquois Confederacy today.

Everyday Life in New France

Habitants

The habitants in New France spent more time clearing and cultivating their farmland than hunting and trapping. They could make a good living as farmers. They built their log homes on the banks of the river. Since there were few roads, the river served as their highway. They cleared and worked their fields and produced enough to meet their needs. Since stores were quite far away, the habitants had to be **self-sufficient**.

The habitants were expected to be loyal to the seigneur who had granted them the land. The Church played an important role in their lives and every habitant paid a tax to the Church to support it.

Since France was at war from 1688 on, it had little time or money to spend on developing the colony of New France. But the habitants and seigneurs continued to work together on the land. They had developed a distinctive way of life in the colony. Traces of their long, narrow farms can still be seen today along the shores of the St. Lawrence River.

Although most settlers lived on the seigneuries, towns expanded in size and importance as more colonists arrived in New France. They became centres for business, transportation, the Church, and government. In general, town life was more sophisticated and comfortable than life on the farms. As well, towns provided markets for the produce the settlers wanted to sell.

Reflecting/Predicting
1. Look through the pictures in this chapter. What do they tell you about life as a settler in New France?
2. How do you think the traders and trappers would have felt about the settlers? Why?
3. What would the habitants have had to do in order to be self-sufficient

This painting by Thomas Davies from 1787 shows a typical farm on the shores of the St. Lawrence River east of Quebec City, in New France. It shows houses, barns, sheds, fields with crops, livestock, and eel traps in the river.

A Day in the Life of an Habitant, 1740

The Dupré family is awakened by the rooster crowing at daybreak. As usual, Marie-Hélène is up first. She calls to her children, "Everybody up. We have a busy Saturday ahead. Remember to say your prayers."

The children crawl out from under their heavy, worn blankets. They kneel down on the cold wooden floor and recite their prayers. Then, everybody dresses quickly in the chilly morning air. Hébert, the father, and Jean-François, the son, pull on brown woollen pants over their long underwear and add long hand-knitted socks. Then, they pull on a thick linen shirt over their heads and put on high leather moccasins, a style borrowed from the Aboriginal peoples. They tie their long hair back and have a quick shave. Marie-Hélène and her two daughters, Claire and Marguerite, wear long, full skirts, blouses, stockings, and thick, rough leather shoes. For doing housework, they add an apron and put a cloth cap over their hair, fastening it with a colourful ribbon.

Morning

Hébert and Jean-François put on jackets, wooden clogs, and red woollen toques before they head out to do the morning chores. There are two cows to be milked. All the animals, including two horses, a bull, a sow and her litter, and seven sheep have to be fed.

In the house, Marie-Hélène, Claire, and Marguerite are also busy. They throw open the windows, hook back the shutters, and let fresh air blow through the house. The mattresses, which are filled with reeds and straw, are taken off the beds and shaken out. The down-filled pillows are fluffed up. Quilts and blankets are carefully folded. The floors of the two rooms are swept and then water is sprinkled on the floors to keep the dust down.

Meanwhile, Marie-Hélène prepares breakfast. Like most habitants, the family works for one or two hours before having breakfast. Then, they sit down to a hearty meal of milk, bread, and pancakes. Over breakfast, the day's work is planned. Hébert will be off to prepare the fields for sowing wheat. Stumps of trees must be burned and pulled out. Rocks and stones must be picked up one by one and hauled away. Jean-François will first help his sisters haul in wood for the bread oven and the fireplace. Then, he will join his father. Even though it is Saturday, the youngest daughter, Marguerite, will walk to a school run by some Ursuline nuns. Claire will stay at home to help her mother. The meal ends with father saying grace and the entire family making the sign of the cross.

Claire is 12. Until she gets married, she shares the household duties with her mother. She cleans up the breakfast dishes and replaces them in one of the pine cupboards. She dusts the few pieces of furniture they own—cupboards, tables, chairs, trunks, and beds, all made of pine. Then, it is time to head out to feed the hens and collect the eggs. Claire spends the rest of the morning digging and preparing the garden.

Marie-Hélène prepares dough for bread. She usually does this about twice a week. When the dough is mixed, she puts it in a warm place by the fire to rise. Then, she takes two water buckets and heads to the river to draw water. This heavy and onerous chore must be done twice every day and more often on wash days. Then, she fires up the bread oven. Like most habitants, Marie-Hélène prefers an outdoor oven for baking bread because it is much larger than the fireplace ovens. Her bread oven is located a few metres from the kitchen door. It is made of stones, mortar, and clay. When the oven is just the right temperature, she bakes several huge, round, crusty loaves. Each loaf weighs about 2 kg.

Afternoon

The ringing of the church bell at noon is the signal for the midday meal. Sometimes, lunches are carried out to the fields if the men are too busy to return to the house. Today, Hébert and Jean-François are working close to the farm-house, so they come in. Marie-Hélène serves everyone before sitting down herself. The meal consists of an omelette made from fresh eggs and cabbage and onions from the **root cellar**. The root cellar is a cool place below the floorboards.

Afterward, the men sit outside smoking their pipes while the women clean up the dishes. At one o'clock, it is back to work. The men return to the fields. The women spend the afternoon planting the kitchen garden. They plant peas, beans, onions, and cucumbers. Vegetables that can be stored over the winter in the root cellar, such as cabbages, onions, carrots, and turnips are especially important. Later in the afternoon, Marie-Hélène and her daughters will try to go to church.

Evening

The main meal of the day is eaten at about eight o'clock, after the evening chores are done. Tonight, it is soup, baked beans, eels, and, of course, the fresh bread that Marie-Hélène has baked. The children drink milk and the adults drink cider. For dessert, there is a slice of bread sprinkled with maple sugar and covered with fresh cream.

When supper is finished, the whole family kneels before a religious picture for prayers. Saturday night is bath night and everyone in the family has a bath. Water is carried in and heated in big kettles over the fire. The hot water is poured into a big tub placed near the fire. The backs of chairs are covered with blankets to hide the bathers from the rest of the family. A big bar of homemade soap is put on the floor next to the tub. One by one, everyone has a turn in the tub.

After their baths, everyone stays up a little longer. The men smoke their pipes. The women try to do their needlework by the flickering candlelight. After nine o'clock, the Dupré family begins to prepare for bed. They all sleep in the same room, but there are curtains around the three beds for privacy. The heavy curtains also help to keep out drafts in the chilly house. The candles are snuffed out. The family snuggles under the covers. Soon, there is no sound but the crackling of the fire and the deep breathing of the sleeping family.

Bread was one of the most important items in the habitants' diet. Outdoor ovens were pre-ferred because of their larger capacity.

Recipe: Habitant Pea Soup

Ingredients
500 g dried green peas
1 large onion, chopped
1 carrot, grated
2 chopped sprigs of parsley
1 bay leaf
10 ml salt
500 g salt pork or salty bacon
3 L cold water

Directions
Soak peas overnight in enough water to cover. Drain. In the morning, bring to a boil in cold water and add onion, carrot, and salt. Reduce heat to a simmer. Add parsley, bay leaf, and chopped salt pork to the soup. Simmer for three to four hours. Add more water if necessary. When done, press the peas against the side of the pot to mash them. Serve with bread and pickles. If you wish, this may be made in a sturdy pot outside over the coals of a fire.

See if you can find some other French Canadian recipes that early French settlers may have used. Prepare a meal for the class using only these recipes.

Netsurfer

www.cmcc.muse.digital.ca/
cmc/cmceng/canpleng.html
This website takes you to
Canada Hall in the Canadian
Museum of Civilization.
Click on Farm Life (#6) for
pictures and stories about
the seigneurial system.
Click on #7, Place de la
Nouvelle-France, for town
life.

The Seigneurial System

The seigneurial system had been in place in New France since the days of Champlain. This system of distributing land was modelled on a system used in France since the Middle Ages. It was understood and accepted by the settlers. The king granted large tracts of land to seigneurs. The seigneurs were usually wealthy and important citizens. Some were retired military officers. Some tracts of land, or seigneuries, were granted to religious orders, including communities of nuns. The seigneuries varied in size from 16 to 160 km^2. The seigneurs kept the biggest lots for themselves and parcelled out the rest to the habitant families.

The rivers in New France were the main means of communication and transportation at that time. So, it was decided that each seigneury should have frontage on a river. The seigneuries extended along the St. Lawrence River and its tributaries. They were long, narrow rectangles that extended back inland from the rivers.

When seigneurs began to grant land to settlers, they used the same system. They offered the settlers farms laid out in long strips. Each farm had access to the all-important waterway. The lots granted to the habitants were not all the same size. One reason is that, when the time came, farms were not divided equally among married children. The widow inherited one half, the eldest son one quarter, and the other children equal shares of the remaining quarters. Very often when children inherited, they would sell their share to one of their brothers or sisters and move to another seigneury.

In 1742, a visitor reported that from the St. Lawrence, it looked like New France was a village strung out along the river. The houses were fairly close to each other. Behind the row of houses were long, thin fields and then nothing but wilderness. Eventually, when the river lots were filled up, a second row of seigneuries developed with no frontage on the river.

Talon's Villages

Jean Talon, the former intendant of New France, had had his own idea about the best layout for a seigneury. He thought it would be easier for the settlers to defend themselves if they lived in villages. He designed three new communities shaped like pies. The homes were in the centre, close together, with fields stretching out behind them like triangular pie wedges. However, the settlers did not like Talon's idea. They all wanted land along the shore of a river.

Rules of the Game

According to the seigneurial system, the seigneur had responsibilities toward the king and toward the habitants, and the habitants had responsibilities toward the seigneur. Here is what the seigneur owed the king:

- kneel before the intendant and swear obedience to the king
- divide the seigneury into lots for the habitants
- report annually how much land has been cleared and how many land grants have been made to habitants
- send all oak trees cut on his land to the king's shipyards
- build a residence, a church or chapel, and a gristmill for the habitants to use

The portraits of this seigneur, Pierre Casgrain, and his wife were painted in 1805. Casgrain purchased his seigneury using money earned as a fur trader.

Here is what the seigneur owed the habitants:
- grant them farms
- promise habitants the right to stay on the land if they honour their contract
- provide protection for them
- build a gristmill for grinding wheat into flour
- provide land for a church and help to build it

The habitants owed the seigneur the following:
- promise to build a house and clear the land for themselves
- pay annual taxes called *cens et rentes*, which could be goods such as pigs, sacks of wheat, or a few chickens
- work three days each year on the seigneur's fields, usually at planting or harvest time
- promise to take their grain to the seigneur's mill and pay him 1/14th of the grain they grind
- give the seigneur a portion of the fish they catch in the river
- give the seigneur some of the wood they cut on the property
- pay a commission if they sell their land
- promise to help build a church and pay the priest
- honour the seigneur with a special pew in the local church

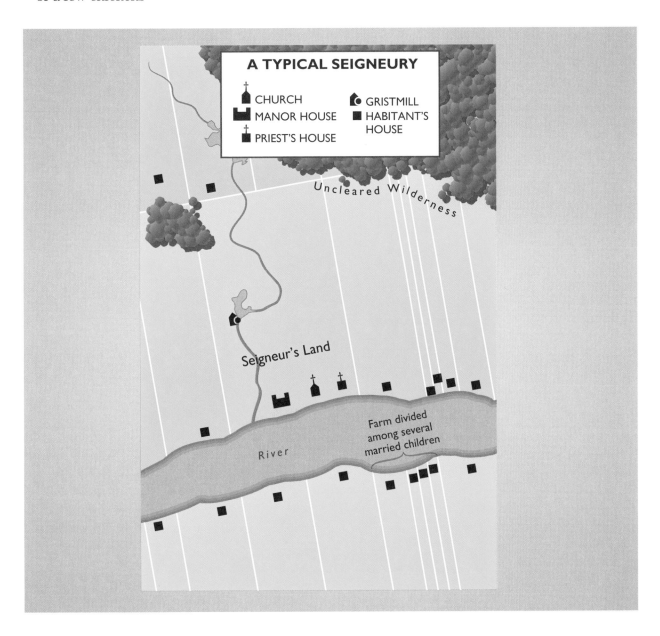

A TYPICAL SEIGNEURY

† CHURCH   🏭 GRISTMILL
▀ MANOR HOUSE   ■ HABITANT'S HOUSE
† PRIEST'S HOUSE

Uncleared Wilderness

Seigneur's Land

Farm divided among several married children

River

Skill Building: Using Pictures or Photographs to Get Information

Pictures and photographs are excellent sources of historical information. Often, we read books to find answers to questions. You can also find answers to questions by "reading" the pictures. There are clues right before your eyes.

How to "Read" a Picture

1. Examine the picture or photograph carefully, like a detective looking for clues.

2. To get started, use the four Ws: What? When? Where? Who?
- What is it a picture of?
- When was it painted or photographed?
- Where does it take place?
- Who, if anybody, is in the picture?

3. What questions come to mind when you look at the picture or photograph?

4. What answers do you find to your questions? Look carefully at the people. What are they doing? What is happening in the foreground? In the background?

5. What are the most important features in the picture? What seems less important?

6. Read the caption, if there is one. The **caption** is a title or a brief description of the picture. It often provides clues to what the picture is about.

7. Sometimes, you might want to check what you have learned from a picture or photograph against information in the textbook or other references.

Try it!

Photo A is of the Yamaska River region of Quebec. A seigneury existed there in the time of New France. Study the photograph carefully to find out information about life in New France more than 300 years ago.

Photo A This photo of the Yamaska River region of Quebec was recently taken from the air. You can still see the outlines of the old farms.

1. Locate the Yamaska River region in your atlas. Which major settlement in New France was in this area?

2. Describe the shape of the farms. Why were they laid out this way?

3. Where are most of the buildings?

4. Why was the river very important to the first settlers in this area? Is it as important now? Why?

5. What difficulty would this shape of field give the farmers?

6. Why did farms get narrower and narrower? What advantages would this have? What disadvantages would this have?

Photo B is of Charlesbourg, Quebec. A seigneury existed there in the time of New France.

1. Locate Charlesbourg in your atlas. What major settlement in New France was nearest to Charlesbourg?

2. Describe the shape of the original seigneury.

3. Describe the shape of a single farm in the Charlesbourg seigneury. Where was the farmhouse?

4. Talon preferred the shape of the Charlesbourg seigneury to that of the Yamaska seigneury. What advantages does Charlesbourg have over Yamaska? What are the disadvantages of its shape?

Photo B This aerial photograph of Charlesbourg shows outlines of old farms.

Culture Link

The Habitant Work Calendar

The habitants were busy from morning to night with chores that needed to be done around the farm. Their tasks varied depending on the season.

Spring

Every year in the spring, the habitants tried to clear a little more land for planting crops. It was hard work. Almost all of it had to be done by hand. Trees were chopped down with axes. The trunks and branches were sawn into logs for the fireplace. Stumps were pulled out or burned. The ashes from burning provided fertilizer for the fields. Rocks and stones had to be picked out of the fields by hand. They were used later for building foundations, fences, and fireplaces.

Louis Hébert, shown here, was one of the first habitants to start farming the land in New France, in the early 1600s. Louis is seeding, a springtime task for the settlers. By the mid-1700s, farming was a way of life for many residents in New France.

Vegetables had to be planted and all family members had to work in the gardens. The gardens were essential because they provided fresh vegetables throughout the summer and food that would be stored for winter use. Strangely enough, the habitants did not eat potatoes. They looked down on the potato with contempt. Marie de l'Incarnation, in one of her letters, described a time of terrible food shortage. She wrote that the people were forced to eat "the buds of trees, potatoes, and other foods never meant to be eaten by human beings."

Wheat was the most important crop that was planted in the spring. It was ground into flour and made into bread. Bread was eaten at every meal. It is estimated that an average man ate 1 kg of bread every day. This would equal two full loaves of bread of the size that we eat today!

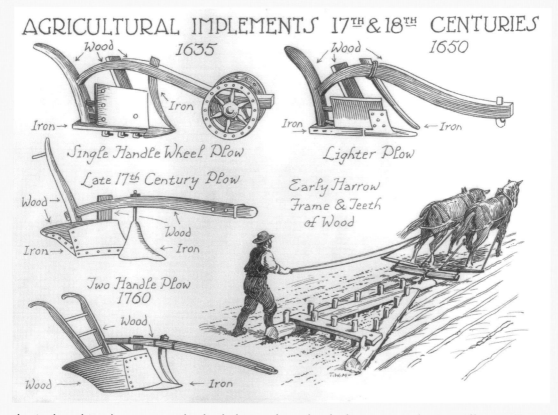

Agricultural implements made the habitants' work a little easier and more efficient. The iron plow was introduced to New France around 1640. Even with the plow, clearing and preparing the soil was a strenuous task. The habitants also used many hand tools. Scythes and sickles with long, thin curving blades were swung over the ground to cut grass or grain. Pitchforks with two prongs were used for throwing hay. Iron pickaxes were used for breaking up hard ground. Hoes were used for weeding.

Summer

Summer brought days of more hard work from dawn to dusk. Hay for the animals had to be brought in and crops had to be tended. The huge vegetable garden always needed weeding and cultivating. Even the children had to help with weeding and hoeing the gardens. Rainy days were a time for sharpening the axes and scythes, greasing the cart wheels, and repairing the tools.

Autumn

In the autumn, the habitants prepared for the long winter. Fruits from the orchard, such as apples, were dried. Wild berries were made into jam. Vegetables, pickles, and jams were stored below the floorboards in the cool root cellar. Herbs were hung to dry by the fireplace. Later, they would help to make food tastier.

When it turned cooler, animals were butchered, placed outside to freeze, and then packed into barrels. Bacon, pork, venison, and moose meat could all be stored this way. Eels from the river were salted and stored in barrels. They were a great delicacy for the habitants.

Loads of firewood had to be cut in the bush and hauled to the house. The family had to stock enough wood to keep the house and barn warm all through the winter. The habitants also had to be sure they had a large supply of homemade candles for the long winter nights.

Winter

When the countryside was covered with deep snow, the habitants made their simple furniture or did a bit of hunting. Fishing through the ice was another popular winter pastime. The habitants usually chopped two holes in the ice and stretched a net between the holes in the direction of the current. The fish caught in the net were a welcome addition to their winter diet. Since the winter months were less busy, it was during this time that many of the family's social activities took place.

---

1. Which season would have been the most difficult for the habitants? Explain why you think so.
2. How did life on an habitant farm differ from life on a farm now? How was it the same?

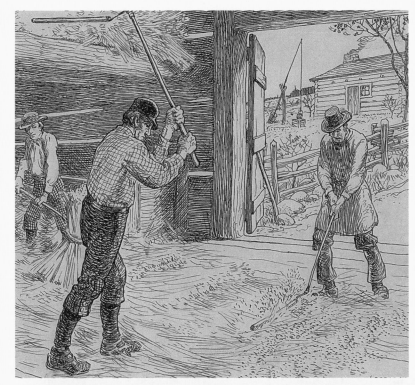

In early winter, the grain is threshed to separate it from the hard stalks. After threshing, the grain is ground into flour at the gristmill.

Winter was a good time to go hunting, since there were fewer demands on the farm. This painting shows a successful kill of a moose.

Tech Link

Sugar Making

The sweet sap of the sugar maple had been known by the Aboriginal peoples for a long time. In the spring, they would set up camp in a sugar bush. The men collected the sap and the whole family helped to carry it to the sugar huts. Each woman had her own sugar hut. The women were responsible for boiling the sap to evaporate the water. This was done by placing hot stones inside the pots of sap. By watching the Aboriginal peoples, the settlers learned how to follow the process themselves.

In the Jesuit *Relations*, there are references to "maple water running from the trees." An average habitant family made 50 or 60 kg of maple sugar from their own trees each spring. Cane sugar, like the sugar we use today, was very scarce in Canada and therefore very expensive. So, maple sugar was important for adding sweetness to the habitants' diet.

A pioneer remembers sugar making:

In early spring, we looked forward to making maple sugar. It meant maple candy and fun for the whole family. Papa chose a place for boiling the sap near the centre of the sugar bush. All of the children helped collect a huge supply of firewood for the boiling. The fire had to burn steadily night and day. We begged our parents to let us stay in the bush all night to tend the fires.

The sap was boiled in big iron kettles. Parents, friends, and relatives all helped to carry the sap from the trees to the kettles. Grand-père had a wooden yoke slung across his shoulders with a pail full of sap hanging from each end. Papa used the ox and the sleigh to bring barrels of sap from the trees.

The sap was boiled until it became a thin syrup and almost ready for "sugaring off." A neighbour brought his fiddle and there was music and dancing right there in the sugar bush. All the children came with spoons and ladles for a taste. To test the syrup, we let drops fall on the snow. If they hardened, the syrup was ready. The hardened drops were wonderful to eat.

Later, the syrup was poured into wooden moulds and left to harden into blocks of sugar. Grand-père, like most habitants, carved the sugar moulds into fancy shapes such as hearts, houses, animals, and books.

The whole family participates in the fun spring event of making maple sugar.

1. Investigate the maple syrup industry today. How is the sugar-making process used today similar to the process used by the habitants? How is it different?

2. Do some research to locate the legend the Aboriginal people tell about how they discovered maple syrup.

Fast Forward

The End of the Seigneurial System

When New France fell to the British in 1760, many seigneurs went back to France. The remaining seigneurs began to demand higher rents and higher fees for ungranted land. They remembered their rights but forgot their duties.

Eventually, it was decided that the old seigneurial system was holding up progress. Railway companies and industries were being charged ridiculously high costs to buy seigneurial land.

In 1854, the Parliament of United Canada abolished the seigneurial system. The seigneurs were paid generously for the land rights they lost. They were allowed to keep their own personal farms. The farmers were obliged to buy their land from the seigneurs. Many farmers could not afford to do so and had to pay rent until 1945. Eventually, their debts were paid through municipal taxes. The last payments were made in the early 1970s.

Social Life on a Seigneury

The habitants of New France worked hard, but they found time for fun and relaxation when their work was done. After the harvest was safely stored in the barns, all the habitants gathered at the seigneur's manor house to pay their annual rents. They arrived with sacks of wheat, barrels of eels, fine chickens and ducks, or bags of wool. In the largest room of the seigneur's house, the habitants greeted the seigneur. They paid him their rents and this was recorded in a big account book. Then, the habitants knelt and received a blessing from the seigneur. A huge celebration followed. The seigneur provided the refreshments. There was music and dancing that lasted into the early hours of the morning.

Often in the winter, the whole family would bundle up in the sleigh and go off to visit a neighbour or a relative. They would stay for a meal, a game of cards, or dancing.

Religion on the Seigneury

Many of the social activities on the seigneuries centred around the Church. The Roman Catholic Church was an important part of people's lives. Most people in New France went to church regularly on Sundays and also on special feast days.

The church served another function. It was a place for the habitants who lived on isolated farms to meet their friends and neighbours and to exchange the latest gossip and news. In the days before radio, television, and newspapers, news had to be sent in letters or passed on by word of mouth. At church, important announcements from the bishop, governor, or intendant were read out to the people.

The church bells provided a structure to the farm community's day. Bells signalled the beginning of morning and evening prayers. The sound of the bell at noon called habitants in from the fields for their midday meal. Bells

Weddings were occasions for celebration. Wedding feasts often lasted two or three days, first at the bride's home and then at the groom's. The banquets that were served always included bacon and mutton. There was plenty of drinking and dancing until late into the night. Births and christenings were also times for celebration.

tolled when people died and pealed in times of emergency.

Important festivals revolved around the Church year. For example, on Christmas Eve, habitant children went to bed early. They were awakened at about eleven o'clock at night. Their parents bundled them into the horse-drawn sleigh and tucked them in with heavy blankets to keep them warm. Then, with sleigh bells jingling, the family drove through the snow to the church for midnight mass. Mass was followed by a huge feast. Unlike Christmas celebrations today, Christmas Day was a quiet time. It was spent singing traditional French carols with the family and enjoying a good dinner. However, families did not exchange their small homemade gifts until New Year's Day.

PLANTING THE "MAI"

On the first of May it was a custom of the Habitants to erect a tree, decked with ribbons before the house of the Seigneur or Captain of Militia.

C.W.JEFFERYS

On 1 May each year, the habitants celebrated May Day to welcome spring. A maypole was planted in front of the seigneur's manor house. This was a tall spruce tree stripped of all its branches except for a few at the top. The seigneur and the habitants took turns blasting the maypole with musket fire until it was blackened. Then, they all danced around it. The habitants joined the seigneur's family in the manor house for a feast. Tourtières (meat pies), eels, smoked meats, baked beans, and maple sugar candy were enjoyed by everyone.

Parish church at Sainte-Anne-de-Beaupré. This church was built in 1660. The church was always an important centre of the community for the inhabitants of New France.

Bienvenue! Welcome to an Habitant's Home

How did the habitants build their houses? Usually, neighbours and relatives would come from near and far to help. Stones were hauled from the fields to build a foundation. Then, squared timbers were laid one on top of another. The ends of the timbers were fitted carefully into upright corner posts. This was called the *pièce-sur-pièce* method of construction. A mortar was mixed of sand, lime, and water. It was used to fill the space between the timbers and to hold them together.

The roofs of these houses were always high and steep so that snow would just slide off in the winter. Usually, the roof was a series of overlapping planks. Later, the habitants might add cedar shingles.

A huge fireplace was often the only source of heat. The chimney was placed close to the middle of the house. Fire was a constant danger. If a fire broke out, there was little the family could do. Water had to be hauled by buckets from the river to try to put the fire out.

Windows were usually small and covered with oiled paper because glass was scarce and expensive. Light could pass through these windows, but no one could see in or out. The windows had shutters to keep out the wind and rain.

Sometimes, the outsides of the houses were given a coat of whitewash to make them look fresh and clean. Most habitants' houses looked much the same, but all were sturdy and fairly comfortable.

Most farmhouses on a seigneury were built of wood because it was cheap and readily available. Also, wooden houses were warmer than those made of stone. However, as the farmers became more prosperous, they often covered their wooden houses with stone.

The Main Room

Imagine you could journey back in time to about 1750 and visit an habitant's home. As you step over the threshold, you enter the large main room of the house. We might call it a family room because this is where the family spends most of its time while inside. The main room is a living room, a kitchen, and a dining room all in one. Cooking utensils hang around the fireplace. A cradle for the baby stands close by. The doors beside the fireplace hide a recessed cupboard.

You glance around the room. To the right of the window is a three-shelf bucket bench where water for drinking and washing is kept. To the left of the window hangs a salt box. Salt is one of the most important seasonings and is taken from the box in pinches between the fingers. A spinning wheel sits in front of the window. A low buffet stands in the corner. Dishes and food are stored in it. The bench on the left serves many purposes. During the day, it is a place to sit. At night, it can be opened up into a bed for the children or visitors. Hanging from the roof beam is a candle lantern that can be used inside or outside.

Most of the furniture is made by the family from wood cut on the farm. Pine and yellow birch grow around the house. Both these woods are good for furniture because they can be cut into long, knot-free planks. Green wood is used for the backs and legs of chairs. Well-dried wood is used for the rungs and rails. As the green wood dries, the grip on the rails tightens up the whole chair, making the use of glue unnecessary.

The furniture is stained dark brown or painted with homemade paint. The habitants seem to favour the colours red, dark green, and blue. The woman of the house knows that red paint is made by mixing buttermilk, red earth from the fields, and linseed oil.

Homespun curtains add a little colour to the room. A rug woven from rags helps to cover the bare wooden floors. The floorboards are made of pine. You can imagine how cold they must be in the winter.

The main room in an habitant home. Can you identify the main pieces of furniture?

The Bedroom

Next, you are invited to peek into the other room of this two-roomed house. This is the bedroom. The whole family sleeps here! This bedroom has the luxury of having its own fireplace. Many do not. There is a four-poster bed in the room. Feel the mattress. It seems to be filled with straw. Pillows are filled with chicken or duck feathers, goose down, or even milkweed. A simple rectangular cradle stands by the bed. It can be rocked by a foot on one of the rockers, or by pushing one of its posts by hand. The tall pine armoire, or cupboard, is firmly held together by pegs. No glue or nails are used. The clothes of the habitants are stored in cupboards like this or in chests. A beautiful hooked rug with an intricate design adds colour and warmth to the room. Sitting on the rug is a pair of the wooden clogs that the habitants wear. The cross on the wall and the religious picture on the shelf remind us of the importance of Catholicism to the people of New France.

An habitant bedroom. Notice the wooden clogs, called *sabots*, by the bed.

Making candles by the dipping method

Lighting the Home

Candles were the only source of light in an habitant home. Usually, they were made in the fall after the animals had been butchered. Animal tallow is hard fat melted down in a large pot. Twisted cotton string wicks were dipped into the liquid tallow. Then, they were hung over a wooden stick while the coating cooled and solidified. The operation was repeated over and over. It took many dippings to make a candle of the required thickness.

Candle making was a messy, painstaking process. But with help from her family, an habitant woman could make 200 candles in a day. There was one problem with tallow candles. Mice and rats loved to gnaw on them! So, the candles had to be stored away safely in candle boxes.

The houses of the seigneurs were much grander and more comfortable than those of the habitants. This one is found on the Ile d'Orléans, an island in the St. Lawrence River near Quebec.

The Towns of New France Around 1750

Not everyone who lived in New France was a farmer or fur trader. By 1750, one in every four people in New France lived in one of the major towns: Quebec, Trois-Rivières, and Montreal. Each of these urban centres had grown in size and importance for different reasons.

Quebec

In 1750, Quebec was the most important town in the colony. Eight thousand people lived there. Perched on a steep rock cliff 100 m high, it controlled the traffic on the great river highway of New France. You can imagine the excitement in the spring when the sails of the first ships were spotted coming up the river. Their arrival brought news and letters from relatives and friends in France. The latest fashions from Europe would arrive to be sold in the shops. Colonists would step down the gangplank to begin new lives in Canada. Soon, the same ships would be loaded for the return voyage to France. They would be carrying cargoes of fur and timber. Quebec was the town that linked the colony to France.

There were two distinct sections to the town. Lower Town was the port area. Inns for travellers and warehouses for supplies were located there. The twisting streets were lined with dozens of shops. Tradespeople and merchants often lived right above their stores. On a typical day, the wooden sidewalks and the dirt roadways came alive with people. The market was located in Lower Town. Habitants carted in their produce and the townspeople came to buy fresh vegetables, meat, butter, cheese, and eggs.

Upper Town, on the heights, was grander. The governor's mansion, known as Château St.-Louis, was here. Nearby, were the Jesuit seminary and important churches and hospitals. Military officers and wealthy merchants built large stone mansions here. It was said that the women of Upper Town were as stylish in their silks and laces as any woman at Versailles, the palace of the French king. A visitor in 1775 noted that the men of Upper Town were vain and pompous. They, too, loved to dress in the latest Paris fashions. They carried swords and wore wigs and beaver hats.

The fortress of Quebec dominated the skyline and controlled the river. It is still an impressive sight for people arriving by ship. Can you identify the upper and lower sections of the town?

Fast Forward

Quebec City

Quebec City, the oldest city in Canada, is also North America's only walled city north of Mexico. The Plains of Abraham lie just outside these city walls. The battle that took place there in 1759 is considered the most important battle in Canadian history. Today, during Carnaval, the annual winter carnival, you can enjoy outdoor activities and French Canadian foods while walking streets that still boast many buildings from the time of New France.

Montreal

Quebec City faced France, while Montreal faced the interior of the Canadian wilderness. Montreal was 250 km up the river from Quebec. By the 1660s, Montreal had grown from the religious community founded by Paul de Maisonneuve and Jeanne Mance as Ville-Marie to become the centre of the fur trade. Each June, fur traders gathered there for the annual fur fair. Voyageurs left from Montreal in huge fleets of canoes on trips to the fur regions of the interior.

Montreal remained a frontier town. Visitors commented that it was friendlier and less "stuffy" than Quebec. All social classes and occupations mixed more easily in Montreal.

In Montreal, you could see the four main features of New France. There were black-robed priests and nuns, reminders that Ville-Marie began as a Catholic community. The presence of soldiers in the streets meant that it was still a frontier town on the edge of Canada's wilderness. Coureurs de bois and Aboriginal people travelling in and out of the settlement were a symbol of the prosperous fur trade. Habitants bringing produce from nearby seigneuries showed the importance of agriculture.

Trois-Rivières

Trois-Rivières was a market town located halfway between Quebec and Montreal on the St. Lawrence River. The town had a governor and a small military garrison. In 1749, about 850 people lived there.

Travellers between Quebec and Montreal often stopped at Trois-Rivières. Of its 25 buildings, 18 were inns. The iron deposits at nearby Saint-Maurice supported a small iron-making industry that made pots, stoves, cannon balls, and a few cannon. Trois-Rivières was also famous as a producer of high-quality birchbark canoes, some of which were 10 m in length and capable of carrying five to eight voyageurs.

A view of Montreal from Ile Sainte-Hélène. The canoe on the river might have been carrying coureurs de bois or Aboriginals coming to Montreal to trade furs.

Transportation in New France

The St. Lawrence River was the main highway for New France. It linked Acadia, Quebec, Trois-Rivières, Montreal, and all the seigneuries along the shore. Canoes and rafts were used on the river in the summer. Sleighs and toboggans drawn by oxen, horses, or even dogs were used for winter travel.

Summer Travel

There were very few roads in the countryside in New France. Not until 1734 was a rough road opened between Montreal and Quebec. It took a month to travel this distance and back by road. The trip by river took only a few days. It was not until the second row of land grants for the seigneuries was opened up that roads became necessary. In the towns, it was another matter. A few roads were paved with cobblestones, but most were unpaved and muddy. The townspeople used elegant two-wheeled, horse-drawn carriages called **calèches** to move around.

Winter Travel

Snowshoes were an Aboriginal invention that Europeans quickly adopted. Without snow-shoes, it would have been impossible for habitants, soldiers, or coureurs de bois to move through deep snow.

One governor of Quebec often hired skaters to deliver important messages to Montreal or Trois-Rivières in the winter. A story is told of one messenger who skated from Quebec to Montreal, a distance of 290 km, in a mere 18 hours!

The large wheels of the calèche were well suited to the muddy roads of the town. Speed limits were established everywhere. In the towns, people were forbidden to "gallop or trot fast." In the country, they were not allowed to gallop in the vicinity of churches.

Heavy stones for the walls of Montreal are being moved on a freight raft called a **cajeu**. This was a heavy barge made of rough pieces of wood nailed together. With sails, it could be used to carry loads of grain, furniture, or even cattle. Cajeux were too heavy to be portaged around rapids. They were just left on the shore when a job was finished. Travellers going in the opposite direction were free to use them.

Law and Order

The intendant had complete responsibility for law and order in the colony. Laws in New France were the same as those in France. The highest court was the Sovereign Council, which dealt with all serious cases. The lower courts handled matters such as the violation of fire regulations. The seigneurs also acted as judges to help solve disputes between habitants.

In England, a person was presumed innocent until proven guilty. But in France and New France, a person suspected of a crime was presumed guilty. At the trial, the accused was expected to prove her or his innocence. The judge pronounced the sentence.

There were prisons in New France. Men were locked up in the Royal Prisons. Women were guarded by nuns in the Hôpital-Général.

The punishment for crimes was severe. Men were sentenced to death very freely. Any thief was subject to hanging. Executions were held in public as a warning to other citizens. If a person was not condemned to death, she or he could be whipped and branded with red-hot irons. People convicted of lesser crimes were paraded out as public examples. The townspeople were then invited to shout insults at the criminals.

Slavery in New France

Slavery became legal in New France in 1709, but there were never very many slaves there compared to the number in the future United States. Slave owners included merchants, traders, governors, bishops, and priests. Most of the slaves came from other colonies or the Caribbean. The majority lived near Montreal and Quebec, where they worked mostly as house servants. Some worked in the schools and hospitals run by the women's religious orders. There were also a few slaves who worked at a French fur-trading post and at the fortress of Louisbourg on Ile Royale, on present-day Cape Breton Island.

The first recorded Black resident of Canada was an eight-year-old boy born on the island of Madagascar. In 1628, he was bought by a local colonist who had him baptized and gave him the name Olivier Le Jeune.

The river could be used as a highway even when it froze in winter. Almost every habitant family owned a homemade sleigh with runners called a **berline**. It was usually pulled by a horse, but poor families who did not own a horse used dog teams. A berline could be fitted with walls of removable planks. The sleigh had no roof. The family had to be tucked in under heavy blankets and furs. Sometimes, heated bricks or stones were placed on the floor to prevent their toes from freezing. When the wall planks were removed, the berline became a work vehicle. It could be used for hauling wood from the bush or food to the cattle.

The Acadian Experience

Since the earliest days of settlement in Acadia, the area had undergone a lot of change and uncertainty. Throughout the 17th century, Britain and France vied for control of Acadia. The area frequently passed back and forth between the two countries. Both nations saw an advantage in owning this North Atlantic gateway, although settling the region was not a priority for either France or Britain. By 1671, the population was only about 400 people. The Acadians were forced to live with this unstable state of affairs. Because of the frequent changes in power, they became accustomed to dealing with both British and French authorities.

Most Acadians were French-speaking Roman Catholics who came from the same region of France. They were a close-knit group, but some English speakers were absorbed into the community. The Acadians soon developed a unique culture. They came to be a people in their own right, distinct from the inhabitants of New France. Regardless of who ruled the colony, the Acadians were able to maintain their own way of life, including their own customs and a unique political and cultural identity.

The Acadian Way of Life

The government situated at Port Royal played only a small part in the lives of the settlers. The European officials were more interested in the struggle with their colonial rivals than with the lives of the Acadians. Under French rule, a seigneurial system supposedly existed. In reality, though, the settlers operated as independent, landowning farmers.

In Acadia, farming, hunting, and fishing were important. Almost all the settlement was along the ocean coastline. The farmers built dikes to help cope with the high tides of the Bay of Fundy. Then, they used the drained marshes as additional farmland. In general, the Acadians had a good standard of living. Most of the people were neither rich nor poor. Hard work was a necessary feature of their day-to-day lives, but their reward was an adequate living.

Acadian farmers irrigated their fields using dikes, or walls of soil. The dikes held water on the field, which was then absorbed into the soil. In this way, the fields were watered with each high tide.

By the 1750s, the Acadian population had grown to about 10 000. Many families had six or seven children, and families with more than ten children were not uncommon. Many people lived to see old age. For some reason, the Acadians had longer life spans than the people in New France. The presence of many old people in their communities helped the Acadians preserve their history and traditions through the generations. Remembering their past would become increasingly important to the Acadians when conflict with the British threatened to destroy their way of life.

Daily Life in Acadia

Life in Acadia was similar in many ways to life in New France. The settlers adapted well to farming, livestock breeding, hunting, lumbering, and fishing. Most of the settlers were farmers whose main crops were wheat, fruit, and vegetables. Livestock was a mainstay of the Acadian economy. Much of this meat was secretly traded to New England, against the

A typical home in Acadia. Examine the picture closely and compare it with the picture of an habitant's home on page 88. What is the same? What is different?

Acadians made the rich soil productive through constant field work.

wishes of the French authorities. Fishing and hunting added to each household's resources.

The Acadians lived in log houses. With the abundance of wood, building a home was easy. The inside walls were covered with clay to make a plaster-like surface. The roofs were likely thatched with hay.

During the winter, the Acadians would spin wool or flax for clothing, tan leather for footwear and harnesses, make candles and soap, and build furniture. In the spring, they made maple syrup and spruce beer. Work in the fields and the woods was usually a community effort. When a young couple got married, the whole village would turn out to clear the land and help build a house for them. Such work would usually turn into a time for socializing.

At social gatherings, the Acadians would tell tales and sing songs of Old France. Fiddlers provided the music. The older members of the community told proud stories of the Acadians' past. The Acadians were fond of smoking—both the men and the women. Most of their clay pipes came from England, but they sometimes made their own with the local red clay.

Trade Relations

Although the settlers were mostly self-sufficient, there were things they could not make or grow themselves. They established trading links with New England and other French settlements. Molasses, cooking pots, axes, gunpowder, and fabrics came through New England. Through Louisbourg, they obtained cottons, thread, lace, firearms, and religious items from France.

A few small fishing villages were located on the outskirts of the main settlements. Dried fish were regularly shipped to France. There were few roads to link the settlements with each other. Canoes and small boats provided most of the transportation. In winter, sleds and snowshoes were used.

Religion was an important part of the settlers' lives. Priests and missionaries served as informal agents of the king and provided

some contact with New France. They gave spiritual and political guidance, made judgements in disputes, and taught the children. The first regular school was founded in Port Royal in 1703. The most prosperous families sent their children to France for schooling.

The Acadians were on friendly terms with their Mi'kmaq neighbours. The Mi'kmaq shared the art of hunting with them and taught them how to use herbs and other plants to make medicines. Unfortunately, contact was not as positive for the Aboriginal people. They became ill with various European diseases and, over time, lost many of their traditional ways.

British Control of Acadia

In 1713, Britain gained control of Acadia again. This time it would be permanent. At first, the Acadians were not alarmed about the situation since they had experienced it before, but frequent conflicts with the English made life insecure. The Acadians became adept at dealing with these conflicts. They were able to abandon their homes very quickly and flee to the woods. The settlers had an edge over the English because they knew all the trails and hideaways in the forests and valleys. Gradually, over the next few decades, the British authorities would become uneasy with their French-speaking population, leading to a disastrous end result.

Newfoundland Settlements

Britain had been active in Newfoundland since the earliest days of European exploration. Newfoundland was an important base for the British fishing industry. English fishermen continued to visit the island for the lucrative cod trade. A French colony was established on the south coast of Newfoundland by the 1660s. By 1713, there were as many French residents as British. Eventually, Britain forced France to give up all claims to the island, leaving the French with fishing rights only. Neither country wanted to set up more permanent settlements. The seasonal fishermen from Europe lived there only in the summer and they did not want competition for the fish from year-round residents.

Newfoundland's population continued to grow anyway. By 1749, Newfoundland had about 7000 permanent residents. These settlers were mainly European fishermen who chose to make Newfoundland their permanent home. Most of the people had come from Britain, but many came from southern Ireland because of the famine there. Even with this population growth, inland areas of Newfoundland continued to be undeveloped. Unlike Acadia to the south, Newfoundland's economy remained completely tied to the sea.

Establishing the Town of Halifax

The British became concerned about the expanding French fort of Louisbourg. They were eager to establish a strong presence along the Atlantic coast in Acadia (which the British called Nova Scotia). So in 1748, they made plans for the settlement of Chebucto, which means "the biggest harbour" in the language of the Mi'kmaq. The British government invested large sums of money to build the settlement. Lord Cornwallis was governor. He organized the fishery, imported manufactured materials from Boston, and had engineers map out the first streets. The new town was renamed Halifax after the Earl of Halifax, the British administrator who oversaw its development from London.

The following year, settlers began to arrive. Disbanded soldiers and sailors were encouraged to immigrate to Halifax, as were artisans from London. At first, the town was primitive. It was far less developed than British advertisements had promised. The first year was unsuccessful and many settlers were disheartened. Some of them died during the first winter and others migrated south to more established areas in New Hampshire, Massachusetts, Rhode Island and Connecticut.

Britain looked to the Protestant countries of Europe to find new sources for settlers. More than half of the people sent to the colony by the British recruiting agents were farmers. Unfortunately, lack of available farmland was a problem. The Acadians occupied much of the best land in Nova Scotia. The recent immigrants were unhappy with this situation. In 1753, Britain tried to deal with the problem by moving the immigrants to the new settlement of Lunenburg. But the tension between the British and the Acadians persisted until the situation came to a head in 1755.

Old Halifax, 1750s. The large home in the centre is the governor's mansion. In contrast to Cornwallis's conspicuous wealth, most people in Halifax earned a meagre living.

Activities

Understanding Concepts

1. Define the following words and enter them in your personal dictionary.

calèche	cajeu	berline
self-sufficient	caption	root cellar

2. Make a sequence of diagrams to show how the lives of the habitants followed the seasons.

3. Imagine you are growing up on an habitant farm in New France. What could you do on a cold day in the middle of the winter for entertainment?

4. Explain why the sleigh and the canoe were so important to the people of New France.

5. In which of the three towns of New France would you have chosen to live—Quebec, Montreal, or Trois-Rivières? Why?

6. In what ways was life in Acadia different from life in New France? What accounted for those differences?

7. How did the Acadians cope with the insecurity of having their land constantly passed back and forth by Britain and France?

8. What made it possible for the Acadians to maintain their unique culture?

Digging Deeper

9. **CREATE** Construct a model of an habitant's farmhouse. Illustrate and explain *pièce-sur-pièce* house construction.

10. **COMPARE** Describe the differences between the life of wealthy people of New France and that of the habitants.

11. **THINK** Describe the "special character" of Montreal in New France.

12. **ROLE-PLAY/WRITE** Imagine you are a person of your age in an habitant family. Describe a day in your life. Include details about your clothing, food, schooling, and work and leisure activities. Tell what you think the future holds for you. What choices do you have?

13. **COMPARE** Use an organizer to compare life in Upper Town and Lower Town in Quebec City.

Making New Connections

14. **RESEARCH** Find out more about habitant handicrafts such as hooked rugs, sugar moulding, furniture making, or woodcarving.

15. **INVESTIGATE/PRESENT** Make a list of items and ideas that the Europeans borrowed or learned from the Aboriginal peoples of North America. Present this information on a bulletin board with text and illustrations.

16. **DEBATE** The habitant families of New France had to do many things for themselves that Canadians today do not. Give some examples. Which way of life is better? Why?

Chapter 5

Conflict and Change in New Franc

News Bulletin

ENGLISH CHALLENGE OUR FUR TRADE

Summer 1670
Quebec, New France

For years, the Iroquois have been threatening our settlements and intercepting our furs. Now New France faces a new problem. The English are competing for our fur trade.

An English company has been granted the right to trade for furs around Hudson Bay. They call themselves the Company of Adventurers of England Trading into Hudson Bay. King Charles II of England has given them a

monopoly on the fur trade in Rupert's Land. This huge territory covers all the lands that are drained by rivers flowing into Hudson Bay.

Two French traitors, Radisson and Groseilliers, are even helping the English develop their posts. These disgruntled Frenchmen, whom the English call "Mr. Radishes" and "Mr. Gooseberry," have sold out New France! Now the English are building small forts all around Hudson Bay and James Bay. The Hudson Bay

posts are log houses roofed with grass or bark and surrounded with pointed log stockades.

Already, hundreds of Cree are paddling to these forts with excellent furs. Ships loaded with furs are sailing directly out of Hudson Bay to England. New France is losing business. This threat posed by the English must end! The competitors must be stopped before they destroy our fur trade!

Radisson (standing) and Groseilliers (seated) seek furs and explore North America.

Predicting
1. What might a British newspaper have said about this issue?
2. Both France and Britain have a lot at stake. What do you think each country will do to preserve its interests?
3. What advice would you give each country about how to resolve these differences?

Rivals: France vs. Britain

France and Britain are friendly neighbours today. They both belong to the European Union. Both French and English people travel back and forth between the two countries all the time. Britain and France have been allies since early in the 20th century. They fought side by side in two world wars. Engineers from both countries recently worked together on a giant project—a tunnel under the English Channel. Now the "Chunnel" links the countries by rail.

However, relations between the two neighbours have not always been friendly. In earlier days, France and Britain were bitter enemies and often at war. They were rivals for colonies in different parts of the world such as the West Indies and North America. Each country wanted to become the colonial "superpower." They were also rivals for military and naval power. Whenever the two countries were at war, their colonies were usually affected too.

In North America, France and Britain were in conflict in three main areas.

Trouble Spot #1: Hudson Bay

In 1670, the British founded the Company of Adventurers of England Trading into Hudson Bay, more commonly know as the Hudson's Bay Company. They built forts where major rivers flowed into Hudson Bay and James Bay. The British hoped to tap the rich source of furs in the northwest. The Chipewyan and the Cree were important trading partners for the Hudson's Bay Company.

The French responded to the threat of British traders at Hudson Bay. They made a series of successful armed attacks on the British posts. But in the end, Britain continued to control the Hudson Bay area.

The French tried another strategy. They built a series of forts along the chain of the Great Lakes, starting at the east end and moving westward. By 1688, they had reached Rainy Lake, near the northwest end of Lake Superior. A few years later, Pierre, Sieur de La Vérendrye, and his sons pushed even further into Aboriginal territory in search of furs. They built posts on Lake Winnipeg and the Saskatchewan River. French traders met the Cree on their way to trade at the Hudson Bay forts and persuaded the Cree to trade with them instead of with the British. In this way, the French were able to choke off much of the flow of furs to the Hudson Bay posts and gain many of the furs for themselves. Cargoes of furs travelled down through the Great Lakes and the St. Lawrence River to Montreal.

Aboriginals trade furs with the Hudson's Bay Company at York Factory. The trading was accompanied by gun salutes, parades, speeches, feasting, and gift-giving. This picture shows red-coated British soldiers parading the chiefs up to the fort.

Differences Between the French and the British in the Fur Trade

French
- French traders go right to the source of the furs. They travel into Aboriginal territory to trade.
- The French government controls the fur trade.
- Settlement is important.
- The French want to convert the Aboriginal peoples to Christianity.

British
- British traders stay at their Hudson Bay forts. They wait for Aboriginal people to bring their furs to them.
- Private individuals invest in the Hudson's Bay Company.
- There is not much interest at first in establishing settlements.
- The British do not try to convert the Aboriginal peoples to Christianity.

Fast Forward

The Hudson's Bay Company

On 2 May 1670, King Charles II of England granted a charter to the Company of Adventurers of England (The Hudson's Bay Company). The trading area granted to the Hudson's Bay Company was known as Rupert's Land. There was a condition in the charter. It said that if the reigning monarch ever visited the area, he or she must be given a tribute of two black elk and two black beaver skins. This photograph shows the Company making good on its promise.

Netsurfer

http://collections.ic.gc.ca/hbc
Visit this website to see some artifacts of the fur trade that were collected by the Hudson's Bay Company. You can see beaver hats, trade goods, and tomahawks.

His Majesty King George VI and Queen Elizabeth received their traditional gifts when they visited Winnipeg in 1939.

Trouble Spot #2: Nova Scotia and Newfoundland

France and Britain often clashed in Nova Scotia and Newfoundland. These regions had been exchanged like pieces on a chessboard during various peace talks. In a 100-year period, control of Nova Scotia had changed hands nine times. In a peace treaty signed in 1713, France surrendered Nova Scotia, Newfoundland, and the Hudson Bay territory. Along the Atlantic coast, France only kept Ile Royale (Cape Breton), Ile St.-Jean (Prince Edward Island), and fishing rights along Newfoundland's north shore. No wonder the colony along the St. Lawrence River felt surrounded by the British. It was being squeezed from the north, the east, and the south.

The Fort at Louisbourg

The French responded by trying to stop any spread of British influence. In 1720, they decided to build a huge fortress at Louisbourg on the shores of Ile Royale. It was built on a natural harbour as a naval base to protect the French fishing fleets on the Grand Banks. Louisbourg would also guard the entrance to the Gulf of St. Lawrence. The St. Lawrence River was the lifeline from New France to France, so it had to be kept open at all costs.

The stone fortress was built like a European castle. No expense was spared. Hundreds of workers were sent out from France. The walls were 10 m high and 3 m thick. The fortress was surrounded by a moat and bastions protected the walls. There were placements for 148 cannon. King Louis XV complained about the skyrocketing building costs, but France was determined to defend its last bit of territory in the Atlantic region.

By the 1840s, this fortified town was the centre of the cod fishing industry. Large quantities of fish were dried and salted here and then sent to Europe. Ships from France, the West Indies, and Canada docked at the many wharves. This was the busiest seaport in New France and one of the busiest in North America. Canada's first lighthouse was built at Louisbourg.

Louisbourg society was different from that of the communities along the St. Lawrence River. There was no seigneurial system; the fur trade was small; the Church had less power, and non-French people (Basques, Germans, and Swiss) lived and worked alongside the French majority. Louisbourg was a complete town, home to government administrators, artisans, fishermen, and innkeepers. There were a number of wealthy residents such as the governor, who lived in the Château St.-Louis. There were also some members of the clergy such as the Brothers of Charity who ran a hospital and the nuns who had a convent and a school. A large portion of the

Ships large and small were always in the Louisbourg harbour. They came from many different countries to fish, to trade, or for military reasons.

population was single young men. Soldiers stationed with the garrison and men in the fishery lived and worked at Louisbourg. It is said that morale among the soldiers was generally low. They complained about the poor food, the cold and barren location, and the uncomfortable living conditions.

The town had stores, homes, straight streets, and its own market. There were many inns and taverns in the harbour area. However, despite the variety of people and occupations at the fort, many supplies had to be imported because the surrounding inland areas were not developed. Nevertheless, Louisbourg became an impressive base that would draw the interest of the English colonies to its south.

Netsurfer

This Parks Canada website lists all the historic sites in Canada. You can find out much more about Louisbourg. You can even take a virtual tour of this reconstructed fortress. http://parkscanada.pch.gc.ca You can find information about life in Old Louisbourg in words and pictures at this site: http://fortress.uccb.ns.ca/behind/html

Fast Forward

Louisbourg Today

In 1961, the Government of Canada began a reconstruction of part of the original town and fortifications of Louisbourg. They recreated what was there in the 1740s. This photograph shows the reconstructed fort.

In the summer, many students work here as interpreters. They dress in authentic costumes of the period to try to recreate the way soldiers and other inhabitants of the fort may have looked.

The original fort at Louisbourg had placements for 148 cannon. Some cannon can be seen here in the reconstructed fort.

Trouble Spot #3: The Ohio River Valley

The third area of French-British conflict was in the Ohio River valley. Both countries saw this area as the key to dominating North America. They raced to see who could be the first to successfully establish themselves and develop the region.

Coureurs de bois had explored this area extensively and had established a chain of forts from the St. Lawrence to New Orleans. This made the English colonies along the Atlantic seaboard feel quite hemmed in. The English colonies had a rapidly growing population of over a million people. By 1750, they needed more farmland. The only possible direction to expand was westward over the Appalachian Mountains. The lands of the Ohio valley were fertile and would attract many settlers. Land companies were formed to divide the land into plots and sell them to settlers. British fur traders, too, set up shop in the area. They built trading posts and made alliances with the local Aboriginal peoples.

The British American colonies wanted the French out of the Ohio area and they were prepared to drive them out by force if necessary. But the French had no intention of withdrawing from the Ohio valley. Just as it did in New France, the British fur trade in the Ohio valley threatened to cut into the profits of France's fur-trading operations. Also, if the English continued to expand southward, they would cut off the main route between New France and Louisiana. This would make communication between the two French colonies difficult.

Governor Duquesne of New France sent troops to reinforce the area. A group of 500 French workers arrived to build Fort Duquesne on the Ohio River. The Aboriginal people in the area joined the French side. There were a number of clashes between French and British. When George Washington moved into the area with British troops in 1754, the government at Quebec acted quickly. A large force was sent to intercept Washington and drive the British out of the Ohio area. Washington surrendered and he and his men were marched eastward, back over the mountains.

The French appeared to be in control of the Ohio valley. However, they had to work hard to keep their Aboriginal allies supplied with trade goods. They also had to feed and support all the French troops stationed in the forts along the Ohio River. It was a long way to bring supplies from the St. Lawrence River to the Ohio River. This became a great drain on the resources of New France.

The Seven Years' War in North America

The French assembled a force of 3000 to send to North America. In June 1755, off the coast of Newfoundland, the British navy attacked and captured two French ships carrying troops. The French were furious and would not continue to negotiate with the British until the ships were returned. Britain refused. On 18 May 1756, Britain declared war on France. On 9 June 1756, France declared war on Britain. In their formal declarations, each country listed its reasons for going to war. Each country blamed the other for the outbreak of war and tried to make it seem like the other country had caused all the conflict. The war that resulted lasted for seven years. But even before the declaration of war, shots had already been fired in North America.

Britain said that
- French attacks in the West Indies and North America had violated the peace treaty
- Britain had to protect its colonies from French expansion

France said that
- the British had violated the terms of the peace treaty
- the British refused to return the two captured ships

Skill Building: Making Predictions

Before the Stanley Cup playoffs, you can try to predict which team will win. You make your predictions based on what you know about both teams, their players, and their past records. In warfare, you can also judge which side has the advantage.

The Situation
France and Britain are at war in the 1750s. Which side do you think has the best chance of winning?

Key Steps
Here are some steps to follow when making predictions.

1.   Find out what you already know. In groups, consider the following questions. They will help you to get started.
a)   How do the two populations compare? Who will have the advantage and why?
b)   New France has the largest territory. Will this be an advantage? Why or why not?
c)   What role would Louisbourg and Quebec play in any war? What role will the interior forts play? Why?
d)   What is **guerrilla warfare**? What role might guerrilla warfare play in this war? Who would have the advantage? Why?
e)   How might Britain use its powerful navy to cripple New France?
f)   Why are the Aboriginal allies important?

g)   How important is a general's experience in commanding a large army? Why?
h)   Which side has the advantage in the area of war supplies? Explain. Why might this become a very important issue?

2.   Make predictions (educated guesses) to answer the questions above. Decide which side has the better chance to win in a war. Write down your predictions and give reasons for your decisions.

3.   Share your predictions with other groups. Vote on each prediction, using the categories "Likely," "Possible," and "Unlikely."

4.   Read the material that follows to confirm your predictions.

5.   Reflect on what you have read. Did you find answers to the questions? What questions are still unanswered? What new knowledge did you gain? How many of your predictions were true?

	New France	**British Colonies**
Population	60 000	1 170 760
Territory	The French had a vast territory to defend, stretching from the St. Lawrence River south to the Gulf of Mexico and north to Rupert's Land.	The British owned territories stretching along the Atlantic seaboard and around Hudson Bay.
Defences	The French had mighty fortresses at Quebec and Louisbourg and a string of forts throughout the interior of their territory.	The British had some forts to protect their territory, especially along the Atlantic coast, for example, in Halifax. These forts would help to keep supply lines open to Britain.
Military strength of the colonists	The French had a large army of part-time soldiers who were very experienced in fighting in the wilderness, canoeing, and surprise attacks. They were supported by regular soldiers from France.	The British colonists were less experienced in wilderness warfare. They were more interested in farming and in business. They were supported by regular soldiers from Britain.
Military strength of the home country	France had the largest and best army in Europe.	Britain had the largest and most powerful navy in Europe.
Allies in North America	The French had many excellent and loyal Aboriginal allies.	The Iroquois were Britain's only Aboriginal allies.
Leadership	General Louis-Joseph de Montcalm was a highly experienced soldier and commander from France.	General James Wolfe came from Britain. At 32, he had little experience commanding a large army.
Supply lines	New France was relatively poor. Food and military equipment had to come from France through the ports of Montreal and Quebec.	The British colonies were rich and prosperous. Their farms, mills, and factories could provide most of the food and military equipment needed.

9 July 1755

Lieutenant General Edward Braddock was sent from England with two regiments of disciplined soldiers who knew how to fight. His orders were to sweep the French out of the Ohio valley and seize Fort Duquesne. Another army would attack Fort Niagara and cut the supply lines between the St. Lawrence River and all the French forts in the Ohio valley.

What followed for the British was a disaster. Braddock managed to get an army of 2200 men and supplies over the Appalachian Mountains. At first, even the French believed that Fort Duquesne was doomed. Braddock marched his soldiers along in lines as they did in Europe. But 200 French and their 600 Aboriginal allies used guerrilla warfare tactics. They hid behind trees and ambushed the red-coated British troops as they stood in the open. French sharpshooters picked off British troops. The British soldiers panicked, broke ranks, and fled. It was a decisive French victory.

One thousand British soldiers were killed, and Braddock himself was mortally wounded. Only a third of the army escaped death or capture. The survivors retreated to a British

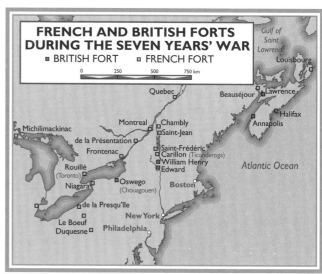

base in Virginia. The French captured their guns, wagons, and supplies. Braddock's secret papers fell into French hands. The papers provided valuable information about British war plans. Among the French and their allies, only 23 were dead and 20 wounded.

In the Atlantic region, however, the situation was reversed.

The Expulsion of the Acadians

Charles Lawrence, the British governor of Nova Scotia, was worried. In 1755, the British had captured Fort Beauséjour on the Acadian border. He was concerned about what he called "the Acadian problem." He found himself in the midst of 10 000 French Acadians. Could he trust the Acadians at a time when Britain and France were at war? Were they a serious security problem? What would happen if a French fleet appeared off the coast of Nova Scotia? Would the Acadians rise up against the British? If they did, there was

General Braddock's British forces were an easy target for the French and their Aboriginal allies. Why did the British suffer so many casualties?

no way that Lawrence and a few British troops could hold Nova Scotia.

The Acadians were generally peaceful and hard-working farmers. They had been living quietly, refusing to get involved on either side of the struggle between Britain and France. Lawrence decided to demand that the Acadians swear an **oath of loyalty** to the British king:

I solemnly swear as a Christian to be faithful to and truly obey His Majesty the King George II, whom I acknowledge to be the Sovereign Lord of Nova Scotia and Acadia. So help me God.

When most of the Acadians refused to take the oath, Lawrence announced that they would be **expelled** from Nova Scotia. They would be moved, by force if necessary, to other British colonies.

British soldiers moved into Acadian villages. They took homes, land, and most possessions from the Acadians. Men, women, and children were herded onto British ships. Many families were separated. When the broken-hearted Acadians looked back, they saw that their houses and barns were in flames.

Ships carrying the Acadians made their way to Georgia, Virginia, Maryland, and other English colonies. Some passengers died when their ships sank on the high seas. Those who survived found themselves among strangers who did not speak their language. They often found themselves living in misery and poverty.

A few Acadians fled into the woods and made their way to Cape Breton and Louisbourg. Some went south to Louisiana, where their descendants are known today as "Cajuns," from "Acadian." Some ended up in France or Quebec. Others stayed in the English colonies and started a new life. Six to eight thousand Acadians had been expelled.

Evangeline Bellefontaine became a heroine of Acadia thanks to a poem written about her life. In 1846, the American poet H.W. Longfellow published a long poem called "Evangeline." It tells how, during the deportation, Evangeline, "a maiden of seventeen summers," was separated from her lover, Gabriel Lajeunesse. She found him again only when he was an old and broken man. He died in her arms.

Today, a bronze statue of Longfellow's heroine stands outside a chapel in the historic park at Grand Pré, in Nova Scotia.

Netsurfer

Find out more about the Acadians at this site: www.schoolnet.ca Choose Digital Collections, then Social Studies to find The Acadian Odyssey.

The Acadians were escorted from their homes by soldiers and put on ships bound for the English colonies.

Fast Forward

The Return of the Acadians

After the Seven Years' War, about 2000 Acadians were allowed to return to Nova Scotia. They found that English-speaking strangers had taken over their farms. The British would not allow them to form large settlements. So, they gradually settled in remote coastal regions, as far away from their enemies as possible. Some settled in the west of Nova Scotia and on Cape Breton. Others preferred to locate east and north of the Saint John River in New Brunswick. Many Acadians also returned to Ile St.-Jean. Today, more than 20 000 people of Acadian descent live on the island.

Some of the Acadians had been put in prison in England. Eventually, they made their way to France. Twenty years later, in 1785, some Acadians accepted the invitation of the Spanish government to settle in Louisiana. About 1500 crossed the Atlantic to join the others who had settled in the bayous along the Gulf of Mexico.

The British attempt to assimilate or absorb the Acadians was a tragic failure. In spite of great suffering, the French-speaking Acadians never gave up their cultural identity. Today, these proud, independent people have increased in population in the Atlantic provinces. The Acadians have chosen their own flag and national anthem. The flag is similar to the French flag to show they remember their roots in France. They value their French language, their Roman Catholic faith, their families and communities, their work, and their culture.

Montcalm's Victories

In 1756, the Marquis de Montcalm arrived in New France. He was a highly experienced professional soldier who had just been appointed commander-in-chief of the French forces. Montcalm wasted no time. He quickly wiped out the powerful British fort at Oswego on Lake Ontario. Four British warships, 200 small boats, 70 cannon, and huge stores of military supplies fell into French hands. The capture of Fort Oswego let the French breathe a little easier because the military route to their western French forts was secure.

The next year, Montcalm took an army up the Richelieu River to the French Fort Carillon. From there, he attacked the British Fort William Henry and won a brilliant victory. Things were not looking good for Britain in North America.

An aerial view of Fort Ticonderoga. Originally named Fort Carillon by its French builders, it controlled the portage route between Lakes George and Champlain. The fort has been rebuilt and restored as a museum.

The British Change Strategy

The British forces were in trouble in North America. Britain needed a new war plan. British Prime Minister William Pitt believed that the best strategy was to attack France's colonies. Fifty thousand fresh British troops were added to the war in North America. New generals were appointed. One was the young James Wolfe.

Pitt ordered three plans of attack:
- capture Fort Duquesne and the Ohio valley
- destroy the forts along Lake Champlain, then break through to Montreal
- destroy Louisbourg and move down the St. Lawrence River to capture Quebec

The British plan began to work. In 1758, Fort Duquesne was captured. It had been a symbol of French dominance in the Ohio River valley. When the French commander saw that

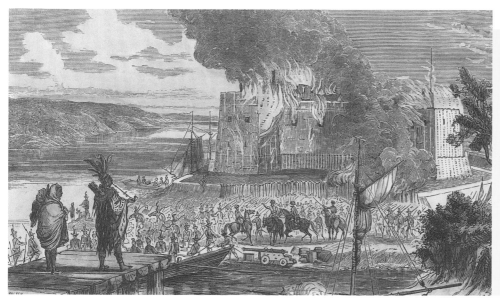

The burning of Fort Duquesne in 1758. The burning of this fort meant the loss of one of the most important French strongholds in the Ohio River valley.

all was lost, he gave orders to blow up the fort. The British built a stockade on the ashes and named it Pittsburgh after William Pitt.

At about the same time, a large British army surprised Fort Frontenac on Lake Ontario. Tons of winter supplies intended for the western fur posts fell into British hands. The gateway to the St. Lawrence was open. The British were in a position to move from the west toward Montreal and Quebec.

Another huge British army was marching toward Montreal from the south. They were slowed down by Montcalm and the French at Lake Champlain. But French troops were forced to fall back to try to protect Montreal.

The Fall of Louisbourg

One hundred sixty British warships appeared off the coast of Cape Breton in June 1758. French warships sitting in the harbour at Louisbourg were sunk. The British bombardment of the French fortress began.

The British ships cut off all French lines of reinforcements. No food, soldiers, or supplies could get to the defenders of Louisbourg. Ammunition and supplies dwindled within the fortress. Then, British soldiers and their cannons landed on the shore. One of the first to leap ashore was James Wolfe.

It took seven weeks of bombardment to convince the French to give up. The people inside the fortress were starving. The walls were crumbling under daily cannon fire. The French fleet had not arrived to relieve them. There seemed to be no chance of rescue. On 26 July 1758, Louisbourg surrendered to the British.

Quebec in Danger

The destruction of Louisbourg was a catastrophe. It was the beginning of the end for the French. The Gulf of St. Lawrence was wide open to the British navy. Quebec was in grave danger. Some British generals thought they should attack Quebec immediately. But it was too late in the year to attack Quebec before winter set in. The British decided to wait until spring.

Quebec was doomed, unless the French fleet arrived first in the spring with soldiers and reinforcements. But the French navy did not arrive; a British fleet appeared on the St. Lawrence River first. In June 1759, James Wolfe arrived with 39 000 soldiers and 25 warships. The British were prepared to capture Quebec, but it would be September until they saw their opportunity.

The weather was stormy and the sea was rough when James Wolfe led soldiers ashore at Louisbourg. Because of his courage and luck at Louisbourg, Wolfe was promoted to lead the British attack on Quebec the following year.

The Siege of Quebec

Thursday, 13 September 1759

It was well past midnight and most of the citizens of Quebec were asleep. However, along the river west of the town, something suspicious was happening. Twenty-four British soldiers had landed at the foot of the steep cliffs. These cliffs were high and so steep that the French believed no army would ever scale them.

All summer long, General Wolfe had bombarded Quebec with cannon fire from across the river. But the city had not surrendered. Winter was coming and Wolfe was desperate. He decided to make one more attempt to capture the fortress.

Wolfe had noticed French women washing clothes on the riverbank. Later, he saw the clothes drying at the top of the cliffs. Wolfe

Taking Quebec. The events shown actually took place over a period of about 12 hours, from late at night until noon the next day. The battle on the Plains of Abraham was not the last battle in the British conquest, but it was the decisive one.

guessed that there must be a way up those cliffs. In the darkness, British soldiers started to scale the cliffs. The attack depended upon darkness, silence, and complete surprise.

Only 30 French sentries were guarding the heights at the top of the cliffs. A sentry called out, "Who goes there?" A British soldier replied in perfect French, "Provisions from Montreal." With quick blows to the head and muffled cries, it was done. No shots had been fired. The British were in control at the top of the cliffs.

A signal light was flashed to the river to the hundreds of British soldiers who had been waiting silently in boats. The troops started scrambling up the cliffs. The place where they climbed up is now called Anse au Foulon. By dawn, more than 4400 British troops were on the heights. They gathered in an open field called the Plains

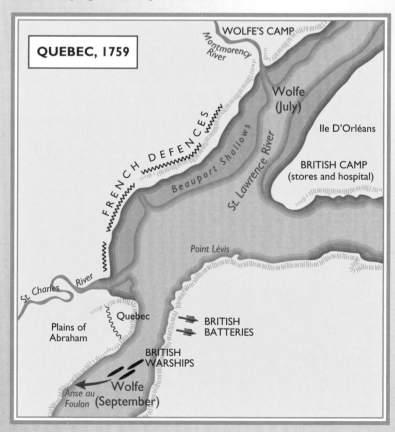

QUEBEC, 1759

WOLFE'S CAMP
Montmorency River
Wolfe (July)
FRENCH DEFENCES
Beauport Shallows
St. Lawrence River
Ile D'Orléans
BRITISH CAMP (stores and hospital)
Point Lévis
St. Charles River
Quebec
BRITISH BATTERIES
Plains of Abraham
BRITISH WARSHIPS
Anse au Foulon
Wolfe (September)

British guns and mortars battered Quebec's Lower Town from across the river. One hundred fifty-two houses were reduced to dust and the church of Notre-Dame-des-Victoires was destroyed.

of Abraham. They were about 3 km from the town of Quebec.

The French general Montcalm was taken by surprise. He knew that he had finally been outwitted. Instead of waiting in the fortress for reinforcements that were nearby at Beauport Shallows, he decided to attack immediately. At eight o'clock in the morning, Montcalm led his army out of the gates and onto the Plains of Abraham.

At ten o'clock, the French army advanced. The British held their fire until the enemy was within musket range. Then, Wolfe ordered his soldiers to fire and British muskets rang out. Before the smoke had cleared, the British reloaded and fired again. French soldiers fell in heaps. When Wolfe ordered the British to charge, the French army retreated into the town.

By noon, the most important battle in Canadian history was over. General Wolfe was one of the 655 British soldiers killed. General Montcalm was also hit by a bullet. As he lay dying, Montcalm said, "I am glad I shall not live to see the surrender of Quebec." A few days later, Quebec was handed over to the British.

The death of General Montcalm

The death of General Wolfe

Profile

Louis-Joseph, Marquis de Montcalm 1712–1759

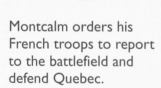

Montcalm orders his French troops to report to the battlefield and defend Quebec.

Montcalm was born into a noble family in the south of France. He was well educated. In 1736, he married Louise Angélique Talon and later became the father of five children.

Montcalm entered the army in 1727. Two years later, at the age of 17, he was promoted to captain. He served in many battles in Europe and was wounded several times. On one occasion, he was captured by the Austrians, but was returned to France in an exchange of prisoners.

Soon after returning to Paris, Montcalm was given an audience with King Louis XV, who promoted him to the rank of brigadier.

In 1756, Montcalm was sent to New France as a major general. In 1758, after his stunning victory at Carillon, he was promoted to lieutenant general and commander of all French forces in North America.

All during the summer of 1759, Montcalm and his troops withstood Wolfe's attacks on Quebec. Montcalm knew that he would not have to fight to win. If the French could simply hold on, avoiding an all-out fight, the freezing of the rivers in winter would drive the invaders away. It was at this point that Wolfe and the British managed to scale the cliffs at Anse au Foulon.

In the short battle on the Plains of Abraham, Montcalm was wounded. He was riding among his soldiers, trying to rally the troops, when two bullets passed through his body. He asked two soldiers to hold him up in the saddle so his injuries did not create more panic among his men. In this way, he rode through the St. Louis Gate to the surgeon. Marquis de Montcalm died early the next morning. He was buried in the convent of the Ursuline nuns, in a hole made by a British shell.

1. If Montcalm had lived, what might he have said about the results of the battle?
2. Do you think Montcalm was a successful military leader? Why or why not?
3. What epitaph would you put on Montcalm's gravestone?

Profile

James Wolfe
1727–1759

James Wolfe was born in England into a military family. Both his father and grandfather were officers in the army. From an early age, he was determined to have a military career. Wolfe joined his father's regiment at age 14. He transferred to the army the next year and saw service in Germany, the Netherlands, and Scotland.

By 23, Wolfe was a colonel. He earned a reputation as a leader and trainer of soldiers. He was a superb battleground commander. After his heroism at Louisbourg, Prime Minister Pitt made the young, ambitious Wolfe the commander of the Quebec expedition.

James Wolfe was a tall, lanky man. Sometimes he wore a wig while at other times he showed his own hair. He was highly emotional and was said to have a very hot temper. His regiment was always one of the best and he never spared himself. Although he was not well liked, Wolfe was respected by all who knew him.

During the summer of 1759, Wolfe and the British camped beside the St. Lawrence River, looking for a way to capture Quebec. Time was running out for the British. The Canadian winter was coming and they couldn't stay anchored indefinitely in the St. Lawrence. Wolfe's officers were getting impatient and they pressured him for a plan of attack. Finally, in September, Wolfe decided to act. His bold idea to strike at the Plains of Abraham saved his reputation but cost him his life.

As Wolfe lay dying on the battlefield, it is said that he heard a messenger cry, "They run. They run." "Who runs?" the general whispered. "The enemy runs away," came the reply. Then, General Wolfe turned on his side and murmured, "I die happy." Wolfe died at the young age of 32. His body was returned to England on the warship *Lowestoft*.

James Wolfe's bold plan and his rigorously trained army won Canada for Britain. Detail from painting by George Townshend.

1. Do you think Wolfe was a successful military leader? Why or why not?
2. What epitaph would you put on Wolfe's gravestone?

The End of French Rule

The battle on the Plains of Abraham was over in a morning. Within a week, the city surrendered. Quebec had fallen. The French tried to hold on for a year at Montreal. However, the British controlled the Atlantic and that meant that any help from France was almost impossible. The next spring, 18 000 British troops closed in on Montreal. They burned the farms along the river as they advanced. The French prepared for a last stand. But Governor Vaudreuil recognized that the French could not win. On 8 September 1760, at Montreal, Vaudreuil surrendered New France to the British. On 9 September, the British marched into the town. The French turned over their guns. The war was over. The fleur-de-lys, which had flown over Quebec since the days of Cartier and Champlain, came down.

The colony was no more. French rule in North America had ended.

After the British Conquest

Can you imagine how the people of New France were feeling in September 1760? They had lost their homeland. Quebec lay in ruins. There were British soldiers in the streets. They would have felt sad, angry, frustrated, and disappointed. But they were also worried. What would become of them? Many of their leaders had returned to France. It seemed like France had abandoned them. They sensed that things were going to be very different for them from that point on. For the French Canadians, the British victory was the worst possible disaster.

French forces surrender Montreal to the British without a shot being fired.

What Were People Saying?

In New France

Habitants:

What will happen to us? Will we be expelled from our land as the Acadians were? Will we lose our homes and our lands like they did? Will we have to stop speaking French and learn to speak English? Will we have to give up our customs and learn to do things the way the British do? Will we be forced to give up our religion? Will the English tax us to death?

French Merchants:

Will the British put us out of business? Will English merchants come in and take over our stock and our shops? If we are allowed to stay in business, will we now have to use English weights and measures? Will our money be useless? Our roots are here in this new country. We can't go back to France now. In France, we would have to start all over again!

Seigneurs:

France seems to have abandoned us. What kind of leadership can we provide for our people? Will we be allowed to keep our seigneuries and our positions in society? We know that the British do not allow Roman Catholics to participate in government. Does that mean we no longer will be part of the Sovereign Council? Worst of all, what if the British decide to scatter us like the Acadians?

Bishop, Priests, and Nuns:

We are very worried about our holy religion. What will happen to the people's faith? The English are not Roman Catholics. Will they allow our religion to continue? Can we keep our churches, schools, convents, and hospitals? Will the Church be permitted to collect tithes to operate all these good services? The survival of the French culture depends on our being able to keep our religion, language, and customs.

The Aboriginal Peoples:

Did we support the wrong side? Should we have been allies with the British? What will happen to us now? Will British colonists move into our land to start farming? Where will we go? Where will we hunt, fish, and trap? How will we maintain our traditional lifestyle?

British Military Leaders:
What shall we do with all these French people? How can we rule a population of over 60 000 that includes less than 1000 British? What if they attempt an uprising? Will we be able to put it down? How can we govern people who speak a different language, practise a different religion, and live by different customs?

In France
French Officials in Paris:
Why worry about losing New France? Was the colony ever self-supporting? No, it was always a drain on French resources. The West Indies are of more use to us because real profits come from the sugar trade. There's nothing in New France but lots of snow!

In the Thirteen Colonies

British Officials:

At last, the war is over and the French threat is gone. Our colonies are no longer going to be hemmed in along the Atlantic seaboard. How soon can we start our westward expansion over the mountains?

British Merchants:

Now we have control of the furs and resources of most of North America. We have a larger market for our goods. How soon can we move into Quebec and set up business? Will we have positions of influence and power in the new colony that Britain has just won? We are the ones who should be asked to join the government and help run the new colony.

Practise the skill of making predictions. New France has fallen to the British. What do you think is now going to happen to the people of New France? What actions do you think the British government will take? Make predictions in groups. Share your predictions with other groups. Then read the material in Unit 2 to see how accurate your predictions were.

The British Make Plans

The conquest of New France presented problems for the British. It was true that Britain was now in control of most of the North American continent. The wealth of furs and forests was theirs. There were also more customers to buy British manufactured goods. But the British were not quite sure what to do with the people in the new colony of Quebec.

Plan 1: Making Canada British

At first, the British tried to change the **Canadiens**. They wanted the habitants and seigneurs to become British. They intended to turn Quebec into a colony like all the other British colonies in North America. This is called **Anglicization** or **assimilation**. Anglicization means that everything had to be done the way the English did it. Assimilation happens when one culture is absorbed by another and the minority culture has to take on the characteristics of the dominant one.

Britain hoped that the French culture and language would soon disappear from Quebec. They thought this would happen automatically as English-speaking settlers moved north from the other British colonies. But very few people in the south wanted to move north to a colder climate where the best land was already taken. Also, English-speaking colonists did not want to live in an area where the French outnumbered them.

Royal Proclamation of 1763

In 1763, the Seven Years' War was officially over. Britain and France signed a peace agreement. When New France became the property of Britain, the British government passed the Royal Proclamation. This Act
- renamed the colony Quebec
- reduced the boundaries to an area along the St. Lawrence River valley and the Ottawa River valley

- closed settlement to all the rest of what had been New France in order to protect the fur trade and the Aboriginal peoples
- made Protestantism the official religion of the colony
- replaced French law with English law
- named a British governor and council to rule the colony
- established English language schools run by Protestants

The Canadiens were expected to adjust to the English language and British laws and customs. But the British government soon realized that they would have to come up with a better plan for Quebec. The French culture would not easily disappear. In fact, the French-speaking population of Quebec continued to grow. Very few English-speaking merchants moved into Quebec. The government of Quebec could not include Roman Catholics. This meant that, in Quebec, a very small English minority had all the power.

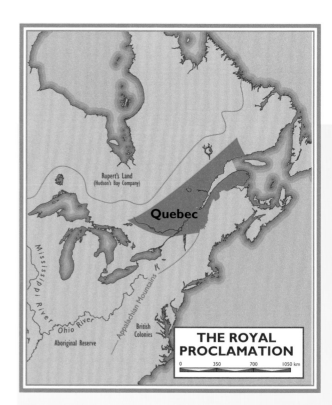

The Royal Proclamation of 1763 drew the borders of the British colony of Quebec.

Plan 2: The Quebec Act 1774

After years of debate about how to treat Quebec, the British government agreed on a new plan. One reason for this was that there was trouble brewing in the English colonies to the south of Quebec. The British North American colonies were growing restless under British rule. The American Revolution would soon break out. The last thing Britain needed was additional trouble with the French colony of Quebec. Therefore, in 1774, the British government passed the Quebec Act. This act was intended to keep the French Canadians happy so they would never attempt to break away from Britain. The act

- gave the territory in the Ohio valley west of the Appalachians to Quebec, returning almost all of what had been New France
- allowed the seigneurs to continue to own their seigneuries and collect rents
- permitted the French to keep their language, customs, and Roman Catholic religion
- allowed the Church to collect tithes
- established two kinds of law—French civil law, which the people were familiar with, and English criminal law with trial by jury
- named a British governor and council to rule the colony, but allowed Roman Catholics to be appointed to the governing council (this was forbidden in Britain)

Which provisions would please the Canadiens? Why? Which provisions would please the English colonists? Why? Would the French be satisfied with the Quebec Act? If trouble broke out in Britain's Thirteen Colonies to the south, would the Canadiens remain loyal to Britain? The British did not have long to wait to find out. Within two years, the American Revolution had begun.

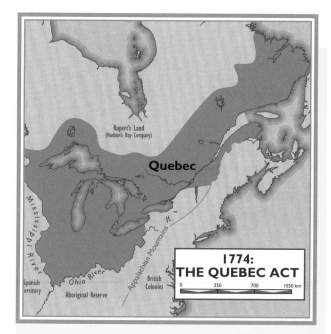

1774: THE QUEBEC ACT

0   350   700   1050 km

With the Quebec Act, Britain expanded the territory of Quebec to include the Ohio River valley.

Fast Forward

Quebec in the 21st Century

French rule in North America ended in 1760. But the French influence will always be felt in Canada. Today, more than 5 000 000 descendants of the early settlers live in the province of Quebec. French culture survives in its people. The **Québécois**, as they prefer to be called, have a culture quite distinct from that of other Canadians. They refuse to be absorbed by the dominant British culture and traditions. They preserve their heritage, language, religion, and traditions. The Québécois feel strongly about their history. If you look at Quebec's licence plates, you will see that they say, "*Je me souviens*," which is French for "I remember." The Québécois remember their history and their culture, and they have continued to develop their own distinctive way of life.

Activities

Understanding Concepts

1. Define the following terms and add them to your personal dictionary.

guerrilla warfare	expel	oath of loyalty
assimilation	Canadiens	Québécois
Anglicization		

2. Describe the differences between the Hudson's Bay Company's trading methods and those of the fur traders from New France. Why would these differences be important in the conflicts between the two countries?

3. Why would the presence of British traders on Hudson Bay be a threat to the colony of New France?

4. Why was the fortress of Louisbourg built?

5. Why did General Braddock lose the battle in the Ohio River area?

6. Make a timeline to show the major events in the Seven Years' War between 1755 and 1760. Decide whether each battle was a French or British victory, and use a colour code to show which was which.

7. On a map of present-day Quebec, Ontario, and Manitoba, mark the fur posts that were owned by the French and the British. If possible, indicate the present-day name of the nearby city or town.

Digging Deeper

8. **RESEARCH** Write a report on the fortress of Louisbourg. Include the reasons for its location, details of its construction (including the materials used), and its military and trade functions.

9. **BRAINSTORM/DISCUSS** What other means might Governor Lawrence have used to handle the question of Acadian loyalty?

10. **DISCUSS**
    a) Did the Acadians deserve the punishment of expulsion?
    b) The Acadians claimed they were neutral. Is it possible to be neutral in the middle of a war?
    c) Should the Acadians have been allowed to move to another French territory?

11. **Construct** Look at the map on page 115 that shows the Battle of Quebec. Create your own model, sketch, or diagram showing the area involved. Include and identify each of the following:
    - the steep cliffs west of Quebec
    - the place where the British climbed up the cliffs
    - the open field where the battle was fought
    - the location of the British cannons used to bombard Quebec
    - the location of reserve French troops that Montcalm might have called to help defend Quebec

    Use your model to describe the events of the battle.

12. **Predict** What might have happened if French ships had arrived in Quebec in 1759 ahead of British ships? Explain.

13. **Discuss** Who do you think was the better general, Wolfe or Montcalm? Explain your answer.

14. **Compare** The Royal Proclamation of 1763 and the Quebec Act of 1774 were both British plans for governing Quebec. How did they differ? Why did they differ?

15. **Think/Write** Why was it so difficult to make Quebec into a colony like all the other British North American colonies?

Making New Connections

16. **Research/Present** Find out more about the history and the culture of the Cajuns who live in Louisiana today. Present your findings to the class.

17. **Think/Discuss** New France fell militarily in 1760. Suggest reasons why the French Canadian culture has survived so strongly to this day.

18. **Investigate/Guest Speaker** Invite French-speaking people from your school or community to speak to your class about French heritage and culture today.

British North America

oronto celebrates Simcoe Day on the first Monday in August in honour of John Graves Simcoe. Simcoe was a British war hero who became the first governor of the British colony of Upper Canada. He arrived in Upper Canada shortly after the American Revolution. This was the time when thousands of United Empire Loyalists were pouring into the Upper Canada wilderness. Like Champlain in New France, Simcoe worked hard to put in place the foundations of Upper Canada—government, laws, courts, and roads.

The Loyalists were the first large group of immigrants to arrive in Upper Canada. They left the United States because they were loyal to Britain. Later, there would be another wave of immigrants, this time from Britain. All these new arrivals had to adapt to the hardships of an isolated environment. They had to learn to co-operate in order to stay alive in the wilderness. They had to respond to the challenge of attack by the United States. In spite of these obstacles, they managed to survive.

The British colony of Upper Canada flourished and grew. By the 1840s, the population had reached one million. The newcomers settled the land. They established schools and churches. They built transportation networks. Their hard work led to economic growth in agriculture and the timber trade. It was the beginning of the future province of Ontario.

1775 – 1783	American Revolution
1783 –	United Empire Loyalists begin arriving in British North America
1791 –	Constitutional Act creates colony of Upper Canada
1792 –	First Legislative Assembly in Upper Canada
1793 –	York is named capital of Upper Canada
1790s –	The Late Loyalists arrive
1803 –	Talbot Settlement is organized
1812 – 1814	War with the United States
1815 – 1850	Great migration of British settlers to Upper Canada
1829 –	Welland Canal links the Great Lakes
1830 on	Slaves escape into Canada using the Underground Railroad
1832 –	Cholera epidemic
1834 –	York renamed Toronto and becomes a city

Focusing In!

After studying this unit, you will be able to answer the following questions.

1. What were the main reasons for the early English settlement of Upper Canada?
2. Who were the United Empire Loyalists and where did they settle?
3. What caused the great migration? How did those settlers change Upper Canada?
4. What part did Canadians play in helping escaped slaves through the Underground Railroad?
5. What were the major causes of the War of 1812 and who were the key players?
6. How did the War of 1812 affect the development of Canada?

The American Revolution and the United Empire Loyalists

Maryland, A British North American Colony, 1763

Samuel Austin was red-faced with anger when he met his neighbour. "A fine way to treat us," grumbled the farmer in Maryland. The news had caught him totally by surprise. Samuel's anger grew as he thought about it. In the Royal Proclamation of 1763, the British government had cut off the Thirteen Colonies from the Ohio valley. "We fought the French for the right to expand across the Appalachians," he said to his neighbour Matthew Butler. "Now Britain, our home country, is going to keep us out of the Ohio and give the country back to the Aboriginal peoples! Why in heaven's name were we fighting to drive the French out of the Ohio?" "They are saying that no settlers will be allowed west of the mountains," Matthew exploded. "You and I have been dreaming for years of relocating our families to new homesteads on the fertile lands in the west, on the other side of the mountains. Now it looks like that is out of the question." "Seems to me, Matthew, that Britain doesn't really care about what happens to the Thirteen Colonies," said Samuel. Both men were extremely bitter.

The British government had just announced the terms of the Royal Proclamation of 1763. The lands west of the mountains that had belonged to New France were now going to be reserved for the Aboriginal peoples. To the colonists, the Proclamation Line was like a barrier built by an unfair parent to keep its

children fenced in and under control. Britain did not give any reasons for the line. Instead, it was announced that there would be 10 000 troops stationed along the line to keep the peace. Britain even suggested that the Thirteen Colonies could help pay the costs!

Many of the colonists in America were as upset and bitter as Samuel Austin and Matthew Butler. They began to murmur that Britain was punishing its long-time colonies. Trouble was brewing in the Thirteen Colonies.

Predicting
1. Why do you think the British made the decision they did?
2. What kind of trouble do you think was brewing? How might the colonists react?
3. How might Britain react to the colonies' expressions of dissatisfaction?
4. Not all colonists agreed with Samuel and Matthew. Why might some think that the Royal Proclamation was a good thing?
5. How might the Aboriginal peoples feel about the Royal Proclamation and the troops stationed along the border?

Britain's Thirteen Colonies

In 1763, the Seven Years' War with France was over. France was no longer a threat to Britain. Now Britain was the most powerful European nation in North America. The British controlled a North American empire that stretched from Hudson Bay to the Gulf of Mexico.

While France was putting down roots along the St. Lawrence River, the English colonies on the Atlantic coast had been developing rapidly. Small groups from Britain had established settlements in Virginia as early as 1607. Since then, the population of these Thirteen Colonies had grown to about 1 500 000. Industries were booming. Shipyards, lumber mills, flour mills, and tanneries were bustling. Prosperous farms were producing surplus food for sale in the towns. The colonies were thriving economically and becoming increasingly self-confident. Sam Austin and Matthew Butler were not alone in resenting the way they were treated by their home country. Many people in the Thirteen Colonies began to feel that they no longer needed ties with Britain.

Between 1763 and 1775, Britain and the American colonies moved further apart. Their differences led eventually to an all-out war called the **American Revolution** or the War of Independence. It lasted from 1775 to 1783. When the peace treaty was finally signed, the American colonies were independent. A new nation was born—the United States of America.

Slavery

Much of the economic growth in the Thirteen Colonies was due to the fact that many large farms, especially in the South, kept slaves. Slaves could be bought and sold as property. Slavery in the United States was not entirely abolished until 1865.

The Boston Massacre was one of the final conflicts leading up to the American Revolution.

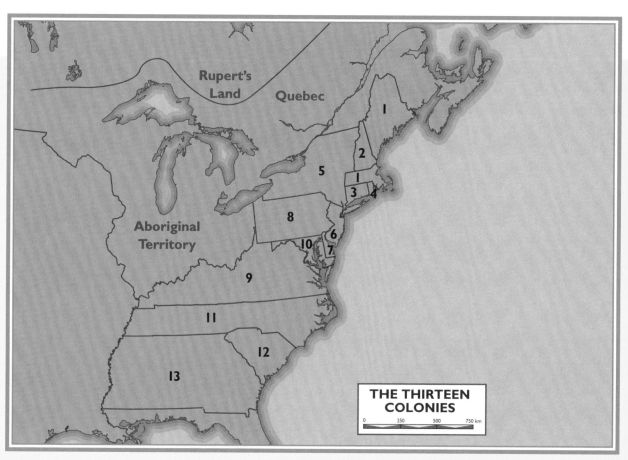

THE THIRTEEN COLONIES

NAME	DATE FOUNDED
NEW ENGLAND	
1. Massachusetts*	1620
2. New Hampshire	1679
3. Connecticut	1665
4. Rhode Island	1663
MIDDLE COLONIES	
5. New York	1664
6. New Jersey	1664
7. Delaware	1664
8. Pennsylvania	1681
SOUTHERN COLONIES	
9. Virginia	1607
10. Maryland	1634
11. North Carolina	1653
12. South Carolina	1670
13. Georgia	1733

* Maine was gradually annexed by the Massachusetts Bay Colony from 1652 to 1658. Maine separated from Massachusetts in 1819.

Skill Building: Recognizing Cause and Effect

All the incidents you are going to read about next can be seen as causes of the American Revolution in 1775. A **cause** is the incident or event that makes something happen. An **effect** is the result or the consequence. For example, if your basketball team does not practise, if your star player is hurt, or if the players do not play well together as a team, your school may lose the championship. Several causes may lead to the final result or effect—the loss of the championship.

At the same time, causes or events may have several effects. All the causes and effects together may eventually lead to a major decision or change. Suppose that someone pulls the fire alarm at your school. The fire department is called, and staff and students evacuate the building. After searching the school and finding no fire, the firefighters determine that it was a false alarm. They suspect that someone set off the alarm as a joke. What effects might this event have? What final change or decision might result? Let's consider the possibilities.

Cause
Someone has pulled the fire alarm at Terry Fox School without cause.

Effects
- The fire department is called to the school to investigate.
- While the firefighters are at the school, they are not available to handle any real emergencies that might occur in the rest of the community.
- Students lose class time during the evacuation and investigation.
- Teachers must assign students extra homework to make up for lost class time.
- Parents, teachers, and students worry that future alarms will not be taken seriously.

Decision
The principal calls an assembly to talk about fire safety and outlines specific punishments for anyone caught setting off the fire alarm as a prank.

Historians study causes and effects to find out how and why major events happened. The American Revolution was a major event. It had many causes and each cause had several effects. All these causes and effects together pushed the American colonists to break away from Britain.

Using a cause and effect organizer can help you understand the complex reasons for the American Revolution. Consider the example below.

The first cause is the Royal Proclamation of 1763. This law angered British North American colonists like Samuel Austin and Matthew Butler. The cause and effect organizer looks like this:

Cause
Royal Proclamation of 1763

Effects
- Colonists are angry because they will not be allowed to expand into the Ohio valley.
- Colonists feel that Britain does not care about them.
- Colonists wonder why they had fought the French for the Ohio lands.

Decision
Some colonists start thinking and talking about breaking away from Britain.

Study the cause and effect organizers on the following pages. Explain how all these events together might lead to the major decision of the American Revolution.

The Sugar Act 1764

Cause
Britain imposes tax on molasses.

Effect
People stop buying and selling molasses.

The Stamp Act 1765

Cause
Britain orders colonists to buy stamps for all newspapers, legal documents, calendars, and playing cards.

Effects
- People make speeches and demonstrate against the Stamp Act.
- Tax collectors are attacked.
- Stamps are burned in the streets.
- Some colonists **boycott,** or refuse to buy, all British goods.
- A group called Sons of Liberty is formed to oppose these new British laws.
- The Stamp Act is withdrawn in 1766.

Stamps were impressions made in paper, like seals on a certificate.

American colonists burn British stamps.

The Townshend Duties 1767

Cause
Britain places a tax on all tea, glass, paper, lead, silk, and paint bought from Britain.

Effects
- Colonists stop buying British goods.
- Merchants who sell British goods have their stores vandalized.
- Britain withdraws all taxes, except the one on tea, in 1770.

The Quartering Act 1768

Cause
Britain orders colonists to pay for food and housing for the British army in North America.

Effects
- Colonists are enraged.
- British soldiers are insulted in the streets.
- Street brawls between troops and citizens take place.

The Boston Massacre 1770

Cause
A Boston crowd clashes with British redcoats. Insults are shouted and soldiers fire into the crowd.

Effects
- Blood is shed for the first time and five colonists are killed.
- The British are accused of firing on defenceless citizens.
- Some colonists become more extreme and vocal in their opposition to the British government.

The Tea Act 1773

Cause
Britain allows the East India Company to sell tea in the colonies without paying the tax. This tea is cheaper than tea sold by colonial merchants, who have to pay the tax.

Effects
- Colonists boycott the imported tea.
- In Boston, 30 to 60 men, disguised as Aboriginal people, board ships in the harbour and dump tea into the water. This event is known as the Boston Tea Party.
- Colonists who oppose Britain start to call themselves "**Patriots**" and call pro-British groups "**Tories**."

The "Intolerable" Acts 1774

Cause

Britain passes the "**Intolerable**
Acts, a series of harsh acts to pun-
ish "the New England fanatics"
(Patriots). These include closing the
port of Boston, placing more troops
in the colony, and outlawing town
meetings.

Effects

- Colonists see these acts as the last straw.
  They are convinced that Britain intends
  to crush them.
- Colonists continue to boycott all British
  goods.
- Patriot leaders meet at the first
  Continental Congress to make a united
  protest to Britain.
- Local fighting militias, called **Minutemen**,
  are armed and ready to fight at a minute's
  notice.

Quebec Act 1774

Causes

- The British government expands
  the border of Quebec to
  include the Ohio valley.
- A governor and a council will
  be appointed by Britain to rule
  the province.
- French Roman Catholics may
  serve in government.

Effects

- Outrage in the Thirteen Colonies spreads
  like wildfire.
- Colonists are furious because they want
  to expand their colonies into the Ohio
  lands.
- Colonists are angry that their former
  enemies, the French Canadians, are being
  treated so generously.
- Colonists are upset that there is no
  elected assembly in Quebec.
- French Canadians will probably stay loyal
  to Britain if there is a war between
  Britain and the Thirteen Colonies.

Conflict at Lexington and Concorde 1775

Cause

Governor Gage of Massachusetts orders British troops to seize arms and ammunition illegally stored by the Minutemen at Concord. Paul Revere warns the Minutemen. At Lexington, British troops are barred by the Minutemen. Eight Minutemen are killed and ten are wounded. The British march on to Concord, destroy the war supplies, and then retreat to Boston. But the Minutemen are expert marksmen and guerrilla fighters. Three hundred redcoats are killed or wounded. The Minutemen lose 85.

Effect

Outbreak of war sets colonies on road to independence.

Paul Revere is pictured here on his midnight ride to warn the Minutemen that the British were on their way to Concord.

Declaration of Independence 4 July 1776

Cause

The second Continental Congress declares the United States of America independent from Britain.

Effects

- The Thirteen Colonies make a complete break with Britain.
- Britain launches a massive attack to crush the revolution.
- Bitter fighting takes place between British forces and the new Continental army under George Washington.

The Americans hoped that the French-speaking people of Quebec would join their revolution. But they refused. In December 1775, the Americans attacked. In Quebec City, a fierce battle was fought on New Year's Eve. Here, red-toqued militiamen and British soldiers are turning back the American invaders. The American invasion of the colony of Quebec failed.

What Was a "Loyalist"?

Not everyone who lived in the Thirteen Colonies wanted independence from Britain. As many as one-third of the American colonists were against it. Colonists who were against the revolution were known as **Loyalists** or **United Empire Loyalists.** They were loyal to King George III of England. They thought there were important advantages, such as trade and defence, in belonging to England. They thought that the idea of using armed violence to overthrow the government was wrong. Other colonists were opposed to all war for religious reasons.

Who Were the Loyalists?

The Loyalists were a mixed collection of people. They came from all of the Thirteen Colonies and represented a cross-section of American society. Some were rich landowners; others were poor and uneducated. Many Loyalists were Anglicans, although some practised different religions. Some were professional people. But about three-quarters of the total were farmers, artisans, shopkeepers, and merchants. Some were recent immigrants. Others had been born in the Thirteen Colonies. There were British officials who had worked in the Thirteen Colonies for the King of England. But not all Loyalists were of British origin. There were also Germans, Dutch, Mennonites, Scandinavians, Blacks, and Aboriginal peoples. Some historians put the number of Loyalists as high as 1 000 000. Others believe it was as low as 450 000. The correct number is probably somewhere between the two.

The Persecution of the Loyalists During the War

Those Americans who called themselves Patriots did not think of the Loyalists, or Tories as they called them, as being loyal in any sense of the word. The Patriots thought they were traitors to the British North American colonies.

Even before the American Revolution broke out, the Patriots set out to terrify anyone they thought was a Loyalist. Anyone who supported the British side was considered an enemy and possibly a spy. After the war began, persecution became even more brutal. Many Loyalists were robbed of their money, land, furniture, and livestock and were driven from their homes. Some were attacked brutally by armed mobs.

Loyalists in Peril

You could be arrested for being a Loyalist for any number of reasons:

- aiding the British in any way
- associating with or hiding Tories
- writing or speaking against the Patriot cause
- drinking to the king's health
- corresponding with the British
- encouraging or taking part in Tory plots

Loyalists who were forced from their homes arrived in Canada. The King's Royal Regiment was made up of displaced refugees who arrived in Montreal from New York. From Canadian territory, they conducted guerrilla raids on the northern states. They burned rebel supplies and freed Loyalists who had been captured.

Others were whipped, abused, threatened, or blackmailed. In this tense atmosphere, people on both sides acted rashly and cruelly toward their neighbours. Loyalists also mistreated Patriots when they got the chance. When Patriots were captured, they were thrown into British prison ships. Many died there.

During the American Revolution, a steady stream of Loyalists fled to Canada. They took whatever possessions they could carry and headed north to the safety of another British colony. Those who could afford it sailed to Britain.

The United States is Born

The war between the Americans and the British officially ended in 1783. At the Peace of Paris, American independence was accepted. Britain retreated and gave up all the territory of the former Thirteen Colonies, which became the United States of America.

The new country refused to give any kind of pardon to the Tories. Americans made it very difficult for Loyalists to come back to their homes and reclaim their property. Loyalists could not vote, hold public office, or even move from place to place freely. Loyalists were required to pay higher taxes than other citizens did. Many Loyalists preferred exile to swearing allegiance to the United States. They were prepared to leave because they were loyal subjects to Britain and wanted to maintain their British connection. From this time on, they were known as United Empire Loyalists.

Carrying what they could, about 100 000 Loyalists said goodbye to the Thirteen Colonies and became **refugees**. Refugees are people who flee their homeland because of war or because they are mistreated. Some boarded ships for the West Indies (Bahamas), Britain, and Nova Scotia. Others set out northward overland for Quebec.

Thousands of Loyalists stayed in the Thirteen Colonies to fight. They joined British regiments as volunteers to fight on the British side against the rebels. Flora Macdonald and her husband Allan were strong Loyalists. Flora helped lead a group of North Carolina Loyalist troops against the Patriots. She rode up and down the ranks shouting encouragement.

United Empire Loyalists

Colonists who fought for Britain and lost their property during the American Revolution were given the right to place the letters "UE" after their names. It was Lord Dorchester, governor general of British North America, who came up with the idea. He suggested it as a mark of honour. The letters stood for "Unity of the Empire." A list of Loyalist families was drawn up. Anyone whose name was on the list became known as a "United Empire Loyalist." Descendants of United Empire Loyalists have the right to place UE after their names.

Fast Forward

A Land of Immigrants

Over the years, many different groups of **immigrants** and refugees have come to live in Canada. Many immigrants have chosen Canada because of the opportunities for a good life that it offers them. Refugees have come here from many different countries to escape political persecution, torture, war, or famine. Although forced to leave their homelands unwillingly, the vast majority of refugees are happy to become Canadian citizens. The immigrants and refugees who have made Canada their home have contributed to the growth and prosperity of the country.

Immigrant Population by Place of Birth, 1996 Census

Place of Birth	Canada
United States	244 695
Central and South America	273 820
Caribbean and Bermuda	279 405
United Kingdom	655 540
Other—Northern and Western Europe	514 310
Eastern Europe	447 830
Southern Europe	714 380
Africa	229 300
West Central Asia and the Middle East	210 850
Eastern Asia	589 420
Southeast Asia	408 985
Southern Asia	353 515
Oceania and Other	49 025
TOTAL	4 971 075

Where Did the Loyalists Go?

In 1783, British North America was made up of the colonies of Newfoundland, Ile St.-Jean (later Prince Edward Island), Nova Scotia, and Quebec. At that time, Nova Scotia included New Brunswick and Cape Breton Island. Quebec included the territory that was to become the colony Upper Canada (later Ontario). Within the same areas, the Aboriginal peoples continued to live in their established communities—and their lives continued to be affected by the expanding European settlement.

Migration to Nova Scotia

At the end of the American Revolution, a great **migration** of Loyalists began. Migration means moving from one country to another. About 35 000 Loyalists gathered around New York City. The British assembled a fleet of ships to evacuate them. Guy Carlton was in charge of the operation. His orders were to remain on duty until every man, woman, and child who wanted to leave the United States was safely moved to British soil.

The British ships travelled in groups to protect themselves. Out on the ocean, American pirates were lying in wait for them. There was danger of the ships being boarded and of the fleeing Loyalists being robbed or even killed. Shiploads of Loyalists were taken up the Atlantic coast to the British colony of Nova Scotia.

Nova Scotia had much to attract the Loyalists. It was the easiest British colony to reach. It was a short voyage by sailing ship from New York to the Bay of Fundy. Halifax was the headquarters for the British fleet in North America and there were thousands of hectares of open land for settlement.

John Parr, the governor of Nova Scotia, was faced with a massive flood of refugees. They had to be sheltered and fed. They had to be given land and help to establish themselves. Parr suggested a site for them at Port Roseway, which had an excellent harbour. Within days, the Loyalists were chopping down trees and laying out the town of Shelburne. For the first months, they lived in a colony of tents and cabins. Salt pork and flour were provided by the British government until the Loyalists could provide their own food from the ocean, forests, and farms. Other Loyalists poured into the area and, by 1784, Shelburne had a population of about 12 000 people. It was the largest town in British North America.

Unfortunately, the land around Shelburne was too poor to grow good crops. When the British government's food rations began to run out, many Loyalists decided to leave Shelburne. They headed to other parts of the Maritimes or to England.

Another 15 000 Loyalists arrived at the mouth of the Saint John River, in what is New Brunswick today. Sarah Frost wrote these nervous words as she sat on the deck of a ship in Saint John harbour on the morning of 29 June 1783:

> **It is, I think, the roughest land I ever saw. We are all ordered to land tomorrow and not a shelter to go under.**

Five weeks later, Sarah Frost and her husband, William, became the parents of a baby girl.

A Loyalist's View

Arriving in the wilderness was so depressing that many Loyalists simply sat down and cried. The Loyalist grandmother of Leonard Tilley, a politician and one of the founders of Confederation, told her descendants about her experience.

> **I climbed to the top of Chipman's Hill and watched the sails disappearing in the distance, and such a feeling of loneliness came over me that, although I had not shed a tear through all the war, I sat down on the damp moss with my baby on my lap and cried.**

Challenges in Nova Scotia

Land along the Saint John River was fertile. But the Loyalists still faced the challenges that all pioneers face. They were living in a wilderness and many were not experienced farmers. In addition, the land had not been surveyed and made ready for the Loyalists. Food and building materials were in short supply. Some had to spend the winter in tents. Some of their children died from cold or starvation. Many eventually returned to the United States or moved to other parts of Canada.

The arrival of such large numbers of Loyalists created other problems for Nova Scotia. Loyalists from the Thirteen Colonies were used to having an elected assembly for their government. They demanded the same in Nova Scotia, but the Quebec Act did not allow for elected democratic government. Within a few months of their arrival, they were demanding their own separate colony. As a result, in June 1784, the colony of New Brunswick was created from the mainland part of Nova Scotia.

In 1784, Cape Breton Island split from Nova Scotia to become a new colony. That same year, the island was almost overrun by a flood of Loyalist arrivals. In the same way, another island, Ile St.-Jean, was sparsely populated before the arrival of the Loyalists. When 800 refugees arrived from New York, the town of Summerside was created and the island was renamed Prince Edward Island.

The Black Loyalists

About 3000 free Black Loyalists were among the groups that arrived in Nova Scotia. Most had been slaves in the Thirteen Colonies. Many had gained their freedom by fighting on the British side during the American Revolution. They had been spies, guides, and bridge builders, as well as Loyalist soldiers in an all-Black regiment called the Black Pioneers.

About 1500 Black Loyalists settled in a new town called Birchtown, near Shelburne. Another 1500 settled around Halifax. They faced more hardships than other Loyalists did. Some of the Black Loyalists did not receive the land grants that had been promised to every Loyalist. Others were given only the poorest land in isolated places. Birchtown was a miserable place filled with struggling people. Many of the Loyalists would not accept the Black Loyalists as equals. However, the Blacks could not risk returning to the United States. If they did, they could become slaves again.

Thomas Peters was a former slave who fought in the American Revolution. He became the spokesperson for Black Loyalists in Nova Scotia. Peters wanted real freedom. He travelled to Britain to plead on his people's behalf. He explained how unhappy they were in the harsh Canadian climate. He complained that they had not received the land and the help that had been promised.

In 1792, the British government offered to transport Black Loyalists to the colony of Sierra Leone in West Africa. About 1200 of the Black Loyalists in Nova Scotia took the free passage to Africa. When they arrived in Africa, they helped to build Free-town, a city on the coast.

There were also Black slaves in Nova Scotia who came with their Loyalist masters. When they arrived in Nova Scotia, they demanded freedom. But it was another 20 years before

LOYALIST SETTLEMENTS IN THE MARITIMES
0   125   250   375 km

Gulf of St. Lawrence

Prince Edward Island

Sydney

New Brunswick

Nova Scotia

Saint John

Annapolis Royal   Halifax

Shelburne

the custom of buying and selling slaves in Nova Scotia ceased. In 1834, slavery was finally abolished throughout the British Empire.

In spite of all the hardships, about 60% of the Black Loyalists stayed in Nova Scotia. They decided to take their chances in the new colony.

Many were skilled as blacksmiths, gardeners, millwrights, carpenters, and coopers. They became successful farmers and tradespeople. Others had skills that allowed them to become cooks, seamstresses, domestic servants, and nurses.

Profiles

Rose Fortune

Born into slavery in the southern United States in 1774, Rose Fortune came north with her Loyalist slave-owners to Annapolis Royal, Nova Scotia, following the American Revolution. There, Fortune gained her freedom.

Some time later, Fortune decided to become the area's policewoman. She was self-appointed, but nobody seemed to mind since she was a promi-nent resident of the town after founding one of its first cartage companies. Her physical strength and dedication helped her keep order in the town and on the wharf, especially among the youth. She was widely respected for her valuable work. Fortune died at the age of 90. She is remembered today as Canada's first female law enforcer.

Daurene Lewis

In 1984, Daurene Lewis, a descendant of Rose Fortune, became the first Black woman to be elected mayor in North America. Lewis grew up in Annapolis Royal, where she later became mayor, and where Rose Fortune worked as a policewoman many years earlier. Lewis's pioneer ancestor was an important role model for her. Before entering politics, Lewis worked as a nurse and was also known as a talented weaver.

1. What character traits would you say Fortune and Lewis have in common?
2. Rose Fortune was an important role model for Daurene Lewis. Do you have any role models in your life? How have they influenced you?

Fast Forward

Black Communities in the Maritimes

Today, the descendants of the Black Loyalists who remained in the Maritimes are working to rediscover, preserve, and promote their culture and their past. As in other parts of the country, they have fought discrimination and prejudice and have overcome many obstacles. They founded their own schools and taught in them. They built their own churches and became ministers for them. Although they were not always allowed to take part in the life of the wider community, they developed a strong sense of their own identity in their communities. Blacks from the Maritimes continue to make significant contributions to arts, politics, sports, and media in Canada.

Migration to Quebec

Several thousand Loyalists arrived in Quebec during and after the American Revolution. Most travelled through the wilderness of New York State to Sorel, east of Montreal. Some made their way to the safety of the British forts at Niagara or Detroit. Men, women, and children came by ox cart or by foot. All had been forced to leave their homes. They carried with them everything that was left of their worldly possessions.

Most of the Loyalists were settled temporarily at Sorel, at the mouth of the Richelieu River. They lived in half-constructed buildings, in tents, and in hastily built barracks. They waited there while Governor Frederick Haldimand considered a permanent solution for them.

The Loyalists' arrival presented serious problems for the governor. The new arrivals were English-speaking Protestants. Haldimand thought they would have difficulty fitting into a Catholic, French-speaking colony. The English were also unfamiliar with the seigneurial land system and French laws.

Haldimand refused to allow the Loyalists to settle in the Eastern Townships of Quebec. He thought this was too close to the American border for safety. A few hundred sailed down the St. Lawrence River and settled in the Gaspé around Chaleur Bay.

Governor Haldimand looked west for a solution to his problems. There was a vast unsettled wilderness along the north shore of Lake Ontario. He thought the "upper country," as it was called, could become a home for the Loyalists.

The land along the north shore of the St. Lawrence River, between the present cities of Cornwall and Brockville, was chosen first. It was surveyed and divided up into eight townships for settlement. Then, another eight townships were laid out along Lake Ontario. These were located between Kingston and Belleville and included the area around the Bay of Quinte.

Netsurfer

The Canada Hall website of the Canadian Museum of Civilization has information about Loyalists arriving in Upper Canada. The site location is www.cmcc.muse.digital.ca/ cmc/cmceng/cal5eng.html

A group of families is shown landing on the Bay of Quinte shore.

Members of a Loyalist family make the journey to their new home.

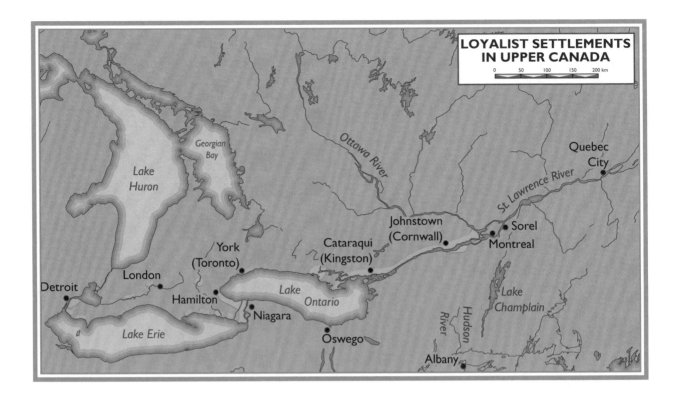

LOYALIST SETTLEMENTS IN UPPER CANADA

0   50   100   150   200 km

Fast Forward

"Indian Affairs"

The first Indian Department in Canada was created in 1755 as a branch of the British Military in North America. The superintendents were responsible for maintaining good relations with the Indians, as they were then called, and securing their allegiance to Britain. This was important for the wars against France and against the American troops. Over the years, the role of this department has changed. Aboriginal peoples are increasingly taking charge of services and programs that the department used to manage.

Before the arrival of the Europeans, Aboriginal peoples had practised their own forms of government for thousands of years. Over the centuries, the authority of those governments was weakened by colonial policies of assimilation and control. Many Aboriginal groups are now negotiating self-government with the Government of Canada. The present-day Department of Indian Affairs and Northern Development is more of an advisory, funding, and supportive body. By re-establishing their own governments, Aboriginal peoples will once again be able to control their own lives and lands.

Profile

Joseph Brant (Thayendanegea)
1742–1807

You can find more information on the life of Joseph Brant at www.indigenouspeople.org/ natlit/brant.htm

During the American Revolution, most Iroquois were loyal supporters of Britain. The Mohawk, Oneida, Seneca, Onondaga, Cayuga, and Tuscarora made up the six nations of the Iroquois Confederacy. Four of the nations were among the first Loyalists to take up arms for the British. Only the Oneida and Tuscarora sided with the Patriots.

Thayendanegea was a Mohawk chief. He had been given the English name of Joseph Brant. He had fought with the British during the Seven Years' War. Though only 15 at the time, he impressed the British. He had gone to school among the colonists in New England and had visited Britain. He had become a Christian and helped translate the Bible into Mohawk.

When the American Revolution broke out, Brant feared that his people would lose their lands if thousands of American settlers poured into the country. He led his people against the rebels. He gambled that the grateful British and Loyalists would help to defend the land and the rights of the Iroquois people.

When the revolution ended, the peace treaty did not include the Aboriginal peoples in any of its terms. The Aboriginal peoples who had fought as faithful Loyalists had been forgotten. Governor Haldimand later corrected this mistake when the Aboriginal allies were invited to choose land that suited them. The British government purchased a tract of land from the Mississauga, located in present-day southwestern Ontario. It was 300 ha of forested fertile land on both sides of the Grand River. A smaller group was given a land grant at Deseronto on the Bay of Quinte.

Joseph Brant led about 2000 Iroquois to the Grand River area. Here, they built a Six Nations community at Brant's Ford, now Brantford, Ontario. Although the original grant has been much reduced, the Six Nations still live there. Brant himself received a land grant in Burlington, as well as a house and a military commission. He lived there until his death in 1807.

1. Why did Joseph Brant remain loyal to the British?
2. Do you think he made the best decision in the circumstances? Why?

Profile

Molly Brant (Konwatsi'tsiaiénni) 1736–1796

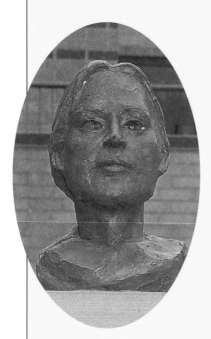

This website has extensive information on Molly Brant's life: http://web.ctsolutions.com/carf/document/brant.html#intro

Who was Molly Brant? She is most often recognized as the sister of Joseph Brant (Thayendanegea), leader of the Mohawk people. However, she is famous in her own right.

Molly Brant was a Mohawk born in 1736. She was a member of the Society of Six Nations Matrons. The Iroquois had a **matriarchal** form of government. This means that, among the Iroquois, it was the women who had authority. Women elected the council that appointed the war chiefs.

Molly Brant married Sir William Johnson, Superintendent of Indian Affairs for the British colony of New York. She was able to help him understand her people. It is said that she ran the affairs of the Indian Department when Johnson was away.

During the American Revolution, Brant sheltered and fed Loyalists. She sent arms and ammunition to those who were fighting. Eventually, the advancing Patriots forced Brant and the Mohawk to flee to Fort Niagara. There, she continued to use her influence to bolster the morale of the Mohawk and keep them loyal to the king.

All through her life, Molly Brant was pro-British and pro-Iroquois. She insisted on speaking Mohawk and dressed in the Mohawk style. She argued on behalf of the Iroquois and complained when she thought the government was ignoring her people.

As a Loyalist, she received a pension and a land grant for her loyalty to the king. She settled at Kingston, where the government built her a house.

Molly Brant was respected by both the British and Aboriginal peoples. Once, when Governor Simcoe was seriously sick with a cough, she recommended a medicine made from a root. The governor got better almost immediately.

Molly Brant raised eight children. She died at age 60 and was buried at Kingston.

---

1. What was unusual about Molly Brant for a woman of her time?
2. If you could ask her three questions, what would they be?

Distributing Provisions

Most of the Loyalists arrived with nothing more than the clothes on their backs. Many were upset when they heard that they were being sent to the wilderness to farm. In 1784, the settlers going to Cataraqui (Kingston) sent a petition to Governor Haldimand. "How can we be frontier farmers without tools?" they asked. "How will we live in the wilderness without food?" Here is a list of what they asked Governor Haldimand to provide.

To His Excellency General Haldimand, Governor General and Commander in Chief:

The Loyalists, going to form a settlement at Cataraqui, ask:

That boards, nails, and shingles be given to each Loyalist family so that they may build houses and other buildings; that eighty squares of window glass also be given each family.

That arms, ammunition, and one axe be given to each male aged fourteen or more.

That the following things be given to each family:

One plow shear and coulter
Leather for horse collars
Two spades
Three iron wedges
Fifteen iron harrow teeth
Three hoes
One one-inch (2.5 cm) and one half-inch (1.25 cm) auger
Three chisels
One gouge
Three gimlets
One hand saw and files
One nail hammer
One drawing knife
One frow for splitting shingles
Two scythes and one sickle
One broad axe

That one grindstone be given for every three families.

That one year's clothing be given to each family.

That two years' provisions be given to each family, enough according to their number and age.

That two horses, two cows, and six sheep be delivered at Cataraqui for each family.

That seeds of different kinds such as wheat, Indian corn, peas, oats, potatoes, and flax be given to each family.

That one blacksmith be established in each township.

Governor Haldimand was shocked at the list. He thought that the Loyalists would be content with an axe and a hoe. But it soon became clear that a great deal of help would need to be provided to them. Since most of the Loyalists had arrived with next to nothing, their needs were urgent.

Each family received a tent. At first, one musket was provided for every five men with 1 kg of powder and 2 kg of lead balls. Later, each family received its own musket. With a musket, families could hunt for food. An axe and a hoe were given to each man. Saws, chisels, and drawknives were provided to groups of families.

Food supplies and clothing were provided for three years. The governor arranged for seeds to be given to the community so that they could grow onions, cabbage, carrots, radishes, parsley, celery, and peas. Since cattle were scarce and very expensive, few were distributed.

Travelling to the Land Grant

The Loyalist immigrants were moved west from Sorel to the land grant. They travelled with their scanty possessions on large, flat-bottomed boats called **bateaux**. The bateau was usually overcrowded with five or six families and all their belongings. There were nearly 200 km of rapids to be navigated. Although the bateau was difficult to capsize, the journey to the land grants was still long and uncomfortable.

A bateau offered no protection from the hot sun or unexpected rain showers. At night, the settlers slept on the shore where they were at the mercy of the weather. There were no inns where travellers could stay overnight. When

What is a Bateau?

An early traveller in Canada in 1793 described a bateau:

> A bateau is a particular type of boat used upon the large rivers and lakes in Canada. The bottom is perfectly flat, and the ends are built very sharp and exactly alike. The sides are about three feet (one metre) high and, for the convenience of the rowers, four or five benches are laid across. It is a very heavy, awkward sort of vessel, either for rowing or for sailing, but it is preferred to a boat for two reasons. First, it draws less water, while at the same time carrying a larger burden; and secondly because it is much safer on lakes and wide rivers where storms are frequent.

they approached rapids or strong currents, everyone had to get off the bateau. The passengers jumped into the chilly water and, using ropes, helped the crew haul the bateau past the trouble spot. Then, dripping wet, they climbed back in and continued the journey.

Bateaux could be propelled by sail, by boatmen rowing or poling along the riverbed, or even by horses along the riverbank.

Distributing the Land

When Britain gained control of Canada in 1763, the Royal Proclamation acknowledged that Aboriginal peoples had a claim or title to their traditional lands. It also stated that only the British government could buy Aboriginal lands or sign treaties with Aboriginal peoples for land. Recent court cases affecting Aboriginal rights to land in Canada still refer to this document. The land that was to be settled by the Loyalists belonged to the Aboriginal peoples. Treaties were signed to obtain the land and avoid a war. The land was then divided up into smaller parcels. Many of the Aboriginal peoples had to relocate further away from the settlers.

When the Loyalists arrived at the new settlement, it was time to receive their land grants. They lined up in front of the surveyor to be assigned their new farms. Lots were assigned by drawing "location tickets" out of a hat. This was the fairest way. Everyone had an equal chance of drawing the best land. This kind of practice is where the terms "lottery" and "drawing lots" come from.

The ticket showed the exact site of the Loyalist's new property. Each head of a family, man or woman, was entitled to 40 ha. For each member of the family, there was an additional 20 ha. The most generous land grants went to members of the military. Junior officers received 200 ha, while senior officers received 400 ha. This was a reward for those who had fought for Britain.

Creating Upper Canada

The territory of the "upper country" that was settled by the Loyalists in 1774 was part of Quebec. The Loyalist settlers soon asked the British government to make their territory a separate colony. They wanted an Assembly where their elected representatives could meet. They also wanted British laws and the British system of holding land. The British government agreed. In 1791, Quebec was divided at the Ottawa River. The western part became Upper Canada (present-day Ontario). The eastern part became Lower Canada (present-day Quebec).

The Constitutional Act of 1791 stated that each province could elect an Assembly, raise taxes, and pass laws. Each colony also had a governor and an appointed council to assist him. The first appointed governor of Upper Canada was John Graves Simcoe.

In this picture, Loyalists are drawing location tickets. There was a great deal of luck involved in obtaining a farm. The best lots would be those along the lakeshore or riverfront.

Activities

Understanding Concepts

1. Define the following terms and enter them in your personal dictionary.

American Revolution	Tory	Minutemen
United Empire Loyalist	refugee	immigrant
migration	bateau	matriarchal
cause	effect	"Intolerable" Acts
Loyalist	boycott	Patriot

2. Explain why the following actions taken by the British government upset many citizens in the Thirteen Colonies:
   a) The Stamp Act
   b) The Townshend Duties
   c) The "Intolerable" Acts
   d) The Quebec Act

3. What is a boycott? Why are boycotts established? What effect would a boycott of British goods probably have had at the time of the American Revolution?

4. List five reasons a person in the British North American colonies might have had for remaining loyal to Britain.

5. Look up "patriot" and "rebel" in the dictionary. Explain how the same person could be called a patriot by some people and a rebel by others.

6. Why did the British government create the colonies of New Brunswick and Upper Canada?

7. What is the difference between an immigrant and a refugee? How would their experiences and feelings about moving to a new country differ? How might they be the same?

Digging Deeper

8. **Discuss** Following the Boston Tea Party, the British decided to get tough with the rebels. Did the rebels deserve this treatment? Explain your reasons.

9. **Role-Play** Imagine that you are a Loyalist family getting ready to flee to Upper Canada. Act out a short dialogue as you decide with your family what to take and what to leave behind.

10. **Map Study** Where did the Loyalists go after the American Revolution? Make a map to show their migration routes.

11. **ANALYZE** Describe the changes in the Maritimes and Quebec that resulted from the arrival of the Loyalists.

12. **DEBATE** Britain should have treated the Loyalists more generously than it did.

Making New Connections

13. **INVESTIGATE/DISCUSS** How are the history and the experiences of the Black Loyalists different from those of the White Loyalists?

14. **INVESTIGATE** Suppose you were going to set up a farm in a frontier area of Canada today. What equipment would you need? Where could you find suitable land? What problems do you think you might encounter? Are these problems greater or smaller than the problems faced by the Loyalists? Explain.

15. **WRITE** Suppose you are a member of an English-speaking family in Quebec. At some point in the future, Quebec decides to separate from the rest of Canada. It becomes an independent country. Your family does not agree with Quebec's decision. You are forced to leave the province. Write a paragraph describing how you feel.

Building a Homestead

19 October 1791
Marysburgh, Upper Canada

To my dear friends in Albany, New York:

It has been many years since you have heard from me. It has been hard for us, but we are happy to be living in a British colony.

Like all the Loyalists, we chose our land grant by lot. We were very lucky to receive a fine, fertile piece of ground close to the lake. After years of hard work, it is beginning to look like a farm.

Robert and our sons first had to clear a place for a shelter. They cut down trees using simple hand axes. They hacked down brush and undergrowth, which I then pulled to a safe place to be burned. Thank God we had good neighbours to help us.

Our next task was to build a rough shanty and some basic furniture. After the first year, we built a better home and a small barn. The shanty was turned over to the pigs and the cow.

Our first crops were planted among the stumps of the small field we cleared. Robert regularly takes our surplus butter and cheese in a bateau to Kingston. He trades them for flour, tea, and salt.

Some years have been more difficult than others. The "hungry year" was 1788–1789. Government rations stopped. Drought, poor crops, and an early, cold winter hit us very hard. Praise God we survived!

We miss our friends in Albany so much and it is very lonely, but we try to stay cheerful. We know that we made the right decision in being loyal to our hearts and our king.

Warmest regards from your friend,
Margaret

Predicting/Reflecting

1. How will the life of Margaret's family change as everyone becomes more settled? What do you think she will be writing about in her letters in another five years?
2. What needs will the colony have to attend to because of the expanding and widespread population?
3. Why do you think people continued to immigrate to Upper Canada even though the conditions were so difficult?

Clearing the Land

The life of the pioneer farmer was one of back-breaking work from dawn to dusk. Most of Upper Canada was forested. Trees had to be cut down with an axe. Then, they were cut with a handsaw, which was slow, difficult work. Some of the cut trees were set aside to build shanties that would house families over the winter. But most were burned. The ashes were carefully collected and used to make soap.

The tree stumps were hard to pull out, even with the help of horses or oxen. Farmers usually left them to rot for up to 10 years. Some stumps, when pulled out, were used to mark boundary lines and can still be seen in some rural areas today. Crops were grown in the places between and around the stumps. The rocks that were pulled out of the fields were used for fences or fireplaces.

The main crops were wheat and corn. Barley and oats were also grown. Farmers raised vegetables for their own use and perhaps had some for trading. Some pigs and a cow were usually kept. Wild berries, plants, and nuts were gathered to add to each family's food supply.

Building the First Home

The first home was usually a **shanty** or cabin. It was simple and cheap to build, but not very comfortable. It had a dirt floor and was not much larger than a small room in an average home today, about 3 m by 4 m. The roof sloped from about 2 m high above the door to 1.3 m at the rear wall. There were no windows, but there was plenty of fresh air because there were always gaps between the logs. A doorway was cut out after all the logs had been notched and fitted into place. For a while, a blanket or rug was used as a door covering.

As soon as they could afford it, the settlers built a better home. The shanty then became a shed for the farm animals.

Clearing the land was hard work. The men cut down trees, which then had to be hauled away, while the women gathered the smaller branches to be burned later.

The settlers' first shelter was a crude shanty built of logs. A fire outside was used for cooking. It was kept burning all night to keep the black bears and wolves at a distance. The smoke also helped to control the hungry mosquitoes. How can you tell that this picture shows the settlers' first year at the homestead?

Building the Second Home

The second pioneer home was much larger than the shanty. Usually, it included more than a single room and there was a small attic for sleeping. Neighbours would work together to build their homes. When the work was done, there was always a party to celebrate.

Often, the house was made of squared logs. Each tree trunk used in the building was squared with an axe or saw. Notches were made at the end so that the logs would fit neatly together. Not a single nail was used. Since the logs were uneven, there were always gaps between them. These were filled with moss or wooden wedges and clay. Sometimes, the roof was constructed from cedar logs that had been cut in half or from overlapping basswood bark. The dirt floor was covered with pine planks. Doors and windows were cut after the walls had been put up. Glass was a luxury. Most people just covered the openings with oiled cloth or paper.

Early houses had a huge fireplace. It was made of stone and could be 2.5 m wide. It was used for cooking and was also the only source of heat for the house. Settlers had to work hard to chop and store enough wood to keep the fires burning. It was a major problem if the fire ever went out. Matches were not invented until 1829. If the family had a flint, they could start a new fire. If they didn't have a flint, someone would have to walk to the nearest neighbour to get burning embers to re-light the fire.

The Loyalists usually made their own tables, benches, and beds. They used pine and maple and sometimes painted these pieces in bright colours with homemade paint. Closets and wardrobes were not common at this time, so clothes were usually hung on pegs on the walls. The Loyalist house was lit with candles made by the family from animal fat. The Loyalists worked hard to establish themselves in the wilderness. They were ready to call Upper Canada home.

The shanty was the first home. It was a very basic structure. When the second, larger home was built, the shanty would become an animal pen or perhaps a henhouse. In later stages, the settlers might add a barn, a storage shed, and a smokehouse for smoking meat.

Danger from Wolves

The threat of wolves was very real for the early settlers. Jane Spring wrote of her experience in 1794:

I think the most exciting time last year was one evening when Father and William were away ... The cattle were in a habit of going a mile or two back into the forest. I set out following an Indian trail. Wolves were plentiful and I was nervous, but I took a heavy club with me ... When almost to the cattle, a wolf near the trail set up a howl and soon a pack of wolves appeared ... A thought entered my head and, as the old cow with the bell passed, I grabbed her tail and hung on ... I depended on that cow to bring me out of the clearing. I took steps ten feet long ... When Father and William saw the trouble I was in, they grabbed their guns and managed to get two or three wolves.

John Graves Simcoe

John Graves Simcoe was the first governor of Upper Canada. He was no stranger to the Loyalists. He had served Britain during the Revolutionary War and fought with the Queen's Rangers in Virginia. Simcoe, his wife, Elizabeth, and their two youngest children arrived in the summer of 1792. Their first stop was Kingston, which was then the largest town in Upper Canada. It had about 50 houses! The Simcoes then moved on to Newark (Niagara-on-the-Lake), the capital of the colony at that time. They were shocked to find that the capital was little more than an outpost in the wilderness.

Simcoe was very excited about his appointment and he brought great energy to his job. He travelled all over Upper Canada. He spent nights in tents and shared hard bread and pork with trappers. He visited the Aboriginal peoples and watched them make maple syrup. He feasted on raccoon, bear meat, and squirrel stew. He called on settlers in isolated cabins to find out first hand about their lives. Simcoe was interested in everything that had to do with the colony.

Choosing a Capital

Simcoe was worried about the location of the capital of Upper Canada. He thought it was too close to the American border. In case of attack, it would be difficult to defend. He thought of moving the capital to the western part of Upper Canada. The site he considered was on the Thames River. He called it London. However, in 1793, the British government decided to establish the capital of Upper Canada at York (Toronto). By the time the Simcoes left York in 1796, it was still a small village with fewer than 12 blocks.

Organizing the Government

Simcoe lost no time in calling an election. In September 1792, the people of Upper Canada would elect their first Legislative Assembly. The government of Upper Canada was headed by a **lieutenant-governor**, often called simply the governor. That was Simcoe. The governor was always a male, always British, and usually a soldier. He was appointed for a term by the king.

The governor chose two different councils to help him run Upper Canada. The first was the **Executive Council**. It included the governor's closest advisors. It had five members who were appointed by the governor for life.

The second council was the **Legislative Council**. It had the power to make laws for the colony. It had seven members who were also appointed for life by the governor. The councillors were usually wealthy and important friends of the governor and their relatives.

The **Legislative Assembly** was made up of elected citizens. They served a four-year term. The people elected members to represent them in the Assembly. This was supposed to give the people of Upper Canada a voice in the running of the colony. So, on paper, the people had a say in government—but it usually only worked on paper, not in practice.

The appointed councils and the governor had enormous power. The councils could refuse to accept any ideas passed by the Assembly that they did not like. The governor generally listened only to the advice of the council members. So in fact, the elected representatives of the people had the least power. The governor and the councils had the most power.

First Legislative Assembly of Upper Canada 1792

The first session of the Legislative Assembly lasted about a month. The members passed many laws. One law granted a reward to anyone who destroyed bears or wolves that were a danger to the settlements. One of the most important decisions the Assembly made was about slavery. Some Loyalists had brought slaves with them. The Assembly decided that no more slaves would be allowed into Upper Canada and that children of slaves presently in Upper Canada were to be freed at age 25. This law meant that slavery would gradually come to an end in Upper Canada.

John Graves Simcoe, the first governor of Upper Canada, arrives at Newark.

Profile

Elizabeth Simcoe
1762–1850

Elizabeth Simcoe as a young woman in Welsh dress, shortly before she accompanied the governor to Upper Canada

Governor John Graves Simcoe brought his wife, Elizabeth, and his two youngest children to Upper Canada. Mrs. Simcoe brought her own chef, maid, jewels, and fine clothes. What a shock it was for her when they arrived at the capital of Upper Canada.

Newark was a small wilderness outpost. Until a house was ready, the Simcoes lived in a portable canvas home that the governor had bought from Captain James Cook, the English explorer. The inside of the canvas home was decorated with wallpaper and paint. It was kept warm with stoves.

Elizabeth Simcoe quickly adapted to her new life in Upper Canada. She spent much of her time studying the country and society of Upper Canada. She loved the Canadian wilderness. She travelled widely, painting watercolours. She sketched scenes, native plants, and leaves.

Mrs. Simcoe and the governor entertained lavishly. Important guests to the colony, such as the Duke of Kent and the explorer Alexander Mackenzie, were welcome visitors. On the king's birthday, the Simcoes held a reception in the morning. Then, from seven o'clock in the evening until eleven, they entertained with a dance, followed by a midnight supper.

Elizabeth Simcoe kept a detailed diary that tells us many interesting things about the colony. It is packed with notes about the social life of the colony, cooking, herbal remedies, and day-to-day events. She frequently recorded gifts or purchases from the Aboriginal peoples.

Tuesday 13 August 1793
An Indian named Wable Casigo supplies us with salmon which the rivers and creeks on the Toronto Bay abound with ... They are best in the month of June.

Sunday 3 April 1796
Some Indians brought maple sugar to sell in birchbark baskets. I gave three dollars for thirty pounds.

When York became the capital of the colony, Elizabeth Simcoe wanted to have a summer house high above the Don River. The house was a sizable pine log structure, 10 m by 16 m. It was built to look like a Greek temple. Huge pillars of peeled pine logs supported porches on both ends.

Mrs. Simcoe called her house Castle Frank after her young son Frank. She used it as a summer house and a country house. The Simcoes would go there in the winter by sleigh up the Don River. In the summer, they travelled by carriage road through the bush. Picnics and dance parties were held at Castle Frank. Although the house was demolished in the 19th century, a Toronto road, a crescent, and a subway stop keep alive the name Castle Frank today.

The Simcoes left Upper Canada in 1796 and returned to England. Elizabeth Simcoe wrote in her diary about that sad day, "I could not eat, I cried all day."

---

1. How did Elizabeth Simcoe's life in Upper Canada compare with that of the women who settled with their families in the wilderness?

2. Why do you think her attitude changed from the time she arrived in Upper Canada to the time she returned to England?

Castle Frank stood on a ridge on the west side of the Don River, south of present-day Bloor Street East in Toronto. It was "built on the plan of a Greek temple," as Mrs. Simcoe explained in her diary.

Organizing the Land

New France had organized the land into seigneuries. Upper Canada organized the land into **townships**. Governor Simcoe introduced the checkered plan of townships.

The typical township was an area of land divided into farms and roads. The Constitutional Act had said that one-seventh of all the land in Upper Canada should be set aside for the use of the Anglican clergy. These were called the **Clergy Reserves**. The British government ordered that another seventh be set aside for the use of the Crown. These were called **Crown Reserves**.

Simcoe's plan was to spread the Crown Reserves throughout the township instead of keeping them all together. They were to be scattered in a checkerboard pattern throughout each township. Simcoe's plan turned out to be a mistake. Most of the Crown Reserves were left as unsettled wilderness. Good farmland was kept out of production. Farmers also complained that Crown Reserves were full of weeds whose seeds blew into their fields. But most of all, the Crown Reserves slowed down road development. Simcoe did not know at the time that the Crown Reserves would create problems before many years had passed.

Clearing land for public roads was a difficult job. If it was not supervised, it was often left undone.

Building Roads

Governor Simcoe hoped to make Upper Canada safe from attack. To do this, he had to have roads to move his troops around the colony. He also needed roads so that settlers could get to their farms.

Simcoe travelled around the colony by canoe, on horseback, and on foot, looking for the best locations for the roads. He planned the beginnings of Ontario's highway system.

His road from Montreal to Kingston was finished in 1796. Kingston Road, from Kingston to York, and Yonge Street, from York north to Lake Simcoe, were ready a few years later. Dundas Street, or the Governor's Road, west from Burlington Bay to the Thames valley was another of Simcoe's roads. The roads were built by the troops of the Queen's Rangers. They were not much better than cleared tracks through the wilderness. But they did make it easier for troops and settlers to move within the colony.

Organizing Settlement

Simcoe dreamed of developing the colony beyond the areas already settled by the Loyalists. He believed that there were many people still in the United States who would be happy to live in a British colony. He wanted them to come to Upper Canada to help populate the region.

To persuade them to come to Upper Canada, Simcoe offered free land. Grants of 80 ha were given away. The British government put up posters in the United States. Loyalists still living there were invited to move to Upper Canada. They had to swear allegiance to the king. They had to promise to clear 2 ha of their land and build a home. They were also responsible for opening a road along the front of their property.

William Berczy from New York State came to Upper Canada in 1794. He wanted to see for himself whether the land bargain was as good as it sounded. He wanted to bring German settlers who had become dissatisfied with life in the United States. Berczy began negotiating for land with Governor Simcoe. He received a grant of 26 000 ha in what would become Markham.

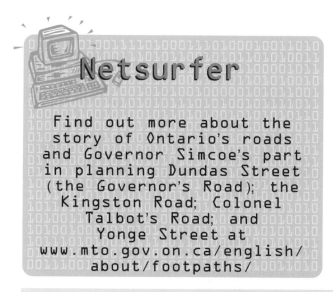

Netsurfer

Find out more about the story of Ontario's roads and Governor Simcoe's part in planning Dundas Street (the Governor's Road); the Kingston Road; Colonel Talbot's Road; and Yonge Street at www.mto.gov.on.ca/english/about/footpaths/

Fast Forward

Highway 401

Highway 401, the Macdonald-Cartier Freeway, was opened in 1965. It was named to honour two of Canada's Fathers of Confederation, Sir John A. Macdonald and Sir George-Etienne Cartier. This highway acts as the "main street of southern Ontario." It serves the majority of the province's population, which is concentrated within 16 km to the north and south of it. The highway runs from the Windsor border with the United States to the western boundary of Quebec. The Greater Toronto Area section is the busiest part of Highway 401. It carries hundreds of thousands of vehicles each day. From the footpaths of the earliest roads of Upper Canada to the building of Highway 401, roads have been the major factor in opening up and developing the economy of the province.

Berczy led 64 families to York. They cut a road and travelled north to Markham in **Conestoga wagons**. The Berczy settlers set up farms along the Rouge River, which flowed into Lake Ontario east of the town of York.

Thousands of families took up Simcoe's offer. Americans came in droves to claim the free land. The new arrivals were called **Late Loyalists**. Many came out of loyalty to the king, but others came for the free land.

Simcoe's policy of welcoming American immigrants contributed greatly to the growth of Upper Canada. In the mid-1790s, the population was about 15 000. By 1812, the population had grown to about 90 000 people.

Governor Simcoe's Contributions to Upper Canada

John Graves Simcoe was the first governor of Upper Canada. Although he spent only four years as governor, he set the pattern for all other governors who followed. He provided wise and energetic leadership. Simcoe put policies into place that would well serve the colony of Upper Canada in years to come.

The property shown here was Jacob Stiver's house. It was part of the Berczy settlement.

A version of the Conestoga wagon. Mennonite families made the trip from the United States to Upper Canada in these wagons drawn by oxen. The wagons could carry heavy loads and were well suited to travel on the rough early roads. The high wheels made it easy for the wagons to ford streams.

Were the Late Loyalists Welcome?

Between 1796 and 1812, thousands of Late Loyalists arrived in Upper Canada. Nathaniel Gamble was one. He brought a large family from Pennsylvania to settle on the newly opened Yonge Street. Gamble swore allegiance to King George III and was given his land. But some of the original Loyalists would have been suspicious about the late arrivals. They questioned how real their loyalty to the king was since they had refused to fight for Britain. Some accused the Late Loyalists of being land-grabbers. In Gamble's case, he proved his loyalty. He fought for Upper Canada against the Americans in the War of 1812. But the growing numbers of American Late Loyalists were a worry to many. By 1812, Late Loyalist families, such as the Gambles, outnumbered the early Loyalists by four or five to one.

Portrait of Col. Thomas Talbot by James Wandesford. Thomas Talbot lived the life of an English country gentleman on his vast estate in the backwoods of Upper Canada. However, he dressed in homespun, cloth made from yarn spun at home, even on journeys abroad. For this picture, he posed in homespun trousers with broad stripes of black and red.

The Talbot Settlement

Thomas Talbot came to Canada in 1792 as the private secretary to John Graves Simcoe. He loved the wild country and, in 1803, he settled on the north shore of Lake Erie. He called the place Port Talbot. He built a house, a gristmill, and a sawmill.

Talbot believed that there was a fortune to be made in land settlement. So, he persuaded the British government to give him 2023 ha of land. In return, he planned to settle colonists on his land. The deal he made with the government gave him additional land every time he settled a colonist. As a result, Talbot gradually became one of the largest landowners in Upper Canada.

During the first years, Talbot built roads and mills on his land. Settlers came slowly at first and were often treated rudely by Talbot. Colonel Talbot was an eccentric man. He lived like a hermit and rarely ventured into the outside world. He interviewed prospective settlers through a window in his house. If he liked them, he would grant them land and treat them fairly. If he disliked them, land was refused and the window slammed shut! Talbot also had strict rules that the settlers had to follow. Each settler had to clear 4 ha of land on the lot and build a house. Each settler also had to clear half of the road in front of the lot. Only then, and after five years on the land, was the certificate of ownership given to the settler.

Because he insisted that settlers help with the building of roads, the Talbot Settlement had the longest and best road in all of Upper Canada. By 1830, the Talbot Road stretched almost 500 km. It opened up much of the southwestern part of the colony to agricultural settlement.

By 1837, Talbot had settled over 200 000 ha of land in 29 townships in the southwestern region. Fifty thousand people were living in the Talbot Settlement, one of the most successful in early Upper Canada.

Skill Building: Making a Mind Map

Do you ever find yourself sketching what is being talked about in class? For example, your class is discussing transportation in Upper Canada. Most students around you are writing down the information in sentences and paragraphs. Your notes consist of sketches of a canoe, a horse-drawn sleigh, and a Conestoga wagon. Don't despair! You have the beginning of a mind map. A **mind map** is a way of recording visually what you have learned. It is a mental picture. It is a good way to organize information because it

- highlights important points
- shows how ideas are connected
- triggers or cues your mind to remember information

How can you prepare a good mind map?

1. Suppose you are reading about John Graves Simcoe. Decide on the main idea or topic of this section. Express it in one or two words. You might settle on Simcoe's policies as the main idea. Print SIMCOE'S POLICIES in capital letters on a page.

    Make a sketch of the main idea or put a square or some shape around it. This is an important step. It helps to make the main idea stand out in your memory. An outline of the head of a British military leader would be one way to illustrate this idea.

2. Next, decide on the sub-topics that support the main idea. There should be no more than six or seven sub-topics. The first sub-topic is Choosing a Capital. Create a label of one or two words for this sub-topic. It could be CHOOSE CAPITAL. Connect it with a line to the main topic.

Sketch the main idea of this sub-topic or put some shape around it. This helps the main idea stand out in your memory. Add a question mark to the label. This reminds you that you want to know more and that you need to fill in more information about the sub-topic.

3. Now skim the section Choosing a Capital in the text. Notice how the information is organized. It tells why Simcoe was worried about Newark, where he wanted the capital, and where the capital ended up.

    Choose the key points and link these details to your sub-topic label. Look at the sample mind map we are creating. Linked to CHOOSE CAPITAL? are the words

- Newark unsafe
- London Simcoe's choice
- York Britain's choice

4. Look at the next sub-topic on the mind map that has been started for you. Each sub-topic is a different colour. This helps you remember. The sub-topic is GOVERNMENT?. There is also a sketch of a parliament building to help you remember. It is linked to the main idea by a line.

5. You see that GOVERNMENT? has several key points—Governor, Executive Council, Legislative Council, and Legislative Assembly. They are linked by lines to the sub-topic. Beside each point add some important details.

    Notice that a mind map shows at a glance the connections between ideas. For example, our mind map tells us that the governor appoints both the councils. Also, the square around Governor, Executive Council, and Legislative Council indicates in a graphic way that these people are separate from the Legislative Assembly.

6. Work in groups or individually to complete the mind map. Add the other sub-topics to SIMCOE'S POLICIES. Read these sections carefully: Organizing the Land, Building Roads, Organizing Settlements, and Organizing the Courts.

Share your mind maps with other groups and learn from each other. Discuss the value of having a visual layout for your notes.

SIMCOE'S POLICIES

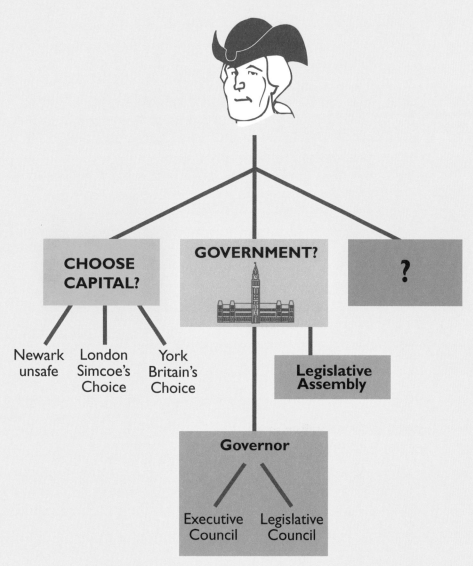

CHOOSE CAPITAL?

Newark unsafe   London Simcoe's Choice   York Britain's Choice

GOVERNMENT?

?

Legislative Assembly

Governor

Executive Council   Legislative Council

Civics & Society

Organizing the Courts

The laws in Upper Canada were based on the laws in Britain. Governor Simcoe set up courts to keep law and order. The courts appointed sheriffs to arrest law-breakers and bring them before the courts. The government appointed **magistrates** or justices to hear cases. The magistrate was much like a judge today. A justice was usually a local citizen appointed to deal with minor offences. A person accused of a serious crime was entitled to a **trial by jury**.

Anyone accused of a crime was brought into court. The charge was read out in front of a magistrate. A jury was selected to hear the facts of the case. The jury decided whether the accused was guilty or not guilty based on those facts. If the verdict was guilty, the sentence would be handed down by the magistrate.

Punishments were very harsh. Crimes such as forgery or stealing a horse were punishable by death. Hangings were public events and people came from a great distance to watch. Not paying bills was another serious crime. For this, a person was put into jail and whipped. The York jail was a cedar log stockade. Prisoners were kept in unheated cells and fed a ration of bread and water.

Sometimes, prisoners were **banished** from the country. They were told to leave Upper Canada. Usually, these people fled to the United States. Anyone caught returning could be sentenced to death.

Flogging of a prisoner at a Toronto jail

1. How would you choose the people on the jury to make sure that it was fair?
2. Courts in Canada today often try to reform criminals through training programs and counselling. In contrast, the courts in Upper Canada only punished criminals. Which approach do you think is better? Why? How would you try to reform criminals if you were an Upper Canada judge?

Tech Link

Potash: The First Cash Crop

Early pioneer farmers produced just enough food for themselves. If they had a little extra, they might trade it for things they needed. Butter, cheese, vegetables, and cream could be exchanged in the towns for tea, sugar, and salt.

Gradually, as farms grew more prosperous, there were products that they could sell. These were sold to British troops stationed in Upper Canada or to fur traders. By 1800, salt beef, salt pork, and flour were being shipped in barrels to markets in Montreal and Britain.

A pioneer makes potash.

The farmers' first **cash crop** was **potash**. It was made from wood ashes, which were plentiful since everyone had a lot of wood. Water was added to the ashes to produce a solution of natural chemicals, called lye. The lye was ladled into iron kettles and boiled over outside fires. This mixture thickened in the kettle and had to be stirred continually. It took about a week to make one barrel of potash. One barrel of potash used about one third of a hectare of timber.

The potash was shipped to Britain to be used to manufacture soap and glass, and to prepare wool for dying. The settlers received cash in return.

The problem with the potash industry was that it did not last long. Once the land was cleared, there were fewer ashes available. But for a short period of time, potash was the industry that brought much-needed cash to Upper Canada.

1. How do you think cash from potash would change the lives of the settlers?
2. What do you think happened to the potash industry? Could it continue forever? Why?

Activities

Understanding Concepts

1. Define the following words and add them to your personal dictionary.

shanty	township	magistrate
Late Loyalist	trial by jury	potash
Executive Council	Legislative Council	Legislative Assembly
Conestoga wagon	mind map	cash crop
banish	Clergy Reserve	Crown Reserve
lieutenant-governor		

2. Make a sketch of a typical pioneer farm in the early days of Upper Canada. Include details about how the land was cleared, the first home, and what crops were planted.

3. What major contributions did Governor Simcoe make to the development of Upper Canada?

4. Name the main parts of the government of the new colony and their functions. How does the structure compare with the structure of our provincial government today?

5. Describe the making of potash by the pioneers. Why was potash very important to the early pioneers? Would you want to make it? Why or why not?

Digging Deeper

6. **THINK/DISCUSS** It is said that the original Loyalist pioneers had to be self-sufficient. Explain what this means and give examples.

7. **THINK/DISCUSS** Why do you think the Legislative Assembly did not abolish slavery all at once?

8. **WRITE** Imagine you are one of the early Loyalists. Write an article for the Upper Canada Gazette explaining what you do not like about the Late Loyalists.

9. **DISCUSS** Why did Simcoe think that roads and settlement should be priorities in the colony? Are they as important today?

10. **ROLE-PLAY** Role-play a group of early Loyalists discussing Governor Simcoe's idea to give Americans free land, as Late Loyalists.

11. **THINK/PRESENT** Imagine you are a person applying for a land grant from Colonel Talbot. Which of his rules would discourage you? Why? Which rules might encourage you? Why? Present your ideas to your group.

Making New Connections

12. **COMPARE/DISCUSS** What qualities did a Loyalist pioneer need to succeed in Upper Canada? What qualities do new immigrants need to succeed in Canada today? In what ways are your lists similar? In what ways are they different?

13. **THINK/WRITE** Toronto City Council has made repeated attempts to have all Ontarians celebrate Simcoe Day on the first Monday in August. In other parts of the province, it is simply called Civic Holiday. Write a letter to the premier of Ontario explaining why all citizens in Ontario should celebrate this day as Simcoe Day.

14. **COMPARE** The fishing industry in Newfoundland, the fur trade in New France, and the potash industry in Upper Canada were similar in many ways. Compare the three in an organizer under the following headings:
    - Why was each industry important for early economic development?
    - Who benefited and how?
    - What happened to each natural resource?

Kingston Gazette

American Troops Capture York

York, Upper Canada

The Americans have captured the capital of Upper Canada! Twelve armed American schooners crossed Lake Ontario carrying 1700 troops. They landed on the beaches west of York.

Major General Sheaffe led 300 British regulars, 300 York militiamen, and about 100 Aboriginal men against the Americans. But his troops were no match for them! Fort York soon fell and the troops retreated into the town. Sheaffe gave the order to blow up the fort as they retreated, killing and wounding many on both sides.

Leaving the town to its fate, Sheaffe and the British soldiers withdrew to Kingston. Defence of York was left to the militia, the Aboriginals, and the citizens. The American invaders quickly captured York. They burned the wooden Parliament Buildings and other government offices. Two ships were destroyed. Thirteen homes and five stores were looted. Some tools, livestock, and silver were reported stolen. Important military equipment was also lost. This victory allows the American navy to strengthen its control of Lake Ontario.

Today, after four days in York, the American invaders sailed away. They appeared to be heading in the direction of Niagara.

Reflecting/Predicting

1. What reasons do you think the Americans had for attacking Upper Canada?
2. How will the British likely react? What problems could this create for the colony?
3. How do you think different groups living in the colony, for example, the settlers, the businessmen, and the Aboriginal people, will respond to another battle with the Americans?
4. How will people living in other British North American colonies react to the news of the capture of York? Explain.

This picture shows the arrival of the American fleet, prior to the capture of York.

Then and Now

"American troops capture York." Can you believe that headline? But as incredible as it sounds to us, the Americans once attacked Canada. Today, the United States is a friendly neighbour. It is our best trading partner. People on both sides of the border travel back and forth quite freely. But for three years, from 1812 to 1815, we were mortal enemies. The border was defended by forts. Red-coated British soldiers and militiamen from the towns and farms fought to protect our property. On the Great Lakes, British and American warships confronted each other with cannons blazing. How did this happen? What were the causes of the War of 1812?

A plaque at Fort York reads:

A FEW YARDS SOUTH OF THIS SPOT, ON WHAT WAS THEN THE LAKESHORE, STOOD THE GRAND MAGAZINE.

DURING THE BATTLE OF YORK 27 APRIL 1813 THE BRITISH FORCES, FINDING THE UNFINISHED FORT UNTENABLE, WITHDREW AND BLEW UP THE MAGAZINE.

THE EXPLOSION KILLED 38 AMERICAN SOLDIERS AND WOUNDED 222, MANY OF WHOM DIED. AMONG THE DEAD WAS BRIGADIER-GENERAL ZEBULON M. PIKE.

SEVERAL BRITISH AND CANADIAN SOLDIERS WERE ALSO KILLED OR WOUNDED.

Causes of the War of 1812

The United States declared war on Britain in June 1812. For the second time in less than 30 years, the Americans and the British were fighting. There were four main causes of the war:
• trade barriers
• Britain's stop-and-search tactics
• Britain's Aboriginal allies
• the American War Hawks

Trade Barriers

The Americans were caught in the middle of a fight between Britain and France. Britain and France had been at war since 1793. The Americans wanted to be able to trade freely with any country they chose. But the war created problems for them. Both European countries were trying to starve the other out. Both warned that any ships sailing to the enemy country would be stopped and their cargoes seized. The powerful British navy was able to enforce the threat. The British stopped, searched, and seized twice as many American vessels as the French

did. The Americans resented this interference with their trade on the high seas.

British Stop-and-Search Tactics

The British navy was **stopping and searching** American ships for another reason. They were looking for runaway British sailors who they believed were hiding on American vessels. In those days, British sailors were treated severely. The wages were low and the food was bad. Many British sailors certainly did desert the navy. But to the Americans, it was an insult to have the British navy stopping and searching their ships. It was the kind of insult that could start a fight.

Britain's Aboriginal Allies

In the US Congress, some American frontiersmen were pushing for a war with Britain. These frontiersmen, known as **War Hawks**, came from the states west of the Appalachians. The War Hawks claimed that the British in Canada were providing Tecumseh, a Shawnee chief, with guns and supplies. They accused the Aboriginal people of attacks on American frontier settlements. They believed that this was a good reason for the United States to go to war with Britain.

The American War Hawks

The War Hawks were anxious for war. They believed it was time to get even with Britain. The United States had been insulted enough by the stop-and-search tactics of the British navy. They were convinced that the British were encouraging Tecumseh to attack American frontier settlements. The War Hawks also believed that the United States would soon control all of North America. An attack on Canada was the first step and it was the easiest way to get at Britain. Canada would make a welcome addition to the territory of the United States.

Not all Americans agreed with the War Hawks. Many dreaded another war with Britain. When the US government voted to declare war, the decision was close. Many eastern states which traded heavily with Britain opposed the war.

The Americans believed that beating the British in Canada would be "a mere matter of marching." For one thing, Britain was too busy in Europe fighting with France to worry about Upper Canada. Secondly, recent American immigrants made up about 60% of the population of Upper Canada. Most Americans thought that these people would not fight in a war against the United States. Thirdly, the population of the United States was 10 times greater than the population of Canada.

Major Events of 1812

General Brock, the British military commander, had the task of defending Upper Canada. He knew it was essential that the St. Lawrence River remain open for supplies and ammunition from Britain. He had only 5000 regular British troops to guard 19 000 km of border. Because Britain was busy at war in Europe, there was no hope of any more help. There were only 100 000 people in all of Upper Canada. Many of them were recent American immigrants, and this worried General Brock. Would these newcomers help him?

Fort Michilimackinac

In the first few months of the war, Brock won some decisive victories. In a surprise attack, his troops captured Fort Michilimackinac between Lakes Michigan and Huron. This fort had been in American hands since 1796.

Fort Detroit

Next, Brock turned on the American fort at Detroit. Tecumseh and his followers joined him. Brock sent a clever dispatch to the American General Isaac Hull at Detroit. In his message to Hull, Brock warned that his Aboriginal allies would be beyond his control the moment the battle started. The Americans were so terrified of Tecumseh and his warriors that they surrendered without a fight. The British captured a large supply of American arms and ammunition.

Tecumseh and General Brock rode together into the fallen fort. Brock knew how much of the victory he owed to Tecumseh. After they arrived at the fort, the general removed his silken scarlet sash and wrapped it around Tecumseh's shoulders. Brock made this gesture in the presence of his own officers and Tecumseh's men. Tecumseh returned the compliment and placed his own arrow-patterned sash around General Brock's waist. Brock wore Tecumseh's sash until his death two months later.

The Battle of Queenston Heights

On 13 October 1812, bad news reached General Brock at his headquarters at Fort George on the Niagara River. The Americans had crossed the Niagara River at Queenston. They had climbed the heights and captured the one British cannon that was guarding the slope. Brock leaped on his horse and sped along the River Road toward Queenston. He gave orders to bring all available soldiers there.

At Queenston, Brock mustered a hundred men and led them in an uphill charge without delay. The general was wearing his scarlet tunic. Around his waist was the sash given to him by Tecumseh. He was an easy target for American sharpshooters. One of them took aim and shot Brock dead.

Eventually, General Roger Hale Sheaffe arrived with 300 redcoats, 50 militiamen, and about 300 Mohawk allies. He brought a battery of guns drawn by farm horses. Sheaffe managed to get up on the heights behind the American line. Sheaffe's redcoats charged with fixed bayonets. The Mohawk, under Joseph Brant's son, closed in from the sides. Many Americans turned and ran. Three hundred US soldiers were killed or wounded at Queenston. Nine hundred fifty were taken prisoner. On the Canadian side, 14 were killed and 57

wounded. General Sheaffe was awarded an honour for his success. But it was General Brock who was the real hero of the Battle of Queenston Heights. He proved that, against all odds, Canada could fight and win.

The battle of Queenston Heights was a proud victory in Canadian history.

BATTLEFIELDS OF THE WAR OF 1812

0   100   200   300 km

BATTLEFIELDS OF THE WAR OF 1812: NIAGARA PENINSULA
(Detail of above map)

0   10   20   30 km

Profile

General Isaac Brock 1769–1812

General Isaac Brock was one of Canada's early war heroes. He was born on the island of Guernsey and joined the British army at age 15. Brock was a tough, bold, daring professional soldier. He was fond of reading, riding, and socializing.

At the beginning of the War of 1812, Brock was the military and civilian leader of Upper Canada. He worried that Upper Canadians were not behind the British in this war. He also questioned the loyalty of the recent American immigrants in the colony. He wanted to give Upper Canadians a reason to side with Britain. General Brock wrote, "Most of the people have lost all confidence." But then he added a revealing remark, "I, however, speak loud and look big." His early victories helped to boost morale and convince Canadians that they had a chance of winning.

General Brock forged an alliance with Tecumseh. Each man admired the skills and abilities of the other. Tecumseh was impressed with Brock's leadership in battle. "Other chiefs say, 'Go'. Brock says, 'Come,'" Tecumseh marvelled. Brock on his grey charger, Alfred, and Tecumseh on a grey mustang made an impressive team together.

Until his death in battle in 1812, General Brock was the main person responsible for Canada's victories over the invading Americans.

1. What did General Brock mean when he said, "I, however, speak loud and look big"? Why was that a "revealing remark"?
2. How did the people of Upper Canada prove their loyalty to Britain?

The tunic General Brock was wearing when he was killed at the Battle of Queenston Heights on 13 October 1812 is on display at the Canadian War Museum.

Netsurfer

"Reliving History: The War of 1812" is probably the most comprehensive website on the War of 1812. It was developed in 1998 for the Thinkquest Internet Contest. You can explore the causes and events of the war, look at pictures and maps, take a tour, and even challenge yourself with quizzes. You can access this website at http://library.advanced.org/22916/exmain.html

This brass compass is said to have been given to Tecumseh by General Brock in 1812.

Profile

Tecumseh
1768–1813

Tecumseh was a Shawnee chief who was born in 1768 in what is now Ohio. One of the greatest North American Aboriginal leaders, he was a genius when it came to planning a strategy and cared passionately about his people.

After the American Revolution, thousands of settlers poured west over the Appalachian Mountains. Increasing settlement alarmed the Aboriginal people, who were afraid that their land and lifestyle would be destroyed. Tecumseh and his brother tried to organize the Aboriginal peoples into a strong confederacy. They wanted to unite all the tribes from Canada to present-day Florida, with the goal of stopping American settlement. Tecumseh preferred to do this peacefully. But if necessary, he would lead members of his confederacy into war.

Tecumseh, his brother, and their Shawnee followers founded a settlement in present-day Indiana. The American settlers feared Tecumseh and his warriors. They were also angry that Tecumseh and his people were trying to block American claims on land in Indiana. These factors led to the Battle of Tippecanoe in 1811. Under the leadership of his brother, called "the Prophet," Tecumseh's people suffered defeat and their village was burned. But Tecumseh was away in the South at the time, so his reputation remained intact.

When the War of 1812 began, Tecumseh joined the British side. He gathered an army of two to three thousand of his followers. It was the largest Aboriginal army the Great Lakes had ever seen. Tecumseh's warriors fought alongside General Isaac Brock in several battles in western Upper Canada. Brock successfully used Tecumseh's plan to capture Fort Detroit.

Tecumseh's last battle with the British was on 5 October 1813. It was the Battle of Thames River near Moraviantown. Tecumseh and his Aboriginals saved the British General Procter, but it was an American victory. Tecumseh, severely wounded, fought until his death.

1. What evidence do you have that Tecumseh was a capable military leader?
2. Do you think he made the right decision in choosing to support the British? Explain.

Major Events of 1813

When winter was over, the Americans were back. This time, their targets were York, Kingston, forts along the Niagara River, and Montreal. There were also naval battles on the Great Lakes.

York

As you read at the beginning of the chapter, in April 1813, the capital of Upper Canada was in flames. The Americans attacked York and burned the wooden Parliament Buildings. Although York was the capital of Upper Canada, the town had no strong fortifications to protect it. When Fort York fell, the town was wide open to attack.

After storing as much loot as possible in their ships, the attackers left York. They even took York's only fire engine. The Americans sailed away to attack British forts near Niagara.

The citizens of York were angry with the Americans. They were also annoyed at General Sheaffe who left them "standing in the street, like a parcel of sheep."

Niagara

At the end of May, the Americans launched another attack along the Niagara River. This was the 52 km frontier that separated Upper Canada from New York State. An American force of 2000 took Fort George. The British abandoned Fort Erie and Fort Chippewa as they pulled their troops back.

By June, the Americans had 5000 troops in the Niagara area. The British commander, Major General John Vincent, led a surprise attack on the American camp at Stoney Creek in the middle of the night. The Americans were caught off-guard and suffered heavy losses. Some important American officers were captured. The Americans began to retreat. This was the first step toward pushing the enemy out of the Niagara area. The British then moved on to Beaver Dam.

Beaver Dam

Later in June, another American force was defeated at Beaver Dam. The Americans were trying to capture a supply depot there. It was at Beaver Dam that Laura Secord became a Canadian legend. She is said to have slipped through enemy lines and warned the British about the American advance. Led by their Six Nations allies, the British attacked the Americans from behind. Within three hours, the Americans had surrendered.

Next, the Americans attacked Newark. Many of the townspeople had already moved away to live with friends and relatives. St. Mark's Church was used by the Americans to store flour, pork, and whiskey. Before they left Newark in December, the Americans set fire to the homes and buildings.

The British troops were furious. They crossed the Niagara River for revenge, capturing Fort Niagara and burning towns along the river. Lewiston, Buffalo, Black Rock, and Youngstown were attacked and burned as the townspeople fled in fear. At Christmas 1813, the Niagara Peninsula was an ugly sight. The blackened, burned buildings contrasted with the white snow. Fort Niagara, Fort George, and Fort Erie were back in British hands.

Naval Battles

Not all the important military engagements in 1813 were on land. Lake Ontario and Lake Erie were the scene of many **naval** battles. Both sides in the war had armed sailing ships made in shipyards on the lakes. Ships could not sail from one lake to the other because of the rapids and falls at Niagara.

An important naval encounter took place on Lake Erie on 10 September 1813. Captain Robert Barclay commanded the British naval squadron on Lake Erie. For a time, Barclay blockaded the harbour where the American ships were anchored. When he left briefly to resupply, the Americans moved their fleet out into the lake. The two navies met at Put-in-Bay on Lake Erie. The Americans were victorious.

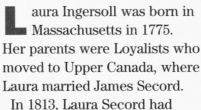

Profile

Laura Secord
1775–1868

Laura Ingersoll was born in Massachusetts in 1775. Her parents were Loyalists who moved to Upper Canada, where Laura married James Secord. In 1813, Laura Secord had Americans camping in her home. She overheard them planning an attack on a supply depot at Beaver Dam. She had to get a message to the British to warn them.

Legend says that Secord took a cow with her so the Americans would think she was on her way to the pasture. She travelled on foot through swamps, fields, and forests. It took her all day to get to the British. She told Colonel James Fitzgibbon what she had heard. The information allowed Fitzgibbon to prepare a defence and defeat the Americans.

Laura Secord's story inspired poets and painters to mark her brave deed. She became a heroine of the War of 1812 in Upper Canada. She showed the same kind of bravery as the women in New France in the days when Madeleine de Verchères defended her village against attack.

There are monuments to Laura Secord in Lundy's Lane, near Niagara Falls, and at Queenston Heights. In 1860, 47 years after her famous walk, the Prince of Wales heard about Laura Secord's loyalty. He rewarded her with a gift of 100 pounds.

1. If Laura Secord had not warned the British, how might the battle at Beaver Dam turned out differently? How might that have affected the course of the war? Why do you think so?

2. If you were Laura Secord, how would you have felt when
   - you had to leave the United States because you were a Loyalist
   - the Americans used your home as a temporary headquarters
   - you overheard the Americans planning the attack
   - you decided to get a message to the British
   - you found the British camp
   - Fitzgibbon defeated the Americans
   - people called you a hero

They captured all six of the British ships defending Lake Erie. Barclay was seriously wounded and taken prisoner. The successful battle on Lake Erie gave the Americans control of the southwestern part of Upper Canada. British troops on land, including Tecumseh and his followers, were forced to retreat eastward.

Moraviantown

The Americans followed the retreating British. The British commander decided to make a stand at Moraviantown in the Thames valley, in southwestern Upper Canada. On the left, he had the Thames River for protection. On the right,

he had thick woods and a swamp. The American attack came in the centre.

The Americans quickly took control at Moraviantown. Only Tecumseh and his warriors seemed to fight with any determination. When their great Chief Tecumseh was killed, the Aboriginals fled. Six hundred British soldiers were captured at Moraviantown.

The battle was a disaster for the British. It came just days after the defeat of the fleet at Put-in-Bay. The British soldiers became very depressed and thought that the Americans might soon win the war.

The Americans carried out a vigorous shipbuilding program on the shores of Lake Erie. When the American fleet sailed out from the harbour, the British fleet was severely defeated. With this victory, the Americans controlled Lake Erie.

Tecumseh died during the Battle of Moraviantown. After his death, the Aboriginals were no longer a large military force in northeastern North America.

It was at this time that Lieutenant-General Gordon Drummond was appointed the new commander-in-chief. He would succeed General Brock. Drummond had been born in Canada but served in the British army overseas. Now he was back in Canada and he set out to revive the fighting spirits discouraged by the American successes on Lake Erie and at Moraviantown.

Montreal

Things were going better for the British at the eastern end of Lake Ontario in 1813. The American leaders decided that they needed to capture Montreal. If they seized Montreal, they could cut off supplies to Upper Canada. They would be able to starve the colony into surrender. To carry out this plan, they sent two armies toward Montreal. One American army headed north from Lake Champlain. The second force moved from the west side of the lake, along the St. Lawrence River. Neither army reached its destination.

Châteauguay

The first American army was halted on 26 October at Châteauguay, just south of Montreal. Lieutenant-Colonel Charles de Salaberry led a French Canadian force of about 800 men, called the **Voltigeurs**. They were greatly outnumbered by the Americans. De Salaberry told his troops to make as much noise as possible when the battle began. He spread his soldiers out so that the trumpet sounds, the war cries, and the gunfire would come from many directions. He wanted the Americans to think that the French Canadian force was larger than it really was. The trick worked. He fooled the Americans into believing they were outnumbered. The American commander abandoned the fight and fled back to the United States. The Voltigeurs had defended Lower Canada and halted the American advance on Montreal.

Lieutenant-Colonel Charles de Salaberry was born in Quebec. His grandfather was the seigneur of Beauport. His father was a member of the Legislative Assembly of Lower Canada. Charles de Salaberry served in the British army and was commissioned to raise a force of French Canadians to fight in the War of 1812. His Voltigeurs met the Americans at Châteauguay. During the battle, de Salaberry stood on a tree trunk. Later, he jokingly wrote that he "rode a wooden horse"!

The American attack on Montreal was stopped at Châteauguay by French Canadian militia under the command of de Salaberry.

Crysler's Farm

The other American army was defeated at the Battle of Crysler's Farm. A huge army set out from an American town on the east end of Lake Ontario. The army formed a procession of 350 small boats filled with thousands of soldiers. They were heading east to capture Montreal. Canadian snipers opened fire from the shores of the St. Lawrence, and British gunboats from Lake Ontario appeared on their heels.

At the rapids of Long Sault, the Americans came ashore. Near the farm of the Loyalist John Crysler, 1800 Americans clashed with the defenders. Canadian and British troops, along with militia and some Aboriginal men, defeated the Americans. The members of the Crysler family huddled in the basement of their house while the battle raged. The Canadian and British force suffered 179 casualties. The Americans lost many soldiers—102 killed, 237 wounded, and 100 taken prisoner. The advance on Montreal had been stopped.

But the war was not yet over. Another year of fighting lay ahead.

Major Events of 1814

By this time, the war in Europe had ended and Britain could turn its attention to Upper Canada. The Americans knew that Britain would be sending additional troops from Europe to join in the fight. The summer of 1814 would be the Americans' last chance for victory.

The Battle at Lundy's Lane

The clash at Lundy's Lane was the bloodiest battle of the war. Americans crossed the Niagara River and turned north. The British went out from Fort George to meet them. The two armies collided just before sunset at Lundy's Lane. Much of the battle was fought in darkness under a thin moon. Both sides charged again and again. The fighting was fierce. Muskets and pistols were fired at point-blank range. The fighting went on for hours in the darkness. Targets could only be seen by the flashing gunpowder of the muskets. Major General Phineas Riall, commander of the British forces in Niagara, was wounded and captured by the Americans.

It is unclear who won at Lundy's Lane. Both sides claimed victory. Both armies were exhausted. The Americans, in need of water and reinforcements, withdrew toward Fort Erie. The British and the Canadians said that they were the winners because they held the field. The following morning, the Canadians buried the bodies of soldiers from both sides.

Fast Forward

Military Re-enactment of the War of 1812

Groups of history buffs and their families get together each summer to re-enact the battles of the War of 1812. Men dress in authentic uniforms worn by soldiers at the time of the battles. Women and children portray activities similar to those they would have been involved in 200 years ago. The re-enactors try to make history come alive by putting on demonstrations for the public.

Today, you can view military re-enactments at many historic sites around Lakes Erie and Ontario. Below are some places you can visit. Tourist boards can provide information about dates and events.

Old Fort York, Toronto, Ontario
Fort George, Niagara-on-the-Lake, Ontario
Fort Wellington, Prescott, Ontario
Fort Erie, Fort Erie, Ontario
Fort Amherstburg, Windsor, Ontario
Old Fort Henry, Kingston, Ontario
Upper Canada Village, Morrisburg, Ontario

Netsurfer

To find out more about military re-enactments, you can visit the website of the Military Re-enactment Society of Canada at www.imuc.org

In August 1814, the British attacked the Americans at Fort Erie. More than 900 British soldiers were killed, wounded, or went missing and the British did not force the Americans out. However, in late September, the Americans began to withdraw across the Niagara River. Both sides were weary of war. Both were running low on men, equipment, and supplies. The casualties in 1814 had been greater than in any other year of the war. The war in the Niagara Peninsula was over.

The Burning of Washington

In August 1814, the British navy carried the war right to the capital of the United States. Major General Robert Ross landed an army and marched on Washington, DC. It was time to get revenge for the burning of York. Government buildings were burned, including the president's mansion. According to legend, the scorched mansion of the president later had to be white-washed to cover the burn marks. From then on, the president's residence was called the White House.

The British attacked Washington, DC on 24 August 1814.

The British fleet was defeated on Lake Champlain in the closing months of the war.

Lake Champlain

An army of battle-hardened British soldiers marched south to attack the United States. They were supposed to be supported by four ships and twelve gunboats on Lake Champlain. The plan was to blow the American fleet of four ships and ten gunboats out of the water. However, the naval battle was a disaster. The British were defeated. The British land army turned in disgust and marched back to Canada.

The War That Nobody Won

By the end of 1814, both Britain and the United States were tired of fighting. There had been no clear winner. Both sides were prepared to end the fighting and sign a peace treaty on Christmas Eve 1814. It was called the **Treaty of Ghent**.

You may find that both 1814 and 1815 are given as the year the war ended. The official end was in 1814. Although peace negotiations were completed by the end of 1814, the war continued into the early months of 1815. The negotiations took place in Europe, so people in North America did not hear about it for some time. Once the treaty was signed, a messenger was sent from Ghent to deliver the news to the armies fighting in North America. Until he arrived, the soldiers and their commanders had no way to know the war was over. News of the treaty did not reach Canada until March 1815.

Territory

The Treaty of Ghent basically put things back the way they were before the war. All the territory seized during the war was returned to the original owner. The treaty did not settle any of the issues over which the United States had declared war.

Britain and the United States agreed on the boundary between the two territories. The 49th parallel of latitude would divide them from the Lake of the Woods to the Rocky Mountains. The boundary line west of the Rockies was not resolved.

Each country agreed to keep only four warships on the Great Lakes—one on Lake Champlain, one on Lake Ontario, and two on the upper lakes. These boats would act as patrol boats to catch smugglers and help make shipping safe. All the other ships would be disarmed. This part of the treaty was called the **Rush-Bagot Agreement**. It was designed to prevent problems that might lead to future wars.

New Unity and Pride in Canada

Canadians, especially those in Upper Canada, had suffered greatly from American raids on their homes, villages, and farms. Also, many lives had been lost. There was a very strong feeling of resentment and hostility toward Americans. After the war, large-scale American immigration to Upper Canada ended. Americans were not really welcome anymore.

The Loyalists in Upper Canada had always had strong feelings of devotion and allegiance to Britain. After all, they had given up everything to live in a British colony. These links were encouraged and strengthened by the War of 1812. After the war, Upper Canada looked more to Britain than to America to provide new immigrants for the colony.

The war brought the people of British North America more closely together. They had fought a fierce battle to protect their homeland. The French and the English had fought shoulder to shoulder to save their country. The colonists were proud of their successes. They were proud to be Canadians. They were beginning to develop a Canadian identity.

The Effects of the War on the Atlantic Colonies

No fighting took place in New Brunswick, Nova Scotia, Prince Edward Island, or Newfoundland. But there were important consequences of the War of 1812 for the Atlantic region. Shipbuilding increased. The timber trade also boomed. Many sawmills were started, especially in New Brunswick. Ships carried tall trees from Canadian forests across the Atlantic to be used for masts for British ships. Keeping the British navy supplied with food and other necessities kept the merchants of Halifax busy and happy.

Canadian ship owners made money as **privateers**. During the war, private schooner owners were granted permission to capture American merchant ships. Maritimers set out in search of American ships loaded with cargo. "Prize money" from captured ships made some captains very rich.

A British warship, the *Shannon*, challenged an American one, the *Chesapeake*, to a fight. The American captain used a phrase that people still use today. He urged his sailors, "Don't give up the ship." Those words soon became the navy's rallying cry. However, the *Shannon* won and towed the *Chesapeake* back to Halifax. It seemed as if the whole town of Halifax turned out to cheer the sight.

The defeat of the *Chesapeake* by the *Shannon* is one of the legendary events of Nova Scotia history. Cheering throngs crowded the Halifax harbour to celebrate the victory.

Tech Link

The Rideau Canal

Shortly after the War of 1812, the British government gave serious thought to the defence of Canada. In case of another war with the United States, Britain had to be able to get soldiers, guns, and ammunition to Upper Canada. There had to be a safe way to travel by water into Lake Ontario. If the Americans blocked the St. Lawrence River to Kingston, Upper Canada would be cut off from all help.

The plan was to build a **canal** so vessels could sail by way of the Ottawa and Rideau Rivers to Kingston. A canal is an artificial waterway for inland navigation. This canal was called a "back way" to Kingston. In 1826, Colonel John By of the Royal Engineers began to build the Rideau Canal. It would link the Ottawa River with Lake Ontario. Thousands of labourers, many of them Irish, toiled to complete the project. It was dangerous work. No one is sure how many workers died from accidents. Men were killed when explosive blasts sent trees or rocks falling on them. Cholera, a deadly disease, swept through the workers' camps, killing many.

The canal was an engineering nightmare. The workers had to hack through almost 220 km of wilderness. There were mosquito-ridden swamps, waterfalls, and places of rough water to be conquered.

At places where there was a difference in level between one body of water and the next, **locks** had to be built. A lock is a section of canal where the level of water can be changed up or down. When completed, the canal would have 47 locks in total. At Ottawa, eight locks had to be built. They formed a kind of staircase down the 24 m drop to the Ottawa River.

How Does a Lock Work?

1. A boat arrives at a lock and wants to go up to the next level.
2. The lockmaster opens the lower lock gates.
3. The boat enters the centre chamber.
4. The gates are closed.
5. The lockmaster opens the valves at the top gates.
6. Water from the other side of the top gates comes through the valves into the lock.
7. The boat naturally floats up as the water rises.
8. The water rises until it is the same level as the water on the other side of the top gate.

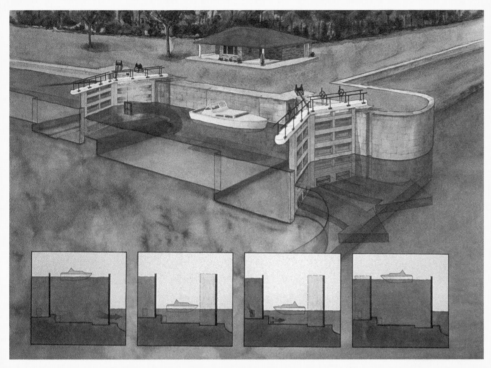

Look carefully at the water levels in the pictures to see if you can figure out what is happening.

9. When the water is the same level as the upper river, the lockmaster opens the top gate and the boat continues along the river.

If a boat wants to go to a lower level, the operation is reversed. Instead of letting water into the centre chamber, water is let out. The boat floats down until it is at the same level as the water below.

A bustling town sprang up around the site of the first lock on the Ottawa River. It was referred to as Bytown. In 1832, the canal was completed. Bytown (Ottawa) became a major port on the Rideau trade route between Montreal and the interior. Boats laden with lumber, cheese, coal, and iron ore passed through the town. All this came to an end in

about 1850 when canals were completed on the more convenient St. Lawrence River, which allowed boats to go around the rapids. Today, the Rideau Canal is used mostly by recreational boats.

A statue of John By, the man who supervised the building of the canal, surveys the Ottawa locks from the edge of a cliff in Major's Hill Park.

1. Why was the opening of the Rideau Canal an important event for Upper Canada?
2. How important is the Rideau Canal today?

The sun sets over the Ottawa locks on the Rideau Canal.

Skill Building: Reading Historical Fiction

Special historical dramas are often presented on television and in movies. They are based on historical events but do not try to be true accounts of real people. When the scenes and characters are created, they give the viewer a real sense of what people in that time period would have been feeling and doing. Historical dramas help to make a time period in history come alive.

Historical novels are like that too. They don't give facts; they are fiction. But authors of **historical fiction** do a lot of research about the time period, the people, and the events they are writing about. They base their story on real people or events. By recreating the events, the writers make you feel like you were there.

An Example

John Ibbitson is a Canadian author who has written a novel called *1812: Jeremy and the General*. It is the story of 15-year-old Jeremy Fields. His parents are dead and his family's farm has been stolen from him. Jeremy sets out for York. Before long, he finds himself in the British army as the batman, or personal servant, to General Brock. He also finds himself in the middle of a war!

The year is 1812, the Americans have invaded Upper Canada, and General Brock must find a way to stop them. Brock holds the future of Upper Canada in his hands, and Jeremy is right there in the middle of it all! Jeremy has to learn what it means to serve and to fight for his country.

In the following passage, Jeremy describes the moment of attack.

All that night I had delivered messages, orders, letters. I returned to Brock's quarters at three to find him slumped over his desk, asleep. I left him there, went to the stables, made sure Alfred was fed and his saddle nearby. I made sure another horse was ready too, one used by messengers riding between forts. Then I threw myself onto my bed. I dreamed of guns and of men dying and of horses screaming and the endless roar of cannon. Over and over again I heard the cannon.

I half awoke. There was a storm outside. Thunder grumbled in the far distance.

I jumped from my bed. The thunder was regular, repeated. It was no dream. It was the sound of cannon.

The Americans had attacked.

Choose one of the following historical novels, or another novel set in Upper Canada:
- *Fire Ship,* by Marianne Brandis
  Young Dan plays an important role during the American attack on York.
- *The Treasure of the Long Sault*, by Monica Hughes
  This story tells the events of 1813 and the Battle of Crysler's farm.
- *Treason at York,* by John F. Hayes
  This thrilling tale tells of Alan Crawford's part in the War of 1812.

Key Steps
The following points will help you study your historical novel.

1. Note the title of the novel and the author.

2. Based on the novel, describe the following:
a) the setting (Where and when does the novel take place?)
b) the theme (What is the novel about? What is the main idea?)
c) the mood (What overall feeling does the story create for you, the reader? For example, is the mood serious or is it lighthearted and funny?)

3. The **protagonist** is the leading character or hero. Name the protagonist or protagonists and describe the role played by each.

4. Choose one character and describe how and why he or she changed over the course of the story. Tell what happens to the character.

5. Describe the most exciting or interesting event in the novel. Why was it exciting?

6. Complete one of the following tasks for a presentation to the class.
a) Create a storyboard for the novel, including one scene for each chapter or main event.
b) Prepare a dramatic reading of your favourite part of the novel in Reader's Theatre style. **Reader's Theatre** involves reading with expression and sound effects, but without props.
c) Work with a partner or small group to dramatize part of the story.
d) Give a brief description or summary of the novel. Then, imagine you were the author and describe any changes you would make to the story.
e) Explain the ways in which this historical novel makes people and events from the past come alive.

Activities

Understanding Concepts

1. Define the following words and add them to your personal dictionary.

Treaty of Ghent	War Hawks	privateer
historical fiction	canal	locks
stop and search	naval	protagonist
Reader's Theatre	Voltigeur	Rush-Bagot Agreement

2. Make a list of America's reasons for declaring war on Britain.

3. Imagine you are British in the years before 1812. How would you defend
   a) your right to stop and search American ships?
   b) your decision to prohibit the Americans from trading with France?

4. Write a headline for a newspaper for each of the following events of the War of 1812.
   a) The Battle at Lundy's Lane
   b) Laura Secord's accomplishment
   c) The Battle of Crysler's Farm

5. Why was the St. Lawrence River an important target for American forces in 1813? Why did the Americans fail to attack and capture Montreal?

Digging Deeper

6. **TIMELINE** Create a timeline mural of the War of 1812. Include the following events on the mural and add any others you think are important.
   • The Americans capture York.
   • General Brock dies at Queenston Heights.
   • De Salaberry tricks the Americans.
   • Stop-and-search tactics are used.
   • The Treaty of Ghent is signed.
   • Tecumseh dies at Moraviantown.
   • Brock captures Fort Michilimackinac.
   • The British defeat the Americans at Niagara.
   • Battle takes place at Lundy's Lane.
   • The Americans capture all of the cannons at Queenston Heights.
   • Brock and Tecumseh exchange sashes in Fort Detroit.
   • The British defeat the Americans at Beaver Dam.
   • The British burn Washington.
   • The Americans are defeated at Crysler's Farm.

7. **WRITE** Imagine you are a resident of York in 1813. Write a letter to a friend telling about the four days when the Americans occupied the town.

8. **MAP STUDY** Examine the map of the battle sites in the Niagara Peninsula on page 177. What reasons might the Americans have had for attacking that part of Upper Canada?

9. **WRITE** Write a newspaper account of Laura Secord's story.

Making New Connections

10. **THINK/DISCUSS** It has been said that the Rush-Bagot Agreement was the beginning of the "undefended border" of which Canada and the United States are so proud today. What is the "undefended border"? Do you think that this statement is true? Explain.

11. **DISCUSS** Who won the war? Americans and Canadians have had friendly arguments about this question since 1815. What do you think? Explain.

12. **PREDICT** In the years following the war, what effect will the war have on how Canadians feel about the US? Why?

Upper Canada Develops

A Difficult Voyage

Quebec City
17 August 1835

To my dear sister Annie,

At last we have arrived, after six weeks at sea. The voyage from Liverpool was a horror. The ship was just a cargo ship. The owner had put in some rough bunks and filled the hold with immigrants like us. You cannot imagine the overcrowding. There were no portholes and no fresh air. Babies were crying constantly and people were quarrelling. The crew was so unfriendly that the men took turns to guard us at night.

The captain handed out only bread and water. We brought our own blankets, towels, dishes, and food. We cooked porridge or potatoes with a bit of salt pork and onions.

Many of the passengers were sick with fever* that spread like wildfire. Their bodies swelled up and were covered with sores. Before we reached Quebec, we stopped at Grosse Island, a quarantine station in the St. Lawrence River. A doctor came on board and examined our tongues for signs of the fever. Those who were sick were put off the ship. They were housed in tents and sheds and had to stay on the island until they got better or until they died. Fortunately, we were declared healthy and allowed to land upriver at Quebec.

We still have a long way to go before we arrive in Upper Canada. I will write you again when we are safely at our new home.

Your loving sister,
Sophie

*Cholera, diphtheria, and typhus were the most common diseases. They were spread by contaminated water.

Conditions faced by immigrants in the steerage section of the ship. How much room does each family seem to have? How much privacy is there?

Predicting
1. Why would so many people be willing to uproot their lives and move to British North America?
2. If you were to interview one of these immigrants, what three questions would you ask them?
3. What effect would so many new settlers in Upper Canada have on the other settlers, the Aboriginal peoples, the towns, and the land?

Immigration to Upper Canada

After the American Revolution, thousands of Loyalists came to Upper Canada in the first wave of immigration. The second wave of immigration started after the War of 1812 and consisted mostly of immigrants from Britain. Between 1815 and 1855, thousands of English, Scottish, Welsh, and Irish crossed the Atlantic to British North America. Historians sometimes call this wave of settlers the **Great Migration**.

Why People Left Their Homes

The trip from the British Isles to North America is about 4800 km. When people left their homes, they often had to leave behind family members. They also left their houses, their possessions, and the places that were familiar to them.

Then there was the challenge of the voyage itself. You have read one person's description of how horrible the experience of crossing the Atlantic could be. Even though the travellers had been told how hard the trip would be, few of them were prepared for the conditions they had to face.

In spite of these obstacles, people continued to emigrate to Canada. The number of newcomers grew until almost one million had landed between 1815 and 1855. Who were these people? Why were they prepared to leave everything and risk the journey to Canada?

Unemployed Military People

The year 1850 marked the end of a war in Europe that had lasted for 25 years. Large

---

Tragedy on the Voyage, 1832

"We had the misfortune to lose both our little boys ... We were very much hurt to have them buried in a watery grave. We mourned their loss; night and day they were not out of our minds. We had a minister on board who prayed with us twice a day. He was a great comfort to us ... There were six children and one woman who died in the vessel."

---

numbers of soldiers and sailors were left without jobs. They had to join the growing ranks of the jobless. The government offered them land in the colonies. They would be able to defend the settlers in case of military attack. Free land and new opportunities made emigrating look inviting. To **emigrate** means to leave your country and move to another.

The Industrial Revolution

The effects of the **Industrial Revolution** were being felt in Britain. People were losing their jobs to machines. Machines powered by water wheels replaced the traditional hand labour of weavers and other skilled workers. A factory full of power looms with a few unskilled workers could produce more cloth than dozens of highly paid weavers. So, these skilled workers also joined the unemployed.

City Slums

Thousands of unemployed people ended up in the growing factory towns searching for jobs. They lived in terrible poverty in dingy, overcrowded slum dwellings. Those lucky enough to find jobs in factories worked for very low wages and in wretched conditions. Even children as young as six were working for pennies a day in factories and coal mines.

It is not surprising that people living in these conditions would consider emigration to British North America.

British Emigrants to Canada

According to the British government of 1847, 87 738 emigrants left for Canada. Of those, 5293 died on the voyage, 3452 died in quarantine, and 6585 died in hospitals.

Clearances and Enclosures

Most British farmers did not own their land. They were **crofters,** or tenants who rented land from large landowners and gave the landowner part of their crops as rent. This system had been in place for generations. Now there was a thriving new market for wool in the factories. Many landlords decided to turn to raising sheep. To do this, they had to enclose the land with fences. They simply turned the crofters off the land and sent them away. In Scotland, many rural areas were almost emptied of people. The movement was called the **Highland Clearances**. In England, it was called the **Enclosure Movement.** Many of the displaced crofters came to Canada.

Famine

The situation in Ireland was even worse. Potatoes were the main food source in rural Ireland. The potato crop failed for several years in a row in the 1840s. A disease called **blight** infected the crop. Damp weather and blight prevented the seed potatoes from growing in the soil. Those that did grow turned black and were unfit to eat. **Famine** struck and starvation spread across the countryside. There was little other food to replace the diseased potato crop.

The potato had provided most of the income for the tenant farmers. Once it was gone, people had nothing. They could not pay their rent and were thrown off the land by the landowners. Their houses were burned so they could not return. Terror filled Ireland. The roads were crowded with wandering beggars searching for food and shelter.

The chance to own land with rich soil in Canada seemed almost unbelievable to many Irish people.

This picture illustrates the conditions that the emigrants in Europe faced before coming to Upper Canada.

British Government Policies

The British government was concerned about the numbers of homeless and jobless in the country. Some officials thought that British North America might be the answer. The British government offered to help poor families who were willing to settle in Canada. Their trip across the Atlantic was paid for by the government or by charities. The program was very successful. Thousands of people took advantage of this opportunity. They settled in the Atlantic colonies and in Upper Canada around Peterborough, Perth, and the Rideau River.

After 1825, this program was cancelled because it was too expensive. However, many settlers already living in Upper Canada sent money to their friends and relatives back home to help them pay for the journey. For example, in 1850, 957 000 English pounds were sent from settlers in Upper Canada to relatives and friends in Britain. It was repaid when the families were settled and earning a living in the New World.

Private Land Companies

Companies were formed specifically to bring settlers to Upper Canada. Private developers were given large sections of Crown Land. In return, they promised to bring settlers to the colonies. They made their profit by selling lots to the settlers. The Talbot Settlement was an early example of a private land company.

Another land company was the Canada Company. It was founded by John Galt in 1826. Galt received a grant of over 400 000 ha called the **Huron Tract**. It stretched from present-day Guelph to Lake Huron. Towns were established at Guelph and Goderich. Roads, mills, a bank, and a school were built before the first settlers arrived. The company advertised widely in Britain with pamphlets that showed pictures of the settlement and the village of Guelph. Agents in Britain made all the travel arrangements. The Canada Company was responsible for settling thousands of people in what is now western Ontario.

The Aboriginal Peoples of Canada

Treaties between the settlers and the Aboriginal peoples began to be negotiated in the late 1700s. These agreements were made between Aboriginal leaders and British officials and then signed in public ceremonies. Initially, there was a lot of trust between the two groups and the terms were agreed to quickly. The Aboriginal peoples usually gave up their rights to part of their territories in exchange for money and goods. Sometimes, they also received a guarantee of a yearly payment. They were allowed to keep their hunting and fishing rights. These treaties allowed European settlement to expand.

After the War of 1812, the British did not need the Aboriginal peoples as allies. The settlers outnumbered them and were less willing to make generous settlements. The British were mainly interested in getting more land while avoiding conflict. A large area had once been set aside for the Iroquois of the Six Nations after they had fought on the British side during the American Revolution. As more and more European settlers needed land, this area was cut to less than a tenth of the original grant.

By 1830, most of present-day Ontario belonged to the British. Each treaty that was signed set aside an area of land for the exclusive use of an Aboriginal group. In this way, the Aboriginal peoples were pushed back by European settlement. They ended up on compact parcels of land called **reserves**.

Skill Building: Learning from Graphs

You have probably seen graphs in books, magazines, and newspapers, and on television news reports. You may even have created graphs on a computer. A **graph** is a visual presentation or summary of information. It shows how different sets of information are related. A graph can clearly show information that would take many words to explain.

A **line graph** is one type of graph. It uses different colours or kinds of lines to display changes in various values. Line graphs are drawn on a grid. They make it easy to compare one thing to another.

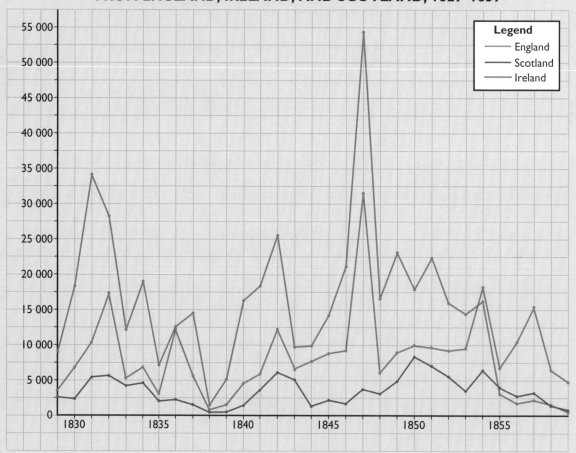

NUMBER OF IMMIGRANT ARRIVALS AT THE PORT OF QUEBEC CITY FROM ENGLAND, IRELAND, AND SCOTLAND, 1829–1859

Legend
— England
— Scotland
— Ireland

Keys Steps

Follow these steps to read a line graph correctly.

1. Read the title of the graph. It should tell you what is being compared. This graph compares the numbers of immigrants who arrived in Quebec from England, Scotland, and Ireland from 1829 to 1859.

2. Locate the **legend**. The legend tells what the lines on the graph mean. The red line stands for immigrants who arrived at the port of Quebec from England. The blue line shows immigrants from Scotland. The green line provides information on the numbers arriving from Ireland.

3. Read the dates along the bottom of the graph. They tell you the time period that is being covered in this graph. It begins on the left with the year 1829. It ends 30 years later on the right in 1859. The other numbers represent the years between 1829 and 1859, measured every five years (1835, 1840, 1845, 1850, and 1855).

4. Examine the numbers along the left side of the graph. The numbers go from 0 at the bottom to 55 000 at the top. They represent the number of people who landed at Quebec each year. Each line on the grid stands for 2500 people.

Locate the year 1830 on the bottom line. Examine the information for the year 1830. Find the line that represents English people coming to Canada. Look at the number on the left side. It indicates that over 6000 immigrants arrived. Find the line that stands for Scottish people coming to Canada. It tells you that about 2500 arrived at Quebec. Find the line that stands for Irish immigrants in 1830. Now you can figure out that over 18 000 immigrants arrived from Ireland in 1830.

5. Study the rest of the graph. What does it tell you? What conclusions can you draw? Consider the following questions.
• Which year marked the highest point of immigration to Canada between 1829 and 1859? Suggest reasons for this.
• In what year did the fewest immigrants come?
• In late 1837, rebellions broke out in both Upper and Lower Canada. What effect did these uprisings have on immigration the following year?
• Which group from Britain contributed the most immigrants to Canada? Suggest reasons for this.

Challenge Yourself!

Brainstorm other types of graphs you have seen. Could these immigration figures be presented in another type of graph? How?

Other Settlers

Not all the people who immigrated to Canada were poor. Not all came because of the advertisements of private companies like the Canada Company. Some left Britain on their own. Educated sons of well-to-do families often found jobs in the colonial government. Successful tradespeople and merchants hoped to earn a better living in Upper Canada. Lawyers, teachers, engineers, doctors, and clergy, too, saw it as a land of adventure and opportunity. As well, not all the families that came to Upper Canada were British. For example, small groups of settlers from Germany settled along the Ottawa River and near Halifax and Lunenburg in Nova Scotia.

The Underground Railroad

"When my feet first touched the Canada shore I threw myself on the ground, rolled around in the sand, seized handfuls of it and kissed it and danced around, till, in the eyes of several who were present, I passed for a madman." This is how Josiah Henson recalled his arrival to freedom in Canada in 1830.

Fighting for Freedom

A number of Black Canadians were involved in the efforts to abolish slavery in the United States and to help slaves when they arrived in Canada:

- Mary Ann Shadd, a freeborn woman of colour, was a well-known teacher, writer, lawyer, and newspaper publisher
- Ruffin Abbott, the first Black doctor born in Canada
- Reverend Samuel Ringgold Ward, publisher of a newspaper dealing with the problems encountered by refugee Blacks
- Henry Bibb, who published a Windsor, Ontario newspaper to help newly escaped slaves

---

Josiah Henson was one of the former Black slaves who came to Canada by way of the **Underground Railroad**. In spite of its name, the Underground Railroad was not a real railroad. The term referred to a network of people and safe houses that helped runaway slaves. The Underground Railroad provided an escape route from the United States to Canada.

Governor Simcoe was a firm opponent of slavery. He had introduced an anti-slavery bill in the first Legislative Assembly in 1792. It did not outlaw slavery, but it did state that no new slaves could be imported to Upper Canada and that no one was to be enslaved for any reason. Slavery was abolished throughout the British Empire by 1834 but continued for a number of years in other parts of the world.

After the War of 1812, Canada gained the reputation of being a safe place for runaway slaves from America. American soldiers returning from the war to their homes in the South talked about Upper Canada. They told of the Canadian government's willingness to defend the rights of Black people. Gradually, by word of mouth among slaves, Canada became known as the "land of promise."

In their efforts to escape, some of the slaves discovered that they could count on the help of a number of people in the northern states. These were often religious people who opposed slavery. They were called **abolitionists** because they wanted to abolish slavery. They were willing to take risks to help runaway slaves get to the safety of Canada.

There was always a need for secrecy because there were bounty hunters looking for runaway slaves. The Fugitive Slave Law in the United States had given owners the right to chase and capture their slaves in any state. Bounty hunters were given rewards by slave owners when they captured and returned the runaways.

To hide and disguise their efforts, the abolitionists used railway terms. The people who led the slaves on foot or horseback or transported them by wagon, barge, or steamer became known as "conductors." The runaways, often hidden in crates, were called "cargo" or "passengers." Hiding places such as barns, cellars, attics, and church towers were called "stations." The people who helped to hide the runaway slaves were "station-keepers."

Messages were sent in code between station-keepers. Can you decipher the true meaning of this one?

> Mr. C. B. C.
>
> Dear Sir,
>   By tomorrow evening's mail you will receive two volumes of the "Irrepressible Conflict" bound in black. After perusal, please forward and oblige.
>
> Yours truly,
> G. W. W.

The web of escape routes was called the "line" or the "track." The final destinations where the slaves arrived in freedom were known as "terminals." The use of these railroad words confused many people. Some Americans thought that there really were trains travelling in underground tunnels all the way from the southern states to Canada!

Several Canadian towns and cities became terminals on the Underground Railroad. One of the most important was Amherstburg in the southwest part of present-day Ontario. Since it was located at the narrowest point of the Detroit River, it was even possible to swim across the river to freedom. Other important terminals were Port Burwell and Port Stanley on Lake Erie. On Lake Ontario, Toronto, Hamilton, and Kingston were terminals. In Niagara, both St. Catharines and Niagara-on-

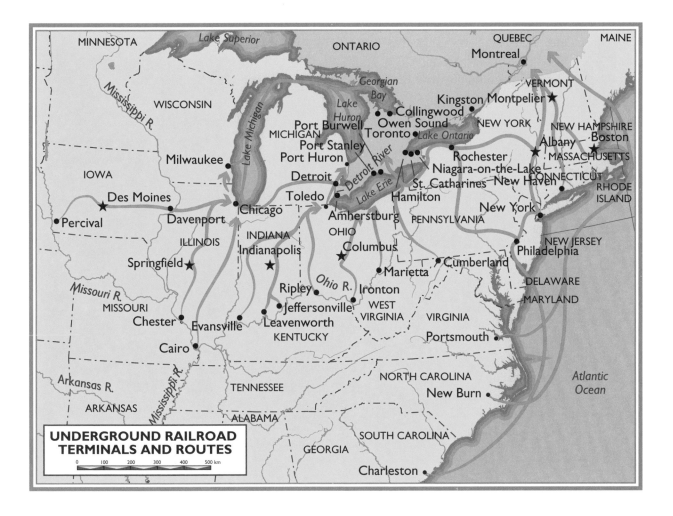

UNDERGROUND RAILROAD TERMINALS AND ROUTES

the-Lake were ends of the line. Sometimes conductors in Chicago put Black refugees on steamers heading for the ports of Collingwood or Owen Sound on Georgian Bay. Passengers coming through New England were sent to Saint John, Halifax, or Montreal.

It is estimated that by 1850, 15 000 to 20 000 runaway slaves had fled to Canada by way of the Underground Railroad. In 1865, all American slaves were freed. About half the Black refugees in Canada eventually returned to the United States. The other Black settlers remained in their adopted country.

Like other immigrants of this period, many former slaves who came by the Underground Railroad became farmers. They often faced racism and were shut out of local society. However, they formed their own strong communities and established farms, schools, and churches.

The most successful self-supporting Black community in Canada was Buxton, near Chatham, Ontario. It was founded in 1849 by the Reverend William King. Freed and fugitive slaves settled on 1720 ha of land. Under King's direction, the settlement prospered. It had a post office, combined sawmill and gristmill, brick yard, and several small industries. Within 10 years, Buxton had reached a population of 1200. Descendants of the first settlers still live in the area.

Netsurfer

The John Freeman Walls Historic Site and Underground Railroad Museum is located in Puce (near Windsor), Ontario. It was an actual terminal of the Underground Railroad. The website is
http://www.web.net/~proverbs/

American slaves escape to Canada by way of the Underground Railroad.

Profile

Josiah Henson

The Reverend Josiah Henson was a slave who escaped to Canada in 1830 with his wife and children. In 1834, he settled near Amherstburg, Ontario. Henson returned to the United States many times to help other escaped slaves reach Canada. In his auto-biography, he reported that he helped 118 individuals escape from slavery in the 1830s and 1840s.

In 1841, Henson moved to Dawn Township, near Chatham, Ontario. There, he helped to start a self-supporting colony where Blacks could live and study. Some of the people worked as farmers. Others worked in the sawmill, the gristmill, or the brickyard. The children and some of the adults attended school. After he left the Dawn settlement, Henson travelled in Canada, the United States, and England, giving speeches and meeting people. Henson's story was recorded in the book *The Life of Josiah Henson, Former-ly a Slave, Now an Inhabitant of Canada*. It is thought that his life was the model for Uncle Tom in the novel *Uncle Tom's Cabin*, written by Harriet Beecher Stowe.

1. Do you think Josiah Henson's establishment of the Dawn settlement was a good thing to do? Explain.
2. Find out more about other Ontario settlements, such as Buxton, that were established by or for Blacks.

The Nazrey African Methodist Episcopal Church was founded by Underground Railroad passengers in Amherstburg, Ontario, where Josiah Henson settled.

Profile

Harriet Tubman

Harriet Tubman was born a slave. She escaped to Canada on the Underground Railroad and settled in St. Catharines, Ontario in 1851. Tubman chose St. Catharines as her headquarters because a large number of Blacks had made their homes there. Also, it was a short distance across the Niagara River to the United States.

Harriet Tubman made many secret journeys to the slave-holding areas in the United States to escort fugitive slaves to Canada. As a "conductor," she helped hundreds of slaves, including her sister and brothers. She never lost a "passenger" and none of the people she helped was ever recaptured. Slave owners offered a $40 000 reward for her capture. This would be equivalent to $1 million today. Although Tubman could not read or write, she was clever enough to outwit her pursuers. The people she helped called her "Moses," after the biblical figure who also led slaves to freedom.

During the American Civil War, Harriet Tubman was a nurse and later a spy and scout for the Union army. After slavery was abolished in the United States, she returned there and used her skills and influence to bring attention to the rights of women. She also established a shelter for elderly and poor Blacks.

---

1. If you were a conductor on the Underground Railroad, as Harriet Tubman was, why would you risk your own life to do this? What would be your greatest worries? Your greatest joys?
2. The Quakers were very involved with the Underground Railroad. Find out why they became involved and what role they played.

The Welland Canal

Most of the Upper Canada settlements were located on waterways. The first highways were the lakes and rivers, originally used by the Aboriginal peoples and later by the Europeans. It was far easier to travel by water than to use the roads, which were largely undeveloped. But there were also serious difficulties with the waterways. Rapids or waterfalls sometimes prevented the passage of boats. Cargo had to be unloaded and portaged around the trouble spots. This created extra costs for the people moving the cargo and was a nuisance for passengers. For example, if you wanted to ship grain between Lakes Ontario and Erie on the Niagara River, you faced a towering obstacle: Niagara Falls was blocking the way!

Construction of the Welland Canal

William Hamilton Merritt, a young merchant from St. Catharines, suggested a solution to the problem of passing Niagara Falls in the 1820s. His idea was to build a canal around Niagara Falls, along a route roughly parallel to the Niagara River. The Americans were building the Erie Canal from Buffalo to the Hudson River. Merritt warned that Canadians must have their own canal. Otherwise, the Americans would capture the trade of the western Great Lakes. He and some other businessmen formed their own company to build the Welland Canal.

During construction of the canal, there were many difficulties that led to huge increases in costs. Most of the problems were caused by the great difference in height between Lake Ontario and Lake Erie. Within the 30 km length of the original canal, 40 wooden locks had to be built to raise or lower ships a height of over 90 m. However, in 1829, the canal was completed. Two schooners, the *Ann and Jane* and *R.H. Broughton*, were the first ships to pass through the new canal from Port Dalhousie on Lake Ontario to Buffalo, New York.

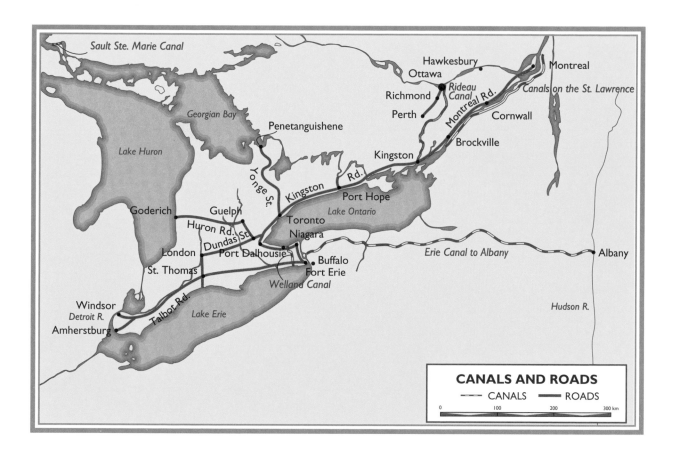

The government of Upper Canada took over the canal in 1841. Since it was so well used, the government had the canal deepened and the locks improved. The wooden locks were replaced with stone locks that could handle larger cargo ships. Villages along the canal such as Welland, St. Catharines, and Port Colborne prospered as more and more Canadian and American ships used it.

In the next few years, several other short canals were completed along the St. Lawrence River south of Montreal. By 1848, steam and sailing ships could pass from the Atlantic Ocean to Lake Superior.

The *Ann and Jane,* out of York, is the first schooner to travel through the Welland Canal. The second, the *R.H. Broughton,* is from Youngstown, New York. The people on the bank are wishing the schooners luck as they pass through the canal.

Fast Forward

The Welland Canal

1870s The Welland Canal was enlarged again.

1932 Major alterations were completed.

2000 The Welland Canal is an engineering achievement on a massive scale. It ranks with the Panama and Suez Canals as one of the largest in the world. Huge ocean-going ships are lifted up and down the Niagara Escarpment by a series of locks. Thanks to the Welland Canal, ships from around the world can move through the Great Lakes to the middle of the continent.

The stone locks of the Welland Canal could handle large cargo vessels.

Profile

William Hamilton Merritt 1793–1862

William Hamilton Merritt was born in New York State in 1793. He moved with his family to Upper Canada at a very young age. After the War of 1812, Merritt settled in what was to become St. Catharines.

Merritt was a merchant and a land agent. He owned gristmills, a salt factory, a potashery, and a distillery. He was always on the lookout for a challenge. That is why he got involved with the Welland Canal Company. Merritt saw the potential of water transportation. He realized that if Niagara Falls could be bypassed with a canal, ships could sail into the heart of the continent. This would be good for business and for the development of Upper Canada.

Merritt and his friends set out to raise the money needed for the job. They appealed to the government and to international bankers. They managed to raise enough money to get the canal started.

Merritt did everything in his power to promote the waterway system. In spite of every difficulty, he kept the project going. He was on the deck of the first Canadian ship that sailed through the canal.

Merritt also headed a company that later built the Welland Railway. The railway was built parallel to the canal. From 1832 to 1862, Merritt was an elected member of the legislature. In 1862, William Hamilton Merritt died aboard a ship while he was inspecting the canal at Cornwall. He was planning to make the canals even bigger and better to make them fit into his dream of a great St. Lawrence Seaway system.

1. William Hamilton Merritt can be described as a "visionary." Define "visionary." What other people do you know of who could be called visionaries? What do they have in common with Merritt?

2. What might have been the effect on the development of Upper Canada if Merritt had not ensured the building of the Welland Canal?

Fast Forward

The St. Lawrence Seaway

William Hamilton Merritt had dreamed of a St. Lawrence Seaway that would make it possible for ships to travel from Britain all the way to the Great Lakes. Merritt described such a plan as "worthy of great minds … Future ages will applaud the wisdom of … (those) who commenced the St. Lawrence Canal on a sufficient scale to ensure its full and complete usefulness."

Few people shared Merritt's vision at that time. Although many canals were built between 1779 and 1932, actual construction on the seaway did not begin until the 1950s. Bridges were modified, new locks were built, and people were displaced from their homes and moved into new towns. In 1959, the seaway was completed. It linked the Great Lakes region to global markets. All this was done jointly with the United States.

The St. Lawrence Seaway extends more than 3700 km, from the Atlantic Ocean to Lake Superior. It takes eight and a half sailing days to travel the full length. The Seaway provides access to 15 major international ports and 50 smaller regional ports. Over two billion tonnes of cargo passed through the seaway in its first 40 years of service. Typical cargo on the seaway includes grain, iron ore, petroleum products, steel, machinery, and mine products. The waterway is open to navigation from late March to late December. This system of locks, canals, and channels has contributed significantly to Canada's involvement in the global marketplace.

The Growing Timber Trade

Next to farming, the most important activity in Upper Canada was the timber trade. Britain needed timber for its wooden sailing ships. White pine for use as masts was in great demand. When Britain's supply of timber from Europe was cut off by war in the early 1800s, shipbuilders had to depend on North America.

The wood was harvested first from the forests of Nova Scotia and New Brunswick. It was exported from the Maritime ports. Later, in the 1820s and 1830s, lumbering became important in the Ottawa valley and the northern parts of Upper Canada. By 1839, wood made up 80% of all exports from British North America.

In the Bush

The axemen carefully selected the trees to be cut down. They looked for tall, straight, knot-free trees. The best white pine might tower 50 m high, and considerable skill was needed to bring these trees down safely. A good axeman could drop a tree on a precise spot. His skill and power were essential if the camp was to be profitable.

Once the trees were felled, they were squared to fit more easily into the timber ships. Rounded edges wasted important space. Squaring was done with an **adze** and a heavy broadaxe that could weigh as much as 5 kg. An adze was a special type of axe with a blade shaped like a hoe. Squaring timber was actually very wasteful. About a quarter of the log was cut away and just left on the ground. In the winter, teams of oxen hauled the logs out of the woods to the rivers.

Rafting the Logs Down River

Spring was the time when the **log drive** took place. The logs were rafted down the river on the high waters of the spring melt. This was the only way to get the logs to the sawmills. The loggers worked furiously to get the logs into the river at the right time.

The drive was the most hazardous part of the loggers' job. Imagine the scene. The loggers worked quickly to tie logs into huge rafts. They used birch and hazel saplings as rope. The log rafts had to be secure or rough water would break them up. Some rafts were 90 m long and 18 m wide! They were so large that a house could be built on them. Each raft had a crew of up to 50 men who lived in tents or cabins right on the raft.

The men skillfully guided the rafts downstream using oars. There was always danger. The rafts were unpredictable. They travelled at breakneck speed through dangerous rapids. The crew had to constantly be on the lookout for rocks and keep the raft away from the shoreline. Many lives could be lost during the spring drives. It was reckless and daring work!

Rafting methods were somewhat different on the Ottawa River. The timbers were put together in smaller rafts called **cribs**. They were not as strong as the St. Lawrence rafts, but they were suited to the Ottawa River and more easily handled. In smooth water, several cribs could be linked together like the cars of a train.

Sawmills also developed as part of the timber trade. By 1854, at the peak of the trade, there were 1618 sawmills in Upper Canada. They produced planks for houses and barns in the settlements. Plank buildings were replacing the old log homes. Boards from sawmills in Upper Canada were also exported to Europe.

Philemon Wright ran the first timber raft down the Ottawa River to Quebec in 1806. It took 35 days to travel from the mouth of the Gatineau River to Montreal. Oars were used at the back, sides, and front to guide the raft through the channels. His son later invented timber slides, which were special alleyways used to get the cribs around waterfalls.

Temporary shelters were built on rafts to house the lumbermen during a log drive.

The Lumber Camp Shanty

Lumbering became a way of life for many people. In the fall, canoes carried the loggers and their supplies to camps in the forests. As the timber trade grew in importance, thousands of men went to live for the winter in the shanties of the lumber camps.

The typical log shanty housed 50 to 60 men. There were tiers of bunks with six or seven sleeping platforms in each tier. Near the door were the grindstones. These were used constantly in the evenings to sharpen the axes. To the other side of the door stood two barrels of wash water and a stand for the wash basins.

The heart of the shanty was the **camboose**. This was a square of logs in the middle of the shanty in which the fire for heating and cooking burned all day and all night. Smoke from the fire escaped through a hole in the roof. Here, the cook prepared all the meals in huge pots and kettles. Each man had a dish, tin plate, and soup spoon. No knives or forks were provided. A logger could buy a small butcher knife for 25¢. This served as both a knife and fork. Between meals, it was stuck in the wall of the owner's bunk.

The food was unlimited in quantity, but it lacked variety. A shantyman in the Ottawa valley described it this way:

The interior of a lumber camp shanty

For breakfast we usually have baked beans, sometimes with a little molasses, bread, and green tea. We take our lunch with us in cotton bags into the woods where we are working. It's usually boiled salt pork and bread and tea. Likely, it's frozen because most of the time we have to bury our lunch in the snow to keep the ravens from getting it. They love to tear open those cotton bags and eat our lunches in the morning while we are working. When lunch time comes we usually sit around an open fire to boil our tea and thaw our sticks of bread by holding them close to the fire.

Supper is the main meal of the day. Each man gets a tea dish, tin plate, and a hunk of bread from the cook's shelves. He takes as much as he wants. There are no tables. He sits on a bench with the plate on his knee and eats with the help of his butcher knife.

For supper, usually there is a huge kettle of fresh boiled beef, and another one of boiled potatoes. There might also be one of salt pork, and there is always lots of bread. For dessert, we might have rice pudding with raisins or stewed dried apples with cinnamon. There is always lots of strong tea which is said to be just right when it is strong enough to float an axe. There is always lots of brown sugar to put in the tea.

The Decline of the Timber Trade

The timber trade in British North America began to decline in the 1850s. After the wars in Europe ended, Britain began to buy more lumber from the Scandinavian countries. Squared timber from Canada was less in demand. It was cheaper for Britain to import lumber from Europe than to import it from Canada. Shipbuilding was also changing. As the century advanced, ships with steel hulls were replacing wooden ships.

Gristmills

The miller was an important person in the settlements of Upper Canada. Mills powered by water were the most effective way to grind grain into flour, saw lumber, and power the spinning and weaving machines that produced cloth. The mills were situated beside a natural site for a dam and a good flow of water. They dotted the streams and rivers of Upper Canada in the 19th century. Often, a village sprang up around the mill.

Running the rapids with a log raft. What safety equipment are these loggers wearing?

Logs float upriver.

Bread was a staple food of the settlers. It was eaten every day. At first, wheat and corn were ground into flour by hand, by pounding the grain with a heavy stone. Soon, the settlers built **gristmills** so that the task could be done faster and with less effort. Flowing water turned a large waterwheel and this turned a shaft that turned a millstone. Underneath, there was another millstone that remained still. The grain was crushed between the two stone surfaces to make flour.

Farmers from the surrounding district used the gristmills for grinding their grain into flour. They brought the grain to the mill by foot or wagon. While they waited, they talked with one another and caught up on local news.

Activities

Understanding Concepts

1. Define the following terms and add them to your personal dictionary.

emigrate	crofter	Enclosure Movement
Highland Clearances	blight	famine
Great Migration	Industrial Revolution	Huron Tract
abolitionist	Underground Railroad	gristmill
log drive	graph	line graph
camboose	adze	crib
reserve	legend	

2. Why did so many immigrants come to Canada from 1815 to 1850? What made Canada a good place to come to?

3. Describe the problems passengers faced on immigrant ships. What do you think was the worst part of the voyage? Explain why.

4. What were the advantages and disadvantages of using the Canadian waterways for transportation?

5. What led to the collapse of the timber trade in Upper Canada?

6. How was the site of a mill picked? Why did settlements often grow up around the site of a mill?

7. The words "immigrate" and "emigrate" are both used to describe the process of leaving one country to live in another. Check the meaning of both words in a dictionary. Describe how to use these words correctly.

Digging Deeper

8. **DISCUSS** During the years 1815 to 1855, many emigrants left Britain.
   a) What groups of people wanted to leave Britain at this time? Why?
   b) How did the British government encourage people to leave? Why?

9. **WRITE** Imagine you are working in the timber trade on the Ottawa River. Write a paragraph for a newspaper describing what you do and the life you live in the lumber camp.

10. **THINK/WRITE** Imagine you are a land developer in Upper Canada in 1822. You have been granted a large tract of land in the backwoods. Draw up a list of rules and regulations for the group of settlers you will bring from Britain.

11. **READ/WRITE** Find and read a fiction or non-fiction book about the Underground Railroad. Write a report on what you learn from the book.

Making New Connections

12. **INVESTIGATE** William Hamilton Merritt predicted that one day ocean-going ships would be able to sail into the heart of the North American continent. Research how the building of the St. Lawrence Seaway in the 1950s fulfilled Merritt's dream.

13. **DISCUSS** "Shantymen" were often farmers as well. How was it possible to combine both occupations? Which type of settler would probably try to do both? Why?

The Pioneers

We often use the word **pioneers** when we talk about the early settlers of Upper Canada. This term refers to people who take the lead, who go first or do something first and pave the way for others. The pioneers in Upper Canada settled a region where few Europeans had lived before. They had to defend their chosen land in battle. They had to learn how to cope in a new, and sometimes hostile, environment. They lived far away from one another and had to be self-sufficient to survive. They were inventive and learned how to make do with very basic materials and supplies.

As Upper Canada grew and prospered, the settlers' lives improved steadily. Towns grew and were able to provide a variety of goods and services for people living within them and in the surrounding areas. Farms became more productive and agriculture became an important part of the Upper Canada economy. The settlers were able to build new and better homes for themselves. They could afford to buy many items to make their daily lives more comfortable. As the pioneer communities became well established throughout Upper Canada, their inhabitants gained many benefits—but they also faced some new problems.

Predicting/Reflecting
Write down what you know about the lives of the pioneers. After you read this chapter, reread what you wrote and answer these questions:
1. What new information did you learn?
2. How is your life different from that of pioneer children? How is it similar?
3. Would you like to have been a pioneer? Explain why.
4. What additional information would you like to find out about pioneers?

The Daniel Stong House at Black Creek Pioneer Village. This log shanty was the family's first home.

A Day in the Life of a Rural Settler in Upper Canada, 1840

The sun is just peeking over the eastern horizon when the Grey family begins to stir. Ruth, the mother, is already in the kitchen stoking the fire in the stove. Her husband, Jacob, is standing at a wash basin in the corner, washing his face and combing his hair.

Ruth goes to the foot of the stairs and calls her children. "Time to get up, boys. Hurry up girls, I need you in the kitchen." Upstairs, Daniel (17), Paul (14), and Will (10) roll out from under the quilt. They stretch and yawn, climb into overalls, and pull on heavy knitted socks. There are chores to be done in the barn before breakfast. In the girls' room, Kate (15) and Mary (12) are hurrying to dress and get downstairs to help their mother.

Before Breakfast

By the time Daniel reaches the kitchen, his father has already left for the barn. He and Paul hurry out to help milk the five cows. They need to muck out (clean out) the stables and strew (scatter) fresh hay over the floor. Meanwhile, Will is starting to carry buckets of water from the well to the trough where the animals drink. It takes Will more than 20 trips back and forth before the cows, horses, pigs, and sheep have all been watered.

Mary goes out to scatter corn for the barnyard fowl. While they are eating, she enters the hen house and collects the eggs. Kate is helping her mother get breakfast ready. When the family comes in from doing chores, everyone is starving! They sit down and, after Jacob says grace, they dive into their morning meal. First, there are bowls of porridge made from their own oats, with thick fresh cream poured on top. Then, there are boiled eggs and slices of fried smoked ham. Thick slices of mother's home-baked bread are slathered with jam made from the wild strawberries they picked in June.

"Children, you won't be able to go to school today." Father is talking to the three youngest children. Daniel and Kate have already finished school and will work at home until they get married and have farms of their own. "Winter is just around the corner. You will have to help Daniel and me finish the harvest. We have to get all the apples picked today, before there is a heavy frost." Father's words make Paul and Will grin. No school today! Farm work is tiring but at least they won't have to trudge 3 km to school and 3 km home again. The Grey children have attended school for only about four months this year. It seems they are always needed to help with some job around the farm. But some of their friends never go to school and can't even read or write their own names.

Morning Chores

After breakfast, Kate and her mother wash dishes, sweep floors, shake out mattresses, and fold quilts. Jacob goes out to harness the horses for some fall plowing. First, he must check the horses' hoofs. A horse could go lame from walking all day with a loose shoe or a stone caught in its hoof. Mary and the boys head down to the orchard. Daniel and Paul climb ladders to pick the apples. Nothing is wasted. Mary and Will pick up all the bruised fruit that has fallen to the ground or been knocked off by the wind. These windfalls on the ground will be taken to Mr. Horner, who owns a small cider press. The juice will be squeezed out and stored in stone crocks until it is ready to drink as cider or be made into vinegar. Daniel and Paul carry the heavy baskets of apples up to the porch. Mother has promised to make apple pies for supper.

If there is going to be pie for supper, Ruth must get the oven heated up. On one side of the fireplace there is a **beehive oven**, or bake oven. It is called a beehive because of its shape. She gets a roaring fire going in the oven. This heats up the bricks and makes them nice and hot for baking. Meanwhile, Kate rolls out dough to make pie crusts and lines tin pie plates with the crust. Ruth peels, cores, and slices the apples and adds lots of brown sugar and cinnamon. She places the apple mixture in each crust and puts on a top layer of pastry. Now she checks her oven. When it is hot enough, she scrapes out the burning ashes. They slide down a chute into the fireplace. Then, she places the four pies she has made on the hot bricks. An iron oven door keeps the heat in. Soon, the smell of pies baking fills the air.

The Midday Meal

At about noon, everybody comes back to the house for the main meal of the day. There are boiled potatoes and carrots from the garden. There is a tasty stew made from rabbits that Paul caught in a homemade trap. There is bread and jam for dessert. Although the boys want to cut into the pies, mother says they are still too hot and that everyone must wait until supper. After an hour or so, the family returns to their work.

Ruth was running out of meat, so about six weeks ago, Jacob butchered two pigs. The meat was cut up, soaked in salt brine, and then carefully dried. Now it is time to hang it in the **smokehouse**. This is a small log building with a fire pit lined with bricks in the middle of the dirt floor. Jacob gets a fire started in the smokehouse. It will be Paul's job to keep the fire smouldering day and night. Jacob reminds Paul to use only hickory or oak logs and to choose green wood that is not too dry. These woods burn slowly and their smoke gives the best flavour to the meat. The smoke fills the building. After about a week of smoking, the meat will be well flavoured and cured to last a number of months.

Evening Chores

At about six o'clock, it is time to start the chores with the animals again. Will is sent to herd the cows back toward the barn. The horses must have their sweaty coats wiped dry and the tangles brushed out of their manes and tails. The sheep must be brought into the safety of the barn. There are a lot of wild animals that could attack lambs or piglets at night. Cows have to be milked and all the animals must be watered and fed.

Notice the beehive oven set in the side of the fireplace. The long-handled, flat, wooden utensil is for placing loaves in the bake oven. On the floor, the door for the oven is propped up, ready for use. Bowls, jugs, a teapot, a coffee grinder, an iron, spoons, lamps, and shakers are kept close at hand.

In the house, Mother and Kate are getting ready for supper. They are frying eggs and potatoes. There will be thick slices of bread and cheese made from milk from their own cows. And, of course, there will be apple pie. The family likes to pour fresh sweet cream over the pie.

When the supper dishes are cleared away, everyone can relax for a while before bed. Will is using a pocket knife to sharpen arrows for the hunting bow he has made. Friends of Daniel and Kate walk over from a neighbouring farm.

They are carrying candle lanterns that they will light to show them the way home. The young people sit on the porch, where they talk and laugh. Mary is stitching a sampler. Ruth is trying to embroider by candlelight, but she gives up as the room gets darker and darker. Jacob dozes in the rocker by the stove. Shortly after nine o'clock, Ruth hustles the younger children off to bed. The others will soon follow because, at first light, they will be up again and will need to be ready for another day on their Upper Canada farm.

Making Soap

Most settlers made their own soap from animal fat and **lye**. Water was allowed to leach (drain) through ashes to produce lye. Lye is very strong and can burn the skin. Even the fumes can burn the nose and throat if they are inhaled, so soap-making was done outside.

Making soap was a lot of work. All the fat was saved when animals were butchered. The scraps of fat were boiled in water and then the lye was added. The melted fat, or tallow, took away the strength of the lye. Ammonia and borax were added for laundry soap. Bayberry, rolled oats, glycerin, or wild ginger leaves were added to make bath soap. Then, the mixture was poured into pans or boxes and allowed to harden. The next day, it was cut into bars, ready for use.

Netsurfer

Discover more about making soap the old-fashioned way. This site contains basic instructions and recipes: www.lis.ab.ca/walton/old/ soapold.html

Sheep provided warm woollen clothing for the settlers in Upper Canada.

The Rural Settler's Work Calendar

A settler's life was always busy. The tasks that needed to be done depended on the time of year.

Spring

Mending fences, plowing fields, and planting new crops were jobs that were done in the spring. There was also a huge vegetable garden to be dug up and planted. This garden would provide food for the family all summer and in the long winter ahead.

Many of the farm animals would be giving birth at this time of year. Men and women had to be on hand to deal with any difficult births. Sometimes, a tiny newborn creature had to be taken inside the house and nursed by hand.

If the family kept sheep, they were washed and then sheared in the spring. The wool had to be carded, or combed, to make sure it was free of tangles. Then, it could be spun into yarn on a spinning wheel. The wool was often dyed using natural dyes such as sumac (orange) and black-berries (purple). After the wool was spun into yarn, it was woven into cloth using a loom.

Horses and improved agricultural tools made plowing, cultivating, and harvest-ing crops much easier. Teams of horses did much of the backbreaking work.

Summer

Summer was a busy time outdoors on the farm. The women and girls looked after weeding and watering the large garden. The men and boys cleared more land and plowed fields for the first time. The growing crops had to be watched carefully for harmful bugs and diseases. Grass and clover were mowed and stored in the hayloft for winter feed for the animals.

Autumn

Autumn was harvest time. Crops had to be cut, gathered, and bound. In the barn, bundles of grain were **threshed**. This means they were beaten with a hinged stick called a flail until the grains were knocked out of the shells. Some-times, the animals were walked back and forth over the grain to perform this same function. Then, the grain was **winnowed**, which means seeds were separated from the lighter covering, or chaff. The grain seeds were then ready to be ground into flour at the local gristmill.

Meat had to be preserved because there was no refrigeration. Pigs and cows were usually butchered in the fall. The cut-up meat was rubbed with salt or stored in a solution of salt and water. Then, the meat was smoked for a week in the smokehouse. Well-smoked meat lasted for many months.

Fruits and vegetables were also stored for winter use. Potatoes, carrots, cabbages, turnips, and onions could be stored in a cold cellar under the floorboards. This was really just a pit dug in the ground and lined with stones. The winter vegetables were packed in layers of straw. Fruit such as strawberries, raspberries, gooseberries, and red currants were made into jam or jelly by adding sugar and boiling the mixture. Other fruit, like apples or peaches, were dried in the sun. When the settlers wanted to use the dried fruit, they poured boiling water over the slices and let them soak until soft and ready to eat. Then, they used the water as a drink. Cucumbers, melons, and onions were often stored by pickling them in vinegar. Vinegar could be made from apples or even maple sap.

Winter

In winter, the farm animals were brought into the barn where they had to be fed, watered, and cared for throughout the cold weather. Fire-wood had to be cut and hauled out of the bush. Wagons, carts, and tools had to be repaired and made ready for spring. But generally, the winter brought a little free time for the settlers in Upper Canada. There was more time for socializing with friends and neighbours.

Grain had to be separated from the chaff. This was a job for windy days. The chaff and the grain were tossed into the air from a blanket. The wind blew the light chaff away and the good grain fell into the basket.

Civics & Society

Working Bees

A barn-raising took the efforts of many people.

"Many hands make light work" is an old saying that was popular in Upper Canada. The pioneers came together to help one another with difficult jobs. When a community gathered to work co-operatively, it was called a **bee**. Bees were held for house building, barn raising, logging, and harvesting. Often, the whole family came to the bee. These times were a chance for **isolated** settlers to help their neighbours and enjoy an outing at the same time.

The person receiving the help was responsible for feeding the workers. Vast amounts of food and drink needed to be prepared and served. Susanna Moodie and her husband held a logging bee. She described the food she had prepared:

> **Pea soup, legs of pork, venison, eel, raspberry pies, with plenty of potatoes and whiskey to wash them down, besides a large kettle of tea were served.**

A group of people could get a lot accomplished in one day. When the work was finished, there was sometimes a dance. It was a chance for everybody to relax. Sometimes, however, these bees resulted in quarrels and even in violence. It could be the early hours of the morning before the neighbours packed their tools and headed home.

Women also got together to work on common tasks. One reason for such a gathering

was a quilting bee. A group of women would meet in someone's home with their materials and a basket of food. They sat around a large quilt frame to sew the quilts. They would enjoy each other's company and share news and problems as they worked. The quilts were made from two layers of cloth filled with cotton or wool. The tops were pieced together and sewn into decorative patterns using small scraps of used or leftover cloth that had been carefully saved. The quilts looked bright and colourful in a pioneer bedroom, but more importantly, they provided essential warmth on cold winter nights.

1. What do you like about working with others?
2. Why did pioneer tasks often require the help of many?
3. Why were working bees such an important part of pioneer life?

Corn-husking bees were a chance for boys and girls to have a good time together. When a boy found a red ear of corn, he was allowed to kiss the girl next to him.

Netsurfer

This website about barn raisings and neighbourhood bees shows how important co-operation was in the lives of the early settlers:
www.mto.gov.on.ca/english/about/footpaths/barn.htm

An Apple-peeling Bee

Before the apples picked in the fall spoiled, the settlers had to peel, core, and dry them for the winter. It was a perfect reason to hold a bee! Friends and neighbours were invited to gather and help. Some peeled apples, some removed the core with a sharp knife, and some cut the fruit crosswise into slices and threaded the slices onto cotton strings. These strings of sliced apples were hung outside in the sunshine to dry. Once the fruit was dried, it would keep for a long time.

Another way to dry fruit was to use a drying screen. These were trays made with a piece of screening stretched across a wooden frame. The slices of fruit were placed on the screen in a single layer and then dried in the sun.

Young people liked to make a game of the apple paring. They tried to remove the whole skin in one long piece. Then, they twirled the apple skin over their heads and dropped it on the floor. Whatever shape it landed in was "read" as the shape of a letter of the alphabet. The letter was supposed to be the initial of the future husband or wife of the person who peeled it. Lots of laughing and teasing would follow for the rest of the day.

Sometimes, apple games were played while lunch was being prepared and laid out. Bobbing for apples in a big tub of water was one favourite game. Another popular game was Snap Apple. An apple was tied to a long string and suspended from a beam. The children held their hands behind their backs. The idea was to see who could take a bite out of the apple while it swung around.

RECIPE: DRYING APPLES

Take four pieces of wood and nail them into a rough frame. Stretch a piece of screening over the frame. Tack the screening onto the frame. Peel, core, and slice the apples into thin slices about 1 cm thick. Place the screen in the oven and bake at a very low heat. Leave the oven door open to let out the moisture. Leave the tray in the oven for several hours until the fruit is completely dry. Makes a great healthy snack!

Outdoor Activities

When they were not busy at work, the settlers enjoyed outdoor activities such as hunting, fishing, horseback riding, canoeing, sailing, and picnicking. Lacrosse and cricket were two popular sports. At local fairs, there were chances to turn working skills into competitions. Plowing matches, wood-chopping contests, horseshoe-pitching, and hay-mowing competitions offered excitement and attracted large local crowds.

Winter was the real time for recreation. Curling, sleigh riding, snowshoeing, and skating were great favourites. Skates made of wood with iron runners were fastened to boots with leather straps. Sleighs were lined with heavy blankets or bear skins to keep the driver and passengers warm. Young people often filled a farmer's sleigh to go out for a ride on one of the backwoods roads.

Indoor Games and Activities

Dancing was a popular indoor activity. At weddings and bees, people of all ages joined in the dancing. Card games such as whist were also popular. Other games such as billiards, backgammon, chess, and checkers were enjoyed indoors. Many hours were spent singing songs in the parlour.

People also found time to read. Books were prized possessions because they were expensive and hard to obtain. Some settlers had brought their favourite books with them and these were read and reread. Books and newspapers were shared and loaned to others who did not have as much reading material.

During moments of free time, a woman might take out her sewing basket. Many of the settlers' clothes and household items, such as curtains, were made at home. Clothing repairs were also the woman's responsibility. Knitting and fancy sewing were common pastimes. Women embroidered pillowcases, dresses, and handkerchiefs. Young girls showed off their embroidery skills by making samplers. Often, these samplers depicted rural scenes and included short verses. Samplers were framed and hung on the wall in the parlour or bedroom.

Religion in Upper Canada

The settlers brought with them the religions they had practised in their homelands. In Upper Canada, there were many different religious groups. These included Anglicans, Methodists, Presbyterians, Lutherans, Baptists, Quakers, Mennonites, and Roman Catholics. The number of non-Christians in Upper Canada was very small. For example, before 1800, there were fewer than 100 Jewish people in Upper and Lower Canada.

The first church services would have been held in someone's house. As soon as possible, the settlers got together to build a church. Often, a church was one of the first public buildings in a community. The settlers wanted to be able to hold church ceremonies for baptisms, marriages, and funerals. People donated their labour and materials, such as planks, logs, and shingles, to put up the church. In isolated communities, the church offered comfort and activities to people who were suffering from loneliness and homesickness.

Sunday was the day of rest for most people in Upper Canada. They put on their best clothes and went to church. After the service, they gathered in small groups to exchange greetings and news. Only essential tasks were done on Sunday. The rest of the day was spent relaxing, singing hymns, or listening to a family member read from the Bible.

The Church of England

From the earliest days, the Church of England (Anglican) was the established church in Upper Canada. That meant that it was the denomination that received land and money from the government. It held a favoured position in society. Until 1798, it was the only church allowed to conduct marriages in Upper Canada. It was also the only church that was given money from the rental or sale of Clergy Reserves. Other churches objected to this policy and asked the government to use that money for education in the province.

The position of the Church of England was strengthened by the presence of John Strachan. He was an important Anglican clergyman and a member of the Legislative and Executive Councils. In 1838, Strachan became the bishop of Toronto. He had a great deal of influence in the government of Upper Canada.

The Methodists

The Methodists were one of the most active religious groups in Upper Canada. They were the most successful in reaching people in rural areas. They sent out travelling preachers to scattered backwoods settlements. The area that each minister covered in his travels was called a **circuit**. The preachers travelled constantly and held religious meetings wherever people could gather. They were called "saddlebag preachers" because they carried hymn books and Bibles in saddlebags flung across their horses. Most settlers, no matter what their religion, welcomed a visit from a saddlebag preacher. They knew that these men had come to bring a Christian message to their family.

Circuit riders organized special camp meetings. The settlers gathered for singing, Bible reading, rousing sermons, and fellowship with their neighbours. These large religious get-togethers could last for several days. It was a chance for the settlers to escape their isolation for a while as well as to worship together.

Quakers and Mennonites

Mennonites and Quakers formed distinct and important communities in Upper Canada. Members of these Protestant sects migrated north to Canada because their **pacifist** beliefs did not permit them to participate in war. Therefore, they could not take part in the American Revolution. Eager to attract diligent farmers, Governor Simcoe encouraged Quakers (who were mainly English-speaking) to come to Upper Canada, promising that their pacifism would be respected. Many settled in the Niagara and Quinte regions, and along Yonge Street north of York. They were outnumbered by the German-speaking Mennonites, who arrived in their Conestoga wagons from Pennsylvania. The Mennonites initially settled mostly on the Niagara Peninsula. By 1800, they had begun a settlement in Waterloo County. Theirs would be the first genuine inland settlement in Upper Canada.

A Methodist circuit rider

Her Majesty's Chapel of the Mohawks, near Brantford, was the first Protestant church built in Upper Canada. It was built in 1785 for the Mohawk, who came to Upper Canada as Loyalists.

Culture Link

A Settler's Home

At first, the settlers lived in a small, uncomfortable log cabin. But as the years passed, they cleared about three-quarters of their original 100 ha. It was hard work. The farm became well established and the family became more prosperous. As soon as settlers could afford it, they built themselves a fine, large house. This was the family's second house.

The house shown below had seven rooms built in two storeys. It was constructed of hand-hewn timbers, some measuring almost a metre in diameter. It was covered with clapboard siding made of planks. The planks came from the sawmill in the village. On the roof were cedar shingles, also a product of the local sawmill. There was even an attic for storage space. The house had two stairways.

In the kitchen was a huge fireplace made of bricks. Bricks are much better for holding the heat than stone and are less likely to crack. So, having a brick fireplace was a sign of the growing prosperity of the family. The family could also afford glass for the windows. There were 13 windows, each with 12 small panes of glass. The second house was light and airy. It was a big improvement over the early log cabin, which was dark and dreary.

Daniel Stong's second house was much larger and finer than his first shanty home.

1. For settlers in Upper Canada, having glass in windows and in more than one room were signs of prosperity. What are some modern signs of prosperity? In what ways have ideas about wealth stayed the same? In what ways have they become different?

2. What other changes do you think would have happened over time to the settler's property, including buildings and farmland?

Welcome to a Settler's House

Imagine you are transported back in time to about 1835 and you visit a settler's home in Upper Canada. You are about to enter the family's second home. You climb the steps to an open but covered porch and enter through the front door. You step into a huge kitchen. It takes up half the ground floor of the house. A stairway leads from the kitchen to the second floor.

The settlers spend most of their time in the kitchen. It is the warmest room in the house. A huge brick fireplace dominates the room. A long table stands in front of the fireplace. It is here that food preparation is done. Meals are also eaten at this table to take advantage of the warmth of the fire.

To one side of the fireplace is the parlour. This is the finest room in the house. It is used mostly on special occasions when important guests, such as the local minister, come to call. Sometimes, women do their embroidery in the parlour and, on Sundays, the family gathers to read the Bible in here. Wallpaper decorates the walls of the parlour and the floorboards are painted.

You can notice many signs of the family's increased prosperity in the second house. The ceilings are much higher, making the rooms harder to heat. But wood is plentiful and free. Throughout the house, there is plank panelling on the walls. The settlers polish it with beeswax until it takes on a high lustre. There are cupboards for dishes. Some of the dishes on the shelves are hand-painted and expensive. There are woven window blinds, curtains, and small rugs on the floor. All these things are signs of increased refinement in the life of this family.

By the 1840s, many Canadian homes had replaced open-hearth cooking with cast iron stoves. The stoves would be set up in front of the closed-in fireplace hearth, still using the same chimney flue. Not only did the stoves provide more efficient cooking facilities, but the stovepipes carried residual heat to other rooms. Most upstairs rooms were heated by simply allowing the warmed air to rise. The cooking stoves had three or four plates over the firebox for direct heat. At the back was an oven for baking or roasting. Notice the ledge at the front of the stove, a good place to keep one's feet warm in the winter.

A large, round mahogany table dominates the center of the parlour of the Lutheran pastor's home. Such parlours were used for important family occasions as well as for greeting and entertaining visitors. On a cozy winter's evening, the whale oil lamp on the table would provide illumination for reading or conversation. The patterned wallpaper with a deep, decorative border and the colourful floral-design carpet were popular at the time.

Bedrooms

There is one bedroom on the main floor. It is referred to as "the borning room" because the babies of the family are born here. This is where the parents and the youngest child sleep. There are two beds, a corner cupboard, chests, a lamp stand, and a washstand in this room. Another staircase leads from the parents' bedroom to the girls' bedroom and the boys' bedroom on the second floor.

The girls' bedroom contains a bed, a chair, a table, a chest, and a linen press, which is a tall cupboard. Each girl has a dowry chest in which she places the things she will need when she marries. These include handwoven blankets, quilts, embroidered place cloths, and perhaps even clothes for the babies she may have. In the boys' bedroom, the furniture is similar, but there are no dowry chests.

Beds

The settlers make their beds of wood and rope. The frame and the legs of the bed are carved from wood. There are no springs or spring-filled mattresses. Instead, holes are bored through four sides of the frame. Then, ropes are strung through the holes to form a kind of strong net. After a while, the ropes begin to sag and have to be twisted and tightened with a special tool called a rope key.

The mattress is made of a large piece of ticking material. It is stuffed with straw, corn-

Some of the things that might have been in a girl's bedroom are laid on the bed.

husks, hay, or goose feathers. Sometimes, the mattress is divided into two parts. Straw is stuffed into one side and goose feathers are placed in the other side. The feather side is turned up in the winter to keep the sleeper warm. In summer, the straw side is turned up to keep the sleeper cool. Insects live in these mattresses. In the morning, people wake up covered with stinging insect bites. Before going to bed, parents say to their children, "Sleep tight. Don't let the bedbugs bite!" This means, "Sleep soundly, so you don't feel any bedbugs biting you."

Some beds are trundle beds. They are low enough to be pushed under a regular bed. They can be pulled out and used when visitors stay overnight. Another type of bed is called a settle or a beggar's bench. By day, it is a bench. At night, the lid is lifted and it becomes a narrow bed. This bench saves space and provides extra seating and sleeping space when needed.

Schools

Most people today view education as the key to a successful, happy life. Every child in Canada expects to go to school until the age of 16. Many students spend years beyond that studying for a specific career.

Few people in the 1800s saw formal education as a key to success in life. Education was a luxury open only to the sons of rich people. Leading citizens in Canada sent their children to private or church schools. They saw no reason for the children of farmers, shopkeepers, or lumberjacks to know anything more than basic reading, writing, and arithmetic since they would never be called on to make important decisions for the country.

Since girls were expected to become wives and mothers, it was thought that they did not need much schooling. Daughters of the rich often got a different education that focused on their skills as future wives and mothers. A number of "ladies' academies" were opened where girls could study housekeeping and needlework along with some spelling, grammar, arithmetic, and writing.

The First Schools

It was not until 1807 that a grammar school (high school) was begun in each of the eight districts of the Upper Canada. Most often, the teachers were clergymen of the Church of England. They taught English, Greek, Latin, mathematics, history, geography, and writing. Since the grammar schools were all in towns, parents from rural areas found it almost impossible to send their children. Unless they could afford room and board in town, rural young people could not attend grammar school. In 1831, only 311 students were enrolled in grammar schools. This was at a time when there were over 200 000 people under the age of 16 living in Upper Canada.

The earliest school buildings were simple log cabins. They each had a wood-burning stove, some student desks, benches made of rough planks, and a desk for the teacher. There were very few textbooks, globes, or atlases. Spellers and Bibles were the most commonly used books. Blackboards, paper, and pens were scarce. The teachers often knew little more than their pupils did. On days when the children were needed to help out at home, they did not go to school.

At first, parents were responsible for paying a few bushels of grain as their contribution to the expenses of the local school. After 1816, the government helped to pay some of the costs of schools. Grants of money were given for part of the teacher's salary and for textbooks. But the students were still expected to bring some wood for the school stove as well as candles if it was too dark.

Ryerson's Advances

The government grants still only provided education for a few. But things changed in 1841, when Egerton Ryerson became Superintendent of Education for what is now Ontario. Ryerson recommended many things we take for granted today:
- teachers must be trained
- the province decides what will be taught
- textbooks written by Canadians should be used

In later years, education was paid for by school taxes. Schools became free and compulsory. Every child had to attend school.

Colleges were established in the 1830s and 1840s. The University of Toronto opened in 1849. From then on, students who wanted a university education no longer had to travel to the United States or Britain.

In a one-room school, children of all ages learned reading, writing, and arithmetic from one teacher. Since paper was expensive, the children wrote on slates similar to blackboards. Notice the dunce cap in the left corner. The child who misbehaved was made to stand in the corner wearing the dunce cap as punishment.

Culture Link

Residential Schools for Aboriginal Children

By the mid 1800s, the government was introducing a residential school system for the Aboriginal peoples. These boarding schools were funded by the government and run by missionaries. Some parents were glad to send their children to the residential schools. They wanted their children to have the skills needed to participate in the new society around them. Other parents tried to hide their children from the people who came to take them away to school.

The schools were often far away from the children's homes. The children were separated from their parents, communities, and culture. Life at the schools was very strict. The children were forbidden to speak their traditional languages. They were punished for practising their traditional spiritual beliefs.

The intent of the Aboriginal schools was to help Aboriginal children become self-sufficient. These schools would also help to assimilate Aboriginal children into mainstream society. The children would adopt the ways of the dominant culture and no longer practise their own ways. Much of the school day was spent on religious instruction, learning English or French, doing chores, and learning some practical skills. The boys were taught farming, carpentry, and blacksmithing. The girls learned household skills such as sewing and cooking. Less than two hours a day was spent on academics. As a result, when the students left the schools, they were poorly prepared for a successful life outside. Unfortunately, many children could no longer fit into the traditional society on the reserves and few could adjust to living in non-Aboriginal society. The residential schools led to an undereducated, unemployable, and poor group of people.

Residential schools were finally phased out in the 1960s. However, they have had a long-lasting impact on the Aboriginal people, their community, and their culture.

---

1. How would life in the residential schools affect the lives of the students?
2. Why did students who had been at the residential schools later find it difficult to fit into their traditional society?

Transportation in Upper Canada

Getting from place to place was one of the greatest problems faced by the early settlers. Where roads did exist, they were very poor. Most of the roads were not much more than rough trails through the bush. In spring or whenever there was heavy rain, many roads became too muddy to travel on. Doctors, mills, and stores were often 50 km away. Getting around was slow and uncomfortable.

Many early settlers had to walk to school, to church, or to visit neighbours. In 1826, Samuel Strickland received word in Peterborough that his wife was seriously sick. She was in Bowmanville visiting her sister. Strickland set out on foot. He managed to cover a distance of 93 km in a single day. (Today, this trip would take one or two hours by car.) On his arrival, he found that his wife had died shortly before. Had the roads of Upper Canada been good, Strickland could have taken a **stagecoach** and seen his wife before she died.

Stagecoach service existed only between important towns. A stagecoach was drawn by two pairs of horses. The horses were changed every 24 km. The coach itself was small and box-like. A coach held nine people—three in the front, three in the back, and three in the middle. Leather curtains hung at the sides and at the back. The luggage was carried on the roof.

There are many accounts by travellers in Upper Canada that tell of the horrors of a coach ride. The roads were so rough that some people ended their journey with bruises, dislocated limbs, and the inability to sit down for a week. One traveller complained that "my hands were swelled and blistered by continually grasping with all my strength an iron bar in the front of my vehicle to prevent myself from being flung out."

Weller's Yellow Stages

William Weller of Cobourg was the most important stagecoach owner in the 1830s and 1840s. His yellow stages and sleighs ran on the most important routes: Montreal-Hamilton, Dundas-Niagara, Toronto-Lake Simcoe, and Cobourg-Peterborough. In 1840, a record run was made between Toronto and Montreal in 36 hours. This was less than one-third the usual time. Weller's stages carried six to ten passengers and mail.

All the coaches were equipped with shovels and axes. Passengers could be called upon to help the driver free the coach from mud or remove a fallen tree from the road. It is no wonder that, on such roads, the speed was only about 4 to 6 km an hour.

The horse ferry was an unusual method of water transportation. It looked like a barge. It had paddles that were propelled by two to five horses walking around and around the deck, pushing a wheel as they went. The movement of the paddles propelled the boat forward. The *Peninsula Packet* was one of the last horse ferries used in Canada. It ran between Toronto and Ward's Island until 1850.

Water Travel

A far better way to travel in Upper Canada was by water. The first settlements were located on the shores of lakes and rivers. The canoe and the bateau were used extensively by settlers. They also had the **Durham boat**.

The Durham boat was a flat-bottomed craft like the bateau. What made it different was its rounded bow and square stern. The bottom was sometimes covered with iron to prevent damage on rocks. Like the bateau, it had sails. The crew used long poles to steer the boat through currents and rapids. Flour, grain, potash, pork, and bales of furs were transported across Lake Ontario and along the St. Lawrence River on Durham boats.

Steamboats

An important change in transportation came with the introduction of steamboats. The *Frontenac*, the first steamboat on the Great Lakes, was built in 1816 at Bath, near Kingston. By the 1820s, steamboats were carrying passengers and cargo back and forth between Niagara and Kingston. Cargo was also towed behind the steamers in Durham boats.

By the 1830s, steamboats were being used on the smaller lakes and rivers. They improved the speed and comfort of travel considerably. However, there were serious difficulties with water transport. In many places, swiftly flowing rapids or waterfalls prevented the passage of the boats. Some rivers were too shallow in the summer months and, in winter, ice made travel by boat impossible.

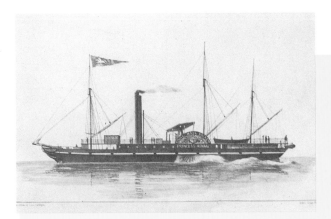

The Princess Royal was one of a number of steamboats carrying passengers and freight between Kingston and Toronto on Lake Ontario.

Winter Travel

The best time for travelling in Upper Canada was winter. In the spring and summer, the roads were poor. In the winter, the settlers could visit their distant friends and neighbours, take their produce to the market, and bring home supplies from stores in remote towns. As surprising as it seems, the cold weather was welcomed by Upper Canadians as a time for travel.

In winter, snowshoes or sleighs were the best ways to travel. Most settlers had a simple sleigh in the form of a box. It was really not much more than two or three boards nailed together and placed on runners. There was a place for a seat and room for barrels of flour or potash in the back. A horse pulled the sleigh.

The settlers in Upper Canada enjoyed winter sleigh parties. The most important thing was to be well-bundled up under bearskins and blankets. Sleighs were also used for visiting friends and neighbours.

This covered sleigh is shown travelling between Toronto and Kingston. Compare this with the picture of coach travel on page 233. Which method of transportation would probably be faster? Why do you think so?

Culture Link

The Voices of Women in Upper Canada

Several well-known female writers have provided us with vivid accounts of life in Upper Canada. Their letters, diaries, and sketches are a gold mine of information about early settlement.

Catherine Parr Traill

Susanna Moodie

Susanna Moodie came to Upper Canada in 1832. She and her husband attempted to carve a farm out of the wilderness. Mrs. Moodie wrote about her experiences as a settler in the backwoods of Upper Canada in a book called *Roughing It in the Bush*.

Susanna Moodie

> **They talk of log houses raised in a single day by the generous exertions of friends and neighbours, but they never ventured upon a description of the dwellings when raised. They were dens of dirt and misery, which would be shamed by an English pigsty.**

Catherine Parr Traill

Mrs. Moodie's sister, Catherine Parr Traill, was also an author. She wrote *The Backwoods of Canada* and *The Canadian Settlers' Guide*. These books are about life in early Upper Canada. Traill's purpose in writing was to try to provide an honest description of conditions in Upper Canada. She believed that the land settlement companies often gave too rosy a picture to prospective immigrants. Then, the settlers were disappointed when they arrived and discovered how hard life really was. She warned that a woman coming to Canada must be:

> **skilled in the arts of ... knitting stockings and mittens, and comforters, spinning yarn on a spinning wheel, and dyeing the yarn ... making clothes for herself, her husband, and her children, for there are no tailors in the bush.**

Anna Brownell Jameson

Anna Brownell Jameson

Jameson was a noted writer and early feminist. She took a keen interest in questions affecting the education, employment, and status of women. Her writings, including the book *Characteristics of Women*, pointed the way for later feminists.

For two years, from 1836 to 1838, she lived in Upper Canada. She journeyed alone through the colony. At this time, it was unheard of for a woman to travel alone. She wrote an account of her experiences called *Winter Studies and Summer Rambles in Upper Canada.* Jameson described her trip along the Talbot Road.

The road was scarcely passable ... pine forest and rank swamp, crossed by those corduroy paths (my bones ache at the mere recollection) ...

the horses paused on the brink of the mud-gulfs and trembled ere they made the plunge downwards. I set my teeth, screwed myself to the seat, and commended myself to Heaven.

Anne Langton

A Gentlewoman in Upper Canada is a collection of journals and sketches created by Anne Langton. Langton settled in the Peterborough area. Like some of the other well-educated people, Anne Langton taught pupils in her home. Private schools were common at that time. Anne Langton tells what it was like:

A sketch by Anne Langton

2 January 1839. I had Menzies' two little girls for a lesson today. I have lately begun to teach them a little. They come for about an hour three times a week; as yet we are not at all perfect in our letters, and I sometimes feel that I shall not accomplish much.

1. The daily lives of these women would have been busy and filled with work and other activities. Why do you think they would take the time to write and draw about their experiences?

2. Why were their writings and drawings important at the time? Why are they important today?

The Role of Pioneer Farm Women

A pioneer farm woman had to fill many roles. She was a housewife and a mother. She had to keep the house clean and tidy without conveniences such as vacuum cleaners and washing machines. She spent hours preparing food to satisfy the appetites of her hard-working family. All the meals had to be prepared from scratch using what she had on hand. There were no supermarkets to go to for supplies. There were no cooking shortcuts like cake mixes or pre-packaged foods. A pioneer farm woman was also responsible for other household tasks such as quilting and making soap, candles, and butter.

The female settler had to be a talented seamstress. She sewed most of the family's clothes. But first, cloth had to be made from flax or wool. She spent long hours spinning, dyeing, and weaving. All the sewing was done by hand and there were few patterns to follow. Most women copied a design from a picture or an old garment, or created their own. The female settler also manually washed and ironed all her family's clothing.

Early families kept their own herb gardens. These herbs are drying for use in cooking or to be made into medicines.

Cloth was woven from local flax or wool and made into clothes for the family.

The pioneer farm woman also tended a huge garden that provided food for her family. She often helped in the fields with the harvest or other heavy work. Assisting at the birth of livestock was another important female task around the farm.

The pioneer wife was a teacher as well as a mother. She tried to teach her children the basics of reading and writing. She also taught them important life skills. She and her husband taught their children the things they needed to know to survive on a farm in Upper Canada.

She had the roles of nurse, doctor, and druggist. Care of the sick and injured was the responsibility of the family. Since doctors and hospitals were often far away, most sick people were treated at home. Women grew herbs, roots, and flowers to be made into traditional remedies. Tea made of dandelion leaves was used for liver problems. A syrup made from the root of spignet cured coughs. A slice of onion soothed a bee sting. Women also learned to set broken bones, pull teeth, and deliver babies.

No wonder an old saying stated, "A woman's work is never done!"

Women in Colonial Society

The newspapers of Upper Canada printed many articles about the role of women in colonial society. Usually, the articles stressed the importance of being devoted to one's husband and children. Young women in Upper Canada were expected to marry and raise a family when they grew up. But some women made different choices. They worked as maids, housekeepers, cooks, and laundresses in the homes of wealthy families. Women also played a role in the education of young children. They took jobs as school mistresses and governesses. Some women owned their own businesses. They operated inns, taverns, and boarding houses. Some opened businesses that made women's hats and clothing. These women entrepreneurs were often called "she merchants."

Urban Communities

Not all settlers in Upper Canada lived on farms in the bush. Some preferred to live in places where they were closer to other people. Some Loyalists settled in communities along Lake Ontario such as Kingston, York, Brockville, Cornwall, Hamilton, and Newark. Port Talbot, London, and Port Stanley grew up in the Talbot Settlement. A little later, the Canada Company developed the towns of Goderich and Guelph. All these communities were along the banks of rivers or the shores of lakes. Water was the only way to move wheat, potash, and lumber easily. These sites also provided the water power necessary to run gristmills and sawmills.

The earliest towns and villages in Upper Canada were founded as military bases or places of government. Others grew up because they were trading centres for their surrounding districts. There may have been a mill there that brought people in. Once the mill was operating, a blacksmith shop might follow. Next might come a general store, a church, or a hotel with a tavern. Eventually, a village was born.

A Typical Village in Upper Canada

Some smaller communities across Upper Canada never grew beyond the size of a village. They consisted of a few shops on the main street. A general store sold food and household articles. You could buy almost anything there, from tea to clothing to door hinges. There was always a mill or tannery that brought in settlers with wheat to be ground or hides to be tanned for leather. Every village had a blacksmith shop. The blacksmith was an essential tradesperson. Not only did he shoe horses, but he also made rakes, shovels, axes, and even carriages and buggies. The hotel or tavern served as a community gathering place. Often, the stagecoach stopped here for meals or a change of horses. Upstairs, there was a large room for political or village meetings.

Most villages had a post office, a school, and one or two churches. If the community was lucky, there would be a doctor living in the village. He usually saw his patients in the front room of his house. The doctor not only examined patients, but mixed his own medicines and pills.

Towns in Upper Canada

In the early 1800s, York and Kingston were the two biggest towns in Upper Canada. Between 10 and 15% of the colony's population lived and worked in them.

Towns were made up of people with different skills and incomes. The wealthiest owned large tracts of land and made money by selling parts of it to others. Doctors, lawyers, bank managers, merchants, and high government officials were also among the wealthy. They lived in fine homes built of brick. Their furniture was often imported from the United States or Britain. Many of them had servants to clean their houses, cook their meals, and drive their carriages.

A second group consisted of shop owners, teachers, ministers, the postmaster, and skilled tradespeople. These people were respected, but earned much lower wages than the first group. Their standard of living was less than that of the wealthy people of the community.

A third major group was made up of people who worked in shops, in factories, or as labourers. Many of these people struggled to have even the bare necessities. Most workers rented small dwellings or a few rooms in cheap row houses. These living quarters were often freezing cold in winter and stifling hot in summer. Outdoor toilets had to be shared with several other families. Disease could spread rapidly through the crowded, filthy streets.

The establishment of towns brought new problems. It was difficult to maintain safety, sanitation, and living standards in the towns. The streets and wooden sidewalks were poorly maintained and accidents were quite common. There was no regular garbage collection, so garbage was commonly thrown into the roads, lakes, and rivers. Many people got their drinking water from these lakes and rivers. Polluted water and lack of sanitation helped spread an outbreak of cholera in 1832. The major towns did not acquire water systems until the 1840s.

Town living also had many advantages. People who lived in towns had more choices for entertainment than those who lived in the country. In towns, there were neighbours close by to visit or to join in a game of cards. Concerts and plays were put on by visiting artists. People could join cricket, lacrosse, or curling teams. Hockey was played on the ice in the Toronto harbour in the 1840s. Horseracing was a popular spectator sport. Several times a year, there were large formal dances for people to enjoy. Most towns and villages held an annual parade of their volunteer firefighters. All the fire equipment was polished and paraded through the streets. Fall fairs and visiting circuses were social highlights.

Town life had much to offer its residents during the 19th century in Upper Canada. There was a sense of community and companionship. Many considered town life preferable to the loneliness and isolation faced by backwoods farm families.

York (Toronto)

The word "Toronto" comes from the Aboriginal word meaning "the carrying place" in the Huron language or "fish weir" in the Mohawk language. For centuries, the Huron and Iroquois had used this place. It was situated at the origin of a canoe-route shortcut between Lakes Ontario and Huron.

Kingston had been important for a long time as a military and government centre. It was the largest city in Upper Canada until 1830, when York's population grew to over 4000.

The city of Toronto in the 1850s. Over 30 000 people lived in Toronto, making it the largest city in the colony.

In 1793, Governor Simcoe decided to make Toronto the temporary capital of Upper Canada. He gave it a British name—York.

York grew very slowly at first. By 1810, there were only 630 people living there. The main buildings were the Parliament Buildings, two blockhouses for defence, a jail, the post office, a customs house, and one church. Business and industry included six hotels, a slaughterhouse, a potashery, a tannery, a wagon factory, and a shipbuilding yard. There was an open-air market, a general store, and a few other stores, including a watchmaker's. There were about a hundred houses.

By the late 1820s, York's population began to grow at a rapid rate. Because of the great migration from Britain, a steady stream of skilled tradespeople and labourers moved into the community. The service industries also grew. Tailors, hairdressers, bakers, lawyers, teachers, and doctors were required for the growing town. There were several weekly newspapers to report the local news. Fine public and private buildings were erected, many of them built of brick and stone. As Toronto grew, roads were gradually improved. A hospital was built and a paid fire department replaced the volunteer fire service.

When the Welland Canal opened in 1829, it linked York to markets in the United States and the West. By 1831, the population was over 4000. In 1834, York became a city and the name was changed back to Toronto. By 1840, the population of Toronto was over 12 000, and by 1851, it was 30 000. Toronto became the largest settlement in the colony, surpassing rivals such as Kingston.

The Growth of Towns

Many centres in addition to Toronto and Kingston grew and became prosperous. Hamilton was well located at the head of Lake Ontario. It became a major port for exporting wheat from the fertile farmland around it. Later, Hamilton became a major producer of iron products. London was another town that grew because of increased wheat production. It also attracted new industries such as the breweries. In the Niagara district, towns like St. Catharines benefited from being close to the Welland Canal. In the eastern part of the province, Bytown (later Ottawa) was a centre of the timber industry. Factories became more common in many cities, but most of them remained small operations with fewer than 100 employees.

By 1851, still only a small percent of the people in Upper Canada lived in communities that had more than a thousand people. Although the towns became more and more important, Upper Canada was still mainly rural. The rural settlers relied on the towns as shipping centres for their produce and other goods. The settlers were also able to buy many things that made life on the farm more comfortable.

Changes for the Aboriginal Peoples

During this time of growth in Upper Canada, the lives of Aboriginal people were changing for the worse.

- The Aboriginal people were not adapting well to life on reserves. Most had no experience in farming and did not want to be settled farmers. They did not want to give up their nomadic life of hunting, trapping, and fishing.
- Missionaries set up schools to teach the Aboriginal children to read and write European languages. They also tried to convince the Aboriginal people that their beliefs and traditions were wrong.
- When the market for furs declined, so did the importance of the Aboriginal people to the fur trade. The demand and supply for furs was no longer steady. Many Aboriginal peoples could not keep up their traditional hunting and gathering lifestyle.
- The Aboriginal people did not have resistance to diseases such as measles and smallpox. Many died from the diseases they caught from the Europeans.

Skill Building: Preparing a Research Report

What would it have been like to live in Upper Canada in the 1840s? What challenges would you have faced? What survival skills would you have needed? Would you like to have lived there at this time? How would life have been different from what it is today?

You can find out more by doing further research and preparing a report. Where would you start? It is easiest to handle a project if you can break it down into some basic steps. Think of your task in five key steps: Purpose, Preparation, Process, Product, and Personal Learning.

Step 1: Purpose

Here is a list of topics you can choose from. You can also brainstorm other possible topics with your class.

Topics

Settlers' foods and recipes
Diseases and traditional remedies
How the settlers celebrated Christmas
A settler's first house
A settler's second house
Transportation in Upper Canada
Pioneer tools
Going to school in Upper Canada in the 1840s
Pioneer games and fun
What the settlers wore
Visiting the general store
Spinning and dyeing wool

Step 2: Preparation

Once you choose your topic, you need to define it more carefully. For example, if you choose to write about spinning and dyeing wool, ask yourself what you really want to know. Try to define three or four major questions that you want to answer.

These focus questions can help to form the outline of your report. Starting with an outline is very important. It helps you to stay on topic, guides your research, and helps you to organize your information so that writing your report is much easier. Here is a sample outline that you can use as a model.

Topic: Spinning and Dyeing Wool

Introduction: States the topic. Outlines what the report will cover.

Body of the Report
A. Shearing the sheep
Who did this job?
When was it done?
How was it done?

B. Getting the wool ready
What does carding do to the wool?

C. Spinning the wool
What are the main steps in spinning?
What is a walking wheel?

D. Dyeing the wool
How was the wool coloured?
Where did the dyes come from?

Conclusion: The conclusion sums up the most important information. It states the most important observation you can make from your research.

Step 3: Process

Now it is time to start your research. Set aside a page for each of the main parts in the body of your report. On that page, create an organizer that outlines the questions you want to answer. This will help to keep your research focused.

Now locate the information. Check the Internet, CD-ROMs, books, encyclopedias, newspapers, magazines, films, pictures, and so on. There are many places to find information. If you need help, ask your librarian or teacher. Pick out the information that answers your questions. Record the information on your organizer in point form. Remember to keep a record of all sources where you found useful information.

Review your information. Have you answered your questions adequately? Do you need to revise your questions? Can you develop a conclusion? Write a sentence or two that states your conclusion. For example, the conclusion here might be: "Spinning and dyeing were time-consuming activities for the settlers. But the thread and yarn were necessary for making clothes."

Step 4: Product

You have organized your information and come to a conclusion based on what you have found. Now you are ready to write the report. Follow the outline and it will not be too difficult. Write an introduction, include a paragraph or two for each of the main topics in the body of your report, and then state your conclusion. Prepare maps, pictures, and illustrations as well, and insert them at the appropriate places.

Step 5: Personal Learning

When you have finished your report, read it through. Does it make sense? Can you follow the ideas easily? Is the information clearly presented? If you find problems, do some revising. Check for spelling, punctuation, or grammatical errors. Give the report a title page. This page should list the title of the report, your name, the date, and the name of your teacher. At the back of your report, give a list of the sources you used. Your report will not be your best work if you overlook these finishing touches.

Finally, think about what you have learned and what you would do differently the next time you prepare a research report.

Activities

Understanding Concepts

1. Define the following terms and add them to your personal dictionary.

pioneer	beehive oven	lye
threshing	winnowing	pacifist
smokehouse	circuit	stagecoach
bee	Durham boat	isolated

2. What was a "bee"? Why were bees held in Upper Canada?

3. Describe the interior of a typical farmhouse in Upper Canada in 1840, or draw and label a floor plan of the house.

4. Compare life on a farm in Upper Canada in 1840 with life on a farm in New France a hundred years before. What is the same? What is different?

5. Why was the Anglican church so powerful in Upper Canada?

6. Who were the Methodists and how did they serve the people of Upper Canada?

7. What factors led to towns and villages springing up in certain places? How did town life differ from rural life?

8. Make models of a settler's first and second house, or sketches of pioneer tools.

Digging Deeper

9. **COMPARE** Develop an organizer to compare the duties and chores of children and adults in Upper Canada. Organize your information into separate categories for indoor and outdoor chores.

10. **CREATE/WRITE** Pretend you have just arrived at your land grant in Upper Canada. Make a journal entry for the first day. Make another entry after one year on your land grant. Make a third entry after 10 years. Share your journal entries with your classmates.

11. **CREATE/WRITE** Imagine you are attending school in Upper Canada. Suddenly you are sent ahead in time 150 years. What would surprise you most about schools today?

12. **CREATE/WRITE** Write stories of the daily life of a fictitious family in Upper Canada.

13. **INVESTIGATE** Investigate the history of your own hometown. What factors were important in influencing its development and growth?

Making New Connections

14. **FIELD TRIP** Plan a visit to a pioneer village or some other historical site. You can learn a great deal about how people lived in the past by carefully observing the site. Keep notes on what you see, hear, and feel. Develop a comparison organizer to list the differences in life then and now. Design a T-shirt to reflect something you learned from your field trip.

15. **INTERVIEW** Invite a member of a local quilting guild to visit the class and demonstrate how quilts are made.

16. **RESEARCH/PRESENT** Plan and hold a settlers' day. Present your projects at this special event.

17. **DISCUSS** How have the roles of men, women, girls, and boys changed since the time of the settlers?

18. **THINK/DISCUSS** What pioneering qualities were most important for success in the 19th century? Which of these qualities will be useful for pioneers in the 21st century? What opportunities for "pioneering" are open to young Canadians in the 21st century?

Conflict and Change

Upper and Lower Canada continued to become better established as the years passed. Daily life was easier and more comfortable. Transportation and communication became faster and more reliable. Immigration continued and the country prospered.

Citizens now began to look for improvements in other areas of their lives. One of the areas they questioned was the way the colonies were governed. The power was concentrated in the hands of a few officials. Average citizens did not feel that they had a voice in the decisions that were made. These decisions affected their lives.

A group of Reformers demanded changes and were prepared to fight for them. They were strongly opposed by those who wanted things to stay the same. The Reformers tried different strategies, including armed rebellion, to change the way the government worked. Although their efforts were not successful at first, changes gradually began to happen. Eventually, the colonies were granted the right to manage their own affairs.

1830s – Growing demand for change in both Upper and Lower Canada

1834 – Assembly of Lower Canada draws up a list of complaints and demands, the Ninety-Two Resolutions

1836 – Sir Francis Bond Head is appointed governor

1837 – Rebellion breaks out in Lower Canada in November
Louis-Joseph Papineau flees to the United States
Rebellion breaks out in Upper Canada
William Lyon Mackenzie escapes to the United States

1838 – Lount and Matthews are hanged as rebel leaders
Rebellion is attempted again in Lower Canada but is crushed
Lord Durham is sent to Canada to report on the troubles

1841 – Act of Union joins Upper and Lower Canada

1846 – Lord Elgin is appointed governor

1849 – The Rebellion Losses Bill is signed by Lord Elgin
Parliament House in Montreal is set on fire
Responsible government is achieved at last

Focusing In!

After studying this unit, you will be able to answer the following questions:

1. Why were some of the people angry with the government?
2. Who were the leaders on both sides? What groups of people supported them?
3. Were any peaceful solutions tried first? What were they? Did they succeed? Why or why not?
4. Why did some people think armed rebellion was the only way to make changes?
5. Why did some people attempt to overthrow the government? When and where did this happen?
6. Why did the rebellions fail or succeed?
7. What major changes affected ordinary Canadians and the future development of Canada?

The Rebellion of 1837

Government Reform

Toronto, Upper Canada
5 November 1837

My dearest son,

I am very concerned about what is happening here in the city. Some people are upset about the government. I really do not understand what the problem is. Governor Bond Head seems to be doing a good job running the province. And he is such a nice man. But I have heard that some of the men are really angry. They say that things have to be changed. They say that the government is not fair and that the people are not listened to. But the government has always been this way and it seems to me to work just fine.

Rebels in 1837 Upper Canada prepare for battle.

Not a day goes by that Mr. Mackenzie's newspaper does not contain some item complaining that we need government reform. He even says they are prepared to fight with weapons for these changes. The men gather in bunches on the streets to argue about it. Sometimes, there are even fist fights when they do not agree. The other night, I heard gunshots and I was very frightened. That is not the right way for these Reformers to make their point. I wish your father were still here to talk about these things with me. He always had a level head and would know what to do. Then, perhaps I would not be so afraid. I know you cannot leave Kingston now to come to Toronto, what with two wee children. And I do not want you to worry about me. I am sure it will all be settled soon and then everything will be quiet and peaceful once again.

With all my love,
Your mother

Reflecting/Predicting

1. Why do you think some of the citizens of Upper Canada are so angry with the government? What changes do you think they want to make?
2. If there is a rebellion, what impact might there be on the people involved? On citizens who are not involved? On the government?

The Battle of Toronto

The Battle of Toronto was the only battle fought during the rebellion in Upper Canada. It lasted four days, culminating in a brief shoot-out at Montgomery's Tavern between the Loyalist troops and the rebels. Although the rebellion was a military disappointment, it did ultimately lead to political change.

Monday Night, 4 December 1837

All night long, the church bells of Toronto sounded the alarm. People were in a panic. Just a few kilometres north of the capital, William Lyon Mackenzie was gathering a small army of rebels at Montgomery's Tavern. The rebels were armed with muskets, rifles, pitchforks, and clubs. They were determined to seize the Parliament Buildings and take the governor prisoner. They would force him to give the people more influence in government.

Just before midnight, the sound of horses' hoofs was heard along Yonge Street. Citizens hurried out as John Powell, an elected official, breathlessly told his news. He described how Mackenzie and a number of armed rebels had stopped him on Yonge Street, about 3 km beyond the city limits. Powell had fired shots at the rebels. He missed Mackenzie, but managed to hit Anthony Anderson. Anderson was one of Mackenzie's few experienced military leaders. Chased by the rebels, Powell hid behind a log. Eventually, he made his way back to Toronto in the dark.

At about the same time, more bad news reached the city. Colonel Moodie was a retired army officer who lived north of Montgomery's Tavern. All day, he had watched with alarm as rebel troops gathered at the tavern. He was determined to get this information to the governor. With three companions, he set out by horse down Yonge Street. When he approached Montgomery's Tavern, the road was blocked. The fiery

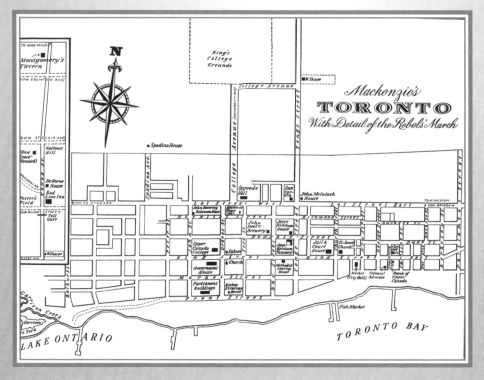

Montgomery's Tavern, Yonge Street, and Bloor Street were the locations of some of the key encounters in the rebellion.

Colonel Moodie roared at the rebels, "Who are you to stop me on the Queen's Highway?" Shots were fired on both sides. When Colonel Moodie tried to charge through the barricade, he was shot and left to die. One of Moodie's companions escaped and brought the news to the city.

Tuesday, 5 December 1837

Alarm grew in the city. Only 300 trained fighters were available to defend Toronto. Most of the troops had been sent to Lower Canada to deal with the trouble there. Rumours spread quickly that the rebel force numbered 5000. The governor of Upper Canada, Sir Francis Bond Head, placed his own family on a steamer in the Toronto harbour for safety.

Sir Francis expected reinforcements from outside the city to arrive. To gain time, he sent officials to bargain with Mackenzie under a white flag of truce. The truce

John Powell was chased by the rebels after he shot at them, but he managed to escape.

party met Mackenzie on Yonge Street at the top of Gallow's Hill. They told him that Governor Bond Head would pardon everyone who laid down his weapon. Mackenzie refused.

At six o'clock, 700 rebels gathered at the Bloor Street tollgate for a night attack on the

Colonel Moodie fired his pistol in the air in an attempt to scare his captors. He was shot from his horse and died.

Rebels march down Yonge Street.

capital. In pitch darkness, they hiked south on Yonge Street with Samuel Lount in the lead. Some rebels were armed with rifles. Others carried nothing more than sharpened sticks, clubs, and pitchforks.

In Mrs. Sharpe's vegetable garden, where Maple Leaf Gardens was later built, Sheriff Jarvis and 27 of his men hid behind a fence. As the rebels approached, Jarvis and his troops ambushed them. There was a great flash and roar as the muskets went off. Both sides panicked. Mackenzie's force turned and headed back to Montgomery's Tavern. Sheriff Jarvis's force fled into the city. After this skirmish, one member of the rebel force lay dead on the road.

Wednesday, 6 December 1837

Reinforcements began to arrive in Toronto. Sixty soldiers came by steamer from Hamilton under Colonel McNab, and one hundred came from Scarborough under Captain Maclean. The main buildings of Toronto—the City Hall, the House of Parliament, and the Bank of Upper Canada—and many private houses were barricaded

with thick planks. Stores closed, making it difficult to buy meat and bread.

On Dundas Street, about 6 km west of Toronto, Mackenzie and Lount held up the stagecoach carrying the mail. They seized money and letters that contained vital information about the defence of the city. Some of Mackenzie's supporters found there were no weapons for them and went home. Two men wounded in Tuesday night's battle died from loss of blood.

Thursday, 7 December 1837

Van Egmond, an experienced soldier, arrived in the morning at Montgomery's Tavern to take control of the rebel forces. He was upset to find out that he had only about 500 poorly equipped troops. Hundreds of Mackenzie's supporters from the outlying districts had not yet arrived.

At noon, Governor Bond Head and Loyalist troops moved north to fight the rebels. About 600 soldiers marched up Yonge Street to the music of two military bands playing "Yankee Doodle Dandy." Two smaller groups of troops moved north through woods and plowed fields to the west and east of Yonge Street. The three companies planned to attack the rebel headquarters at Montgomery's Tavern.

At one o'clock, rebel scouts sent word to Mackenzie that the government forces were marching up Gallow's Hill. Van Egmond and about 200 armed soldiers took up position in the woods south of the town. They were on the west side of Yonge Street. Another 60 hid behind a rail fence east of Yonge Street. The unarmed rebels remained at the tavern.

As the rebels opened fire, Loyalist troops set up their two cannon and aimed into the woods. One of the rebels, Joseph Gould from Uxbridge Township, described the scene.

They fired over us into the tops of the trees cutting the dead and dry limbs of the hemlocks which, falling thickly among us, scared the boys as much as if cannon balls had been rattling around us. The other gun was fired low. One of the balls struck a sandbank by my feet and filled my eyes with sand, nearly blinding me.

The rebel flag. Two white stars on a deep blue background represent the two new Canadian "states."

At that moment, the Loyalist troops advancing through the woods on the west side of Yonge Street closed in behind the rebels. The rebels dropped their rifles and ran. Then, the cannon were moved up and pointed directly at the front of Montgomery's Tavern. A couple of cannon balls passed right through the tavern. The rebels inside poured out like bees from a hive and headed into the surrounding woods.

BATTLE OF MONTGOMERY'S FARM.

At the Battle of Montgomery's Tavern, the rebels were outnumbered and were poorly armed. After less than an hour of fighting, the rebellion was crushed.

Governor Bond Head ordered a thorough search of the tavern. In one room, the soldiers found Mackenzie's papers, including a list of the names of all rebel supporters. Then, the tavern was burned to the ground.

The fighting lasted less than half an hour. One rebel died immediately. Eleven were wounded, four of whom later died. Five Loyalists were wounded, but none of them seriously. The rebellion was crushed. Mackenzie and other rebel leaders rode off swiftly to the north to avoid being taken prisoner. Sir Francis Bond Head offered a reward of 1000 pounds for the capture and return of the rebel leader, William Lyon Mackenzie.

PROCLAMATION.

BY His Excellency SIR FRANCIS BOND HEAD, Baronet, Lieutenant Governor of Upper Canada, &c. &c.

To the Queen's Faithful Subjects in Upper Canada.

In a time of profound peace, while every one was quietly following his occupations, feeling secure under the protection of our Laws, a band of Rebels, instigated by a few malignant and disloyal men, has had the wickedness and audacity to assemble with Arms, and to attack and Murder the Queen's Subjects on the Highway—to Burn and Destroy their Property—to Rob the Public Mails—and to threaten to Plunder the Banks—and to Fire the City of Toronto.

Brave and Loyal People of Upper Canada, we have been long suffering from the acts and endeavours of concealed Traitors, but this is the first time that Rebellion has dared to shew itself openly in the land, in the absence of Invasion by any Foreign Enemy.

Let every man do his duty now, and it will be the last time that we or our children shall see our lives or properties endangered, or the Authority of our Gracious Queen insulted by such treacherous and ungrateful men. MILITIA-MEN OF UPPER CANADA, no Country has ever shewn a finer example of Loyalty and Spirit than YOU have given upon this sudden call of Duty. Young and old of all ranks, are flocking to the Standard of their Country. What has taken place will enable our Queen to know Her Friends from Her Enemies—a public enemy is never so dangerous as a concealed Traitor—and now my friends let us complete well what is begun—let us not return to our rest till Treason and Traitors are revealed to the light of day, and rendered harmless throughout the land.

Be vigilant, patient and active—leave punishment to the Laws—our first object is, to arrest and secure all those who have been guilty of Rebellion, Murder and Robbery.—And to aid us in this, a Reward is hereby offered of

One Thousand Pounds,

to any one who will apprehend, and deliver up to Justice, WILLIAM LYON MACKENZE; and FIVE HUNDRED POUNDS to any one who will apprehend, and deliver up to Justice, DAVID GIBSON—or SAMUEL LOUNT—or JESSE LLOYD—or SILAS FLETCHER—and the same reward and a free pardon will be given to any of their accomplices who will render this public service, except he or they shall have committed, in his own person, the crime of Murder or Arson.

And all, but the Leaders above-named, who have been seduced to join in this unnatural Rebellion, are hereby called to return to their duty to their Sovereign—to obey the Laws—and to live henceforward as good and faithful Subjects—and they will find the Government of their Queen as indulgent as it is just.

GOD SAVE THE QUEEN.

Thursday, 3 o'clock, P. M.
7th Dec.

☞ The Party of Rebels, under their Chief Leaders, is wholly dispersed, and flying before the Loyal Militia. The only thing that remains to be done, is to find them, and arrest them.

R. STANTON, Printer to the QUEEN'S Most Excellent Majesty.

A proclamation from Sir Francis Bond Head offered a reward of 1000 pounds for the capture of William Lyon Mackenzie.

The Causes of the Rebellion

What is a rebellion? A **rebellion** is an armed uprising against the established government. In some cases, the leaders of a rebellion try to establish a new and independent organization in place of the existing government.

Money in Upper Canada

When British North America was first formed, the British pound became the official currency of Upper Canada. But people continued to use many different kinds of money for almost a century. For example, there were American dollars and gold coins, Spanish dollars, Nova Scotia provincial money, and "army bills" issued by the government to pay for war supplies. All these different currencies made things very complicated. The government put a value on each kind of money by comparing it to the British standard. In the 1850s, the decimal system used in the United States was adopted. Eventually, the government began to print and issue its own money and the currency became standardized.

It is difficult to know what one thousand pounds in 1837 would be worth in today's money. However, we can get a general idea by making some comparisons. The following figures come from the Upper Canada government's budget in 1819:

- salary of governor: 2000 pounds
- salary of chief justice: 1100 pounds
- salary of attorney general: 300 pounds
- salary of sheriff: 100 pounds
- salary of naval officer: 100 pounds

In those days, an aristocrat in England needed about 10 000 pounds each year to support his lifestyle. A lower-middle class income was about 150 pounds per year. So, a 1000-pound reward for William Lyon Mackenzie in 1837 would have been a very large sum indeed!

For a few days in December 1837, rebellion raged in Upper Canada. Toronto, the capital, was a city with a population of between 10 000 and 12 000. It was under attack by a force of between 500 and 1000 armed colonists. The rebels marched on the city to overthrow the government and bring about changes they considered important. Why would formerly law-abiding citizens take such a desperate step? Why did this rebellion fail?

How the Colony Was Governed

In the early 1800s, Upper Canada was part of British North America. British North America was made up of six colonies and two territories. The colonies were Upper Canada, Lower Canada, New Brunswick, Prince Edward Island, Nova Scotia, and Newfoundland. The territories were Rupert's Land, owned by the Hudson's Bay Company, and the North-Western Territory.

As you read in Chapter 7, each British colony in North America had an Assembly of elected colonists. The colony was divided into voting districts, and each district elected representatives to the Assembly. At Assembly meetings, the elected representatives made plans for the colony. When these plans were formally written down, they were called **bills**. However, before a bill could become a law, it had to be approved by the governor and the councils.

Each colony had Executive and Legislative Councils whose members were appointed by the governor. Often, the governor and the small group of people he chose to advise him did not approve of the Assembly's bills. When this happened, they could simply toss the bills aside and ignore the wishes of the Assembly. Since the councils were chosen and not elected, they did not necessarily worry about carrying out the wishes of the people as the representatives to the Assembly did.

Those Who Ruled the Colony

The governor was at the head of the government in the colonies. He was sent from Britain as the personal representative of the reigning monarch. He was told that he was responsible to no one but the king or queen for his actions.

Usually, the governor came to North America for a short stay only. He was often totally unfamiliar with the people and the way of life in the colony. Therefore, he depended a great deal on the advice of the executive and legislative councillors. The problem was that the advisors in these councils were always chosen from among the wealthy and influential people of the colony—judges, clergy, bankers, lawyers, military officers, and leading business people. A few were English immigrants, but most were members of United Empire Loyalist families who had lived in the colony for many years. These people felt that they had proven their loyalty to Britain by coming to British North America during the American Revolution instead of fighting the British. They had also fought the Americans in the War of 1812. They believed this loyalty gave them the right to govern. The people who were advising the governor were, in most cases, close friends or related to one another.

The colonists nicknamed this small group of Loyalists the **Family Compact**. They did not all come from the same family, but they all did belong to the highest social class. They thought that because they were wealthy and better educated, they could govern the colony much more effectively than ordinary people could.

Fast Forward

The Governor General Today

Today, in Canada, the governor general represents the British monarch. She or he must formally approve all laws passed by the Parliament of Canada. But the people who advise the governor general are chosen from the population's elected representatives in Parliament. The governor general listens to the advice of these elected members. Thus, she or he is "responsible" to the wishes of these members and, through them, to the people of Canada who elected them.

BRITISH NORTH AMERICA, 1837

0   250   500   750 km

Alaska (Russia)

The North-Western Territory (British)

Newfoundland

Rupert's Land (Hudson's Bay Company)

Oregon Territory

Lower Canada

Upper Canada

Prince Edward Island

Nova Scotia

United States

New Brunswick

Mexico

Special Privileges for a Few

The governor had the right to appoint all officials. He selected council members, judges, sheriffs, and justices of the peace. He also named coroners, customs officers, postal officials, immigration officers, and Indian Affairs officials. As head of the military forces, he appointed the officers. He could make land grants and spend crown money for pensions to reward faithful supporters.

Obviously, the British governors relied heavily on the advice of the Family Compact when naming people to positions. It was said that a person could not obtain a government job unless he was a member or related to a member of the Family Compact. Farmers and their families were not included among these privileged few.

Aboriginal Peoples and the Government of Upper Canada

The Aboriginal peoples had no say in what the government of Upper Canada did. By 1837, most of them had been relocated to reserves or other areas away from the settlements and towns. The governor, Sir Francis Bond Head, believed that the Aboriginal peoples were a "doomed race." In 1836, he suggested that they should all be shipped to Manitoulin Island where they could be protected. He convinced some of the Aboriginal peoples to move to reservations in the Georgian Bay area. That is why we do not often read about the involvement of the Aboriginal peoples in the Rebellion of 1837.

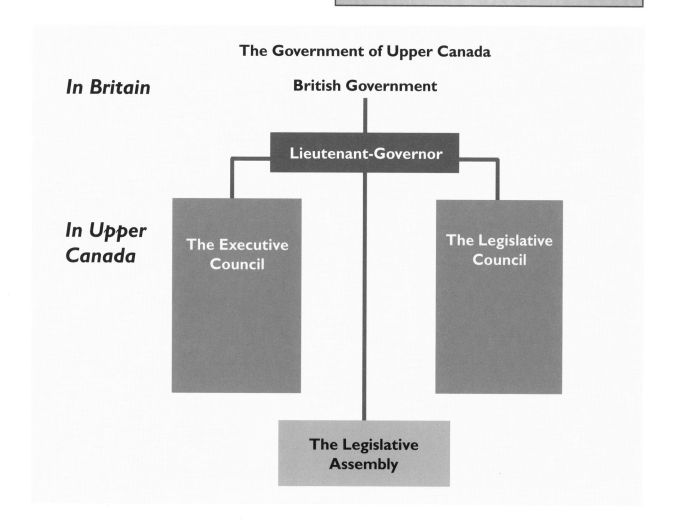

The Government of Upper Canada

In Britain   **British Government**

Lieutenant-Governor

In Upper Canada   **The Executive Council**   **The Legislative Council**

The Legislative Assembly

Profiles

John Strachan   1778–1867

One of the most powerful members of the Family Compact was John Strachan. Strachan arrived in Upper Canada from Scotland in 1799. He was an Anglican clergyman who later became the bishop of Toronto. Strachan was also a member of both the Executive and Legislative Councils.

Strachan insisted that the Anglican Church should have special privileges and position in the colony. For example, until 1831 only Anglican clergy were licensed to perform marriages even though the majority of the colonists belonged to other churches. Strachan was also interested in education. In 1827, he founded an Anglican university, King's College, which later became the University of Toronto. Even after the Family Compact lost its power after the Union of 1841, Strachan remained influential in religion and education. When the Reformers made King's College non-denominational in 1849, Strachan opened the rival Trinity College in 1852 as a strictly Anglican alternative.

John Beverley Robinson   1791–1863

Another prominent member of the Family Compact was John Beverley Robinson. He had been one of Strachan's pupils. Trained as a lawyer, Robinson eventually became a chief justice of Upper Canada. The **chief justice** was the head judge and head of the law courts in Upper Canada. In this position, Robinson was able to exercise a great deal of power in the councils and with the governor. As long as the Family Compact could persuade the governor to listen to its advice, the elected representatives in the Assembly would not have much say in government.

1. John Strachan and John Beverley Robinson held a lot of power in the areas of religion and law. How did this kind of power translate into political power? Do you think that lawyers and clergy today have political power?
2. Would you object to a government that was ruled by a handful of men like Strachan and Robinson? Explain.

The Problem of Land

A major cause of discontent among the people of Upper Canada was the unfair way in which land was granted to settlers. The best farming areas were often given to members of the Family Compact or their friends and favourites. The result was that less than one-tenth of the land in the colony was producing crops. Most of the best farmland was in the hands of people who had neither the skill nor the intention to farm it. They were simply waiting for the land to go up in value so they could sell it at a handsome profit.

Farmers also objected to the government practice of granting one-seventh of all surveyed land to the Anglican Church. People said that it was not fair that other Protestant churches, such as the Presbyterian, Methodist, Baptist, and Lutheran, were not given equal grants. But more important, they complained because these church lands were left uncleared for years while new settlers had to be content with poorer land. A large uncleared church grant would often be between a settler and the nearest neighbour. It held up settlement because no roads were built through it. It harboured weeds that contaminated the crops and wolves that attacked the settler's flocks and herds.

It seemed to the farmers that they were being treated unfairly by the government's land policies. No wonder there were so many farmers in the ranks of William Lyon Mackenzie's rebellion!

The Problem of Roads

Farmers need roads if they are to get their products to market. But in Upper Canada, roads were terribly inadequate. For most of the year, even the main roads were impassable. Only in the winter, when they were frozen over, were many roads easily travelled.

Another complaint was about toll roads. Beginning in 1805, many main roads were made toll roads. People had to pay to use these roads. Tollgates were set up every 6 to 8 km and were looked after by a sentry. Toll charges varied from booth to booth, depending on what the operator wanted to charge. The operators were supposed to use the fees to keep the roads well maintained. However, many of them ignored their responsibilities. As the roads got worse, the settlers became angrier. Some tollbooths were burned to the ground to protest against the high rates and the deplorable conditions of the roads.

The government, however, did spend large amounts of tax money to build canals. These canals benefited the merchant members of the Family Compact and their business friends. To farmers, it seemed that the government granted money to everyone but them. They found it almost impossible to borrow money to buy land, improve their farms, or buy new farm tools. Bankers and merchants grew prosperous while the farmers struggled just to keep their farms going.

To make roads passable, settlers laid trunks of trees side by side across the roadway. The people named the roads corduroy roads because they resembled the coarse ribbed cloth called corduroy.

Fast Forward

Toll Roads Make a Comeback in Ontario

Toll roads existed in Ontario from 1805 to 1926. They were re-introduced in 1997 when Highway 407 opened. It is one of the world's first all-electronic toll highways. Individual vehicle transponders, video camera surveillance, and electronic accounting replace the tollgates.

Staff in the Highway 407 control room monitor traffic. The screens show the major exits and intersections along the highway.

Profile

William Lyon Mackenzie
1795–1861

The most famous Reformer in Upper Canada was William Lyon Mackenzie. He was also the most outspoken. He was born in Scotland in 1795. His father died when he was only three weeks old, leaving his mother Elizabeth Mackenzie with very little to live on. Through sheer hard work, Elizabeth Mackenzie supported herself and her son, but there was never money for luxuries in their home.

Young William was a keen reader. He kept notes on the many books he borrowed from libraries. Between 1806 and 1819, he read 957 books. In later life, he was always able to quote famous authors to back up his opinions.

In 1820, Mackenzie set sail for Montreal. Two years later, he was joined in Canada by Isabel Baxter, who soon became his wife. Over the years, the Mackenzies had 13 children. Five died in infancy and one at the age of 13. Five daughters and two sons lived to be adults.

From the time he arrived in the colony, Mackenzie had been complaining about the government. In York, he set up his newspaper, the *Colonial Advocate*. Now his complaints could be read by a large number of people. In the *Advocate*, he attacked the Family Compact and even the governor. He dragged out family scandals and gossip about the Family Compact and printed them in his paper for the entire colony to read.

Late one night, some sons of Family Compact members decided to end Mackenzie's attacks on their parents once and for all. They broke into his newspaper office, smashed his press, and threw the type into the bay. Mackenzie learned the names of the young law-breakers and brought them to court. He won the case. With the money he received from his lawsuit, he bought a better press and renewed his attacks on the governor and the Family Compact.

In 1827, Mackenzie was elected to the Assembly as one of the representatives for York. He represented the people who lived in the area that went from Lot Street (now Queen Street) in Toronto to Lake Simcoe. In the Assembly, Mackenzie continued his fiery attacks on the government. He was only 165 cm tall, but people listened to him when he spoke. He was completely bald and wore a flaming red wig that he would sometimes toss into the air in front of the startled Assembly. He had bushy eyebrows and his piercing gaze from his deep-blue eyes made his enemies nervous.

Five times Mackenzie was expelled from the Assembly for his attacks on the government. Each time, the people voted Mackenzie back into the Assembly, where his attacks on the government continued. In 1834, York became the city of Toronto and honoured Mackenzie by making him its first mayor. By late 1837, however, Mackenzie felt that publishing and politics were not enough to achieve the reforms he desired. Mere words would no longer be his weapon of choice. He turned to armed rebellion as a last resort.

---

1. What words would you use to describe Mackenzie's personality? Why?
2. Why is Mackenzie an important figure in Ontario history?

Mackenzie's newspaper, *The Colonial Advocate,* launched fierce attacks on leading Tories.

Tech Link

Newspapers in Upper Canada

Newspapers, magazines, and pamphlets were very important to the settlers. From these, they could get up-to-date information about what was happening in the colony and the rest of the world. Printing presses were rare in Upper Canada when the province was founded. The original presses were wooden ones imported from the United States and Britain. By the 1830s, more modern iron presses were being used. By 1833, William Lyon Mackenzie owned two iron presses and his old wooden one.

The first newspaper, the *Upper Canada Gazette*, was established in 1793. But it was not until the 1820s and 1830s that most major towns had their own paper. The printing industry continued to grow. There were more and more readers because of immigration and because more people could read and write. By 1833, York had eight print shops. Printing presses were also in smaller towns. Newspapers were becoming influential in politics. People began to use them to demand changes in the government. Reformers like Mackenzie used the press to promote their views and win new followers, and so did their conservative opponents.

Printing a newspaper was hard work and very time-consuming. Each individual letter had to be chosen and placed in order in a frame to make words and sentences. Then, ink was rolled onto the letters and one sheet at a time was pressed down on it to print the impression. As improvements to the printing press were made, papers could be printed and distributed faster. Information became more and more accessible to the readers.

Although most newspapers had a small circulation, they reached a wide audience. Each copy was read by many people. Most people would read the newspaper in a public place such as a pub. It was also common for one person to read the paper aloud to others.

1. What role do newspapers play in people's lives today? How and why has that changed since Mackenzie's day?
2. Where do you get news about what is happening in the world?

The printing press used by the Radical Reformer William Lyon Mackenzie is preserved at Mackenzie House in Toronto.

Who Were the Tories?

Friends and supporters of the Family Compact were known as **Conservatives** or **Tories**. Tories wanted to "conserve" or keep the existing form of government more or less as it was. Conservatives might say, "We don't want any changes. Things are fine the way they are right now in the colony." The Tories approved of England's way of governing its colonies. They claimed that the governor should be responsible only to the king or queen. Needless to say, members of the councils were nearly always chosen from among Conservatives. Many people in the colony supported the Tories.

Who Were the Reformers?

Reformers wanted the system of government changed or "reformed" so that ordinary people would have more influence. More and more colonists began to disagree with the Family Compact. Most Reformers were moderates. **Moderate Reformers** might say, "Many things are unjust in the colony. However, changes will not happen overnight. We must attack the problem but realize that it may take many years to bring about any change."

Reformers claimed that the governor should be responsible for carrying out the wishes of the majority in the Assembly. This approach would be known as **responsible government**. The colonies should be allowed to grow up and manage their own affairs.

Early Reformers included Robert Gourlay, a Scotsman who had settled in Upper Canada in 1819. He pointed out the need for roads and denounced abuses in the method of granting land. Gourlay was arrested, accused of stirring up the settlers, and banished from the country.

Susanna Moodie Comments on the Rebellion

Susanna Moodie was a loyal Tory whose husband served with the government troops helping to put down the Rebellion of 1837. Here is an excerpt from her diary, written at the time of the rebellion.

Buried in the obscurity of these woods (north of Peterborough) we knew nothing, heard nothing of the political state of the country, and were little aware of the revolution which was about to work a great change for us and for Canada ...

A letter from my sister explained the nature of the outbreak and the astonishment with which the news had been received by all the settlers in the bush. My brother and my sister's husband had already gone off to join some of the numerous bands of gentlemen who were collecting from all quarters to march to the aid of Toronto, which it was said was besieged by the rebel force. She advised me not to permit Moodie to leave home in his present weak state; but the spirit of my husband was aroused, he instantly obeyed what he considered the imperative call of duty and told me to prepare for him a few necessaries that he might be ready to start early in the morning ...

This honest backwoodsman, perfectly ignorant of the abuses that had led to the present position of things, regarded the rebels as a group of monsters, for whom no punishment was too severe, and obeyed the call to arms with enthusiasm. The leader of the rebels must have been astonished at the rapidity with which a large force was collected, as if by magic, to put down the rebellion.

William and Robert Baldwin, also Moderate Reformers, worked out their own plan for responsible government for Upper Canada. Put simply, the governor should not be allowed to have his own way. He should do what his council advised him to do and he ought to pick that council from the largest party in the Assembly. In this way, the governor would be carrying out the wishes of the largest number of voters. Upper Canada would then have responsible government as it was practised in Britain itself.

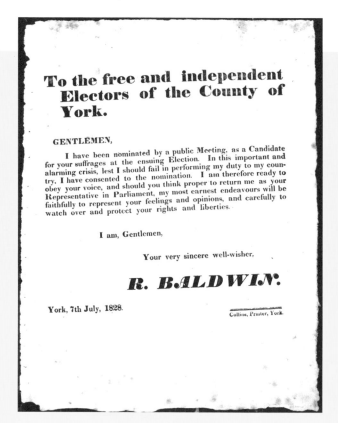

To the free and independent Electors of the County of York.

GENTLEMEN,

I have been nominated by a public Meeting, as a Candidate for your suffrages at the ensuing Election. In this important and alarming crisis, lest I should fail in performing my duty to my country, I have consented to the nomination. I am therefore ready to obey your voice, and should you think proper to return me as your Representative in Parliament, my most earnest endeavours will be faithfully to represent your feelings and opinions, and carefully to watch over and protect your rights and liberties.

I am, Gentlemen,

Your very sincere well-wisher,

R. BALDWIN.

York, 7th July, 1828.   Collins, Printer, York.

Election poster of Robert Baldwin, 1828, Upper Canada

Dr. William Baldwin and his son Robert were among the most influential Moderate Reformers in Upper Canada. The Baldwins were a wealthy York family. Both father and son were well-educated professionals. Although they were members of the Anglican Church, they were not Tories. The Baldwins believed strongly in reform, though they did not want Upper Canada to break away from Britain. They simply wanted more people to have influence in running the colony.

Who Were the Radical Reformers?

As time went on, some of the Moderate Reformers in Upper Canada grew more radical. A **Radical Reformer** might say, "We want changes in our colony and we want them now. We will use all methods to bring about these changes, including violence if necessary."

Mackenzie and others began to lose hope that the people would ever gain the right to make their own laws. He came to doubt that Upper Canada could remain a British colony. He began to speak of breaking away from Britain as the Americans had done in 1776. When he started talking about independence, Mackenzie lost the support of many Moderate Reformers. Men like Baldwin were as loyal to Britain as the governor himself. They feared that Mackenzie had gone too far!

Election Day, 2 January 1832

Early on the morning of 2 January 1832, sleigh bells were heard on Yonge Street. It was election day in York. Since daybreak, voters had been heading to the Red Lion Inn. An election had been called because there was a vacant seat in the Assembly of Upper Canada. The people's hero, William Lyon Mackenzie, had been thrown out of the Assembly for criticizing the government. Now a by-election was necessary and excitement was in the air.

By ten o'clock that morning, a large crowd had gathered around the hustings. Mackenzie was ushered onto the hustings to the sound of bagpipes. A loud cheer went up from the crowd. Mackenzie and his Tory opponent, Mr. Street, were introduced to the voters. Each candidate had a chance to make a speech.

Shortly after one o'clock, the polls opened and voting began. Person after person mounted the hustings and announced his vote. By three o'clock, 119 votes had already been cast for Mackenzie. Only one person had voted for Mr. Street. So, Street withdrew from the unequal

contest and conceded the election. It was all over in two hours. Mackenzie had won! He had been re-elected to his seat in the Assembly. If the election had lasted for four or five days, as it often did in those days, Mackenzie could have polled as many as 5000 votes!

The crowd that elected Mackenzie now pushed into the tavern. They had a victory to celebrate! Inside, Mackenzie's supporters presented him with a large gold medal and chain. On the medal were the words "King and Reform." They believed those words described Mackenzie's ideals. The voters of York hung their gift around Mackenzie's neck. It was a proud moment. That gift remained one of Mackenzie's most prized possessions until the end of his life.

After dark, a torchlight parade of sleighs set off with Mackenzie through the streets of York. The parade stopped in front of the Parliament Buildings. Mackenzie's supporters let out a defiant cheer. They had re-elected their member to the Assembly. He would be the people's representative no matter how much it annoyed the governor and the Family Compact! Finally, late at night, Mackenzie was driven by sleigh to his home and carried into his house in triumph on the shoulders of his supporters.

A New Governor

In 1836, a new governor, Sir Francis Bond Head, arrived in Upper Canada. He knew nothing about Canada and little about politics. There is a story that his appointment was an error and that his cousin Edmund Head was the person intended for the post. As far as the Reformers were concerned, Bond Head's appointment *was* a mistake. They felt that in sending Bond Head as governor, Britain was saying that there would be no self-government or reform in the colony. Sir Francis considered all Reformers, including the Moderates, disloyal traitors to Britain.

During the election of 1836, Sir Francis Bond Head went around the colony urging people to vote for the Tories. "A vote for a Reformer," he warned, "is a vote against Britain!" The Tories won the election, and Mackenzie and many other Reformers lost their seats in the Assembly. Today, no governor or governor general would ever promote one party or candidate over another.

Mackenzie's Call to Arms

The time had come, Radical Reformers decided, to take up arms. If they could not get reform by peaceful means, they would fight for their beliefs. In late November 1837, Mackenzie published a bold call for independence from Britain. Throughout the colony, people read his pamphlet.

Canadians! Do you love freedom? … Do you hate oppression? Do you wish perpetual peace? … Then buckle on your armour, and put down the villains who oppress and enslave our country … The bounty you must pay for freedom is to give the strength of your arms to put down tyranny at Toronto.

Up then, brave Canadians! Get ready your rifles and make short work of it; … with governors from England we will have bribery at elections, corruption, villainy, and continued trouble in every township. But Independence would give us the means of enjoying many blessings.

This pamphlet was Mackenzie's call to arms. In the backwoods and in the Tory stronghold of Toronto, colonists shouldered their muskets. They intended to march down Yonge Street to scare the government into surrendering. The time had come to overthrow the government of Upper Canada.

As you have read, the rebellion in Upper Canada was short-lived. In a few days, it was put down by Sir Francis Bond Head and Loyalist troops. After the burning of Montgomery's Tavern, William Lyon Mackenzie fled toward the American border at Niagara. For much of the way, he travelled on foot. He waded across Sixteen Mile Creek up to his neck in icy water. Even with a price of 1000 pounds on his head, all along the way his supporters risked their lives to hide him from government search parties. These supporters were proud to help their hero escape. One person who aided

Sir Francis Bond Head was a former soldier who had no political experience before he was appointed governor of Upper Canada in 1835. He left Canada in 1837.

Mackenzie ordered these words to be printed on his own gravestone:

> **Up the hill stood the home of Samuel Chandler**
> **He guided Mackenzie to Buffalo**
> **And here they had supper**
> **Dec. 10, 1837**

Four days later, exhausted and nearly frozen, Mackenzie was rowed across the Niagara River where he stepped to safety on American soil.

From Navy Island in the Niagara River, Mackenzie tried to keep his rebellion alive. With about 200 supporters, he conducted raids along the border. When the officials of Upper Canada protested, the American government arrested Mackenzie. They put him in jail at Rochester, New York, for 18 months.

Some Rebels Hang

Two of Mackenzie's leading supporters were not as lucky. They were Samuel Lount, a blacksmith from Holland Landing, and Peter Matthews, a farmer from Pickering. They had been captured after several days in hiding, while attempting to escape to the United States. They were both convicted and sentenced to hang on 12 April 1838 for their leading roles in the rebellion.

Following the 1837 uprisings, many rebels fled to the United States. They joined forces with some Americans to launch raids across the border. This scene shows an attack near Windsor, Ontario.

Civics & Society

Elections in Upper Canada

Elections in Upper Canada were times of great excitement. People came to the voting centres from their farms on foot and horseback, or by sleigh in the winter.

Each political group set up headquarters, usually in a local tavern or inn. Outside, they built a platform of rough boards. The platform, called the **hustings**, was covered with a slanted roof to protect the speakers from the weather. On the morning of the election, crowds gathered around to hear speeches by the candidates. Heated discussions often followed. Some people tried to convince others to vote for their favourite candidate, sometimes offering whiskey, free sandwiches, or even small amounts of money.

Voting was public at that time. When it was time to vote, each person climbed onto the hustings and announced who he was voting for. So, everyone knew how each person had voted. The clerk then wrote down the vote.

Sometimes, fights broke out between rival political groups. If the crowd did not like the way a person voted, he could end up with a bloody nose or a broken jaw. If employers did not like the way their workers voted, the employees could be fired. Since all the voting took place in the open, candidates could make sure that people voted the way they had promised.

This kind of voting meant that the elections were not always fair. Sometimes, people were afraid to vote the way they really wanted to. For that reason, in 1874, the government decided to make all voting secret. It decided to give people pieces of paper called ballots and allow them to mark down their choice in secret. This way of voting is called the **secret ballot**.

In the early 1800s, only men were allowed to run for political office at all levels of government. Women were expected to make home and family their priority and were not encouraged to participate in public life or political debate. In most areas, women who owned property were allowed to vote in municipal elections, but few women actually came to the elections.

In 1844, a law was passed that clearly barred women from voting. This happened after several women had voted in a riding. The losing candidate said that women had no right to make political

Chapter 11: The Rebellion of 1837

decisions. He stated that the proper place for women was at home. At the time, many people also thought that women were mentally and physically inferior to men., even though many pioneer women did traditionally male tasks such as clearing land and building farms. It would not be until the next century that women were granted the right to participate in the political process by voting.

1. What types of candidates would benefit most from the introduction of the secret ballot?

2. How might life in Ontario be different today if women could not vote?

3. Why do you think that, when there is an election, only a percentage of the people who can vote actually do?

Fast Forward

Women Finally Gain the Right to Vote

In 1874, the law allowing people to vote by secret ballot was passed. Two years later, in Toronto, Emily Howard Stowe, the first female doctor in Canada, founded the first suffrage society. It was devoted to the advancement of women's rights. **Suffrage** means the right to vote. All across the country, women met in similar groups to work toward change. Unfortunately, they were not supported by all women and had the support of only some men.

Province	Date
Manitoba, Saskatchewan, Alberta	1916
British Columbia, Ontario	1917
Nova Scotia	1918
New Brunswick	1919
Prince Edward Island	1922
Newfoundland	1925
Quebec	1940

Over a period of 24 years, women were finally granted the right to vote in provincial elections. The Wartime Elections Act of 1917 gave women in the military and female relatives of men in the military the right to vote federally. In 1918, the federal vote was granted to all female citizens in Canada aged 21 and over. In 1919, women gained the right to stand for election to the House of Commons.

Emily Howard Stowe faced many obstacles in her struggle to become a doctor. She had to attend medical school in New York because no Canadian college would accept a woman student.

Many people gathered to watch public hangings such as those of Matthews and Lount. They were hanged on 12 April in front of the jail in Toronto.

Monument to Samuel Lount and Peter Matthews

Elizabeth Lount's Plea

Elizabeth Lount, Samuel's wife, was not prepared to accept the death of her well-respected husband without a fight. This brave woman visited the governor and begged on her knees for her husband's life. She collected the signatures of 30 000 people. The petition urged the government to spare the lives of Lount and Matthews. The governor refused to accept the pleas of Elizabeth Lount. The execution was carried out at the Toronto jail. Peter Matthews left a widow and 15 children and Samuel Lount left a widow and 7 children.

The government refused to turn over the bodies of the rebels to their families. They were buried in unmarked graves near the intersection of Yonge and Bloor Streets in Toronto. In 1859, William Lyon Mackenzie and others moved the bodies of Lount and Matthews to the Toronto burial ground known as the Necropolis. In 1893, a monument was erected that carries the following inscription:

This monument is erected to the memory of Samuel Lount of Holland Landing, County of York, Born 24th September 1791, Died 12th April 1838, and of Peter Matthews of Pickering, County of Ontario, Born 1786, Died 12th April 1838. Erected by their friends and sympathizers, 1893.

Two months after the execution of her husband, Elizabeth Lount wrote, "Canada will do justice to his memory. Canadians cannot long remain in bondage. They will be free."

Aftermath of the Rebellion

It is estimated that in the year following the rebellion, 25 000 people left Upper Canada for the United States. Their hopes of seeing change in Upper Canada had been dashed. At a time when the total population of Upper Canada was 300 000, this loss of 25 000 hard-working citizens was a serious blow to the colony.

For many years after the uprising, it was difficult for a reform movement to operate. Fear of another rebellion or a rebel-led invasion from the United States made many Tories distrustful. Anyone who talked about reforming the government was immediately branded as a rebel.

One-way Ticket to Australia

Ninety-two rebels were given a one-way ticket to the convict settlements of Australia. They were sent to Van Diemen's Land, now called Tasmania. This was a British prison colony off the southeastern coast of Australia. At first, the exiles were kept in prison camps where they were poorly housed, clothed, and fed. Eventually, the prisoners were sent out into the community as cheap labour for farmers. Several attempted to escape. In 1844–1845, the Canadian exiles were granted pardons. Some of the former rebels returned quietly to Canada. Others, who were soured by the way they had been treated, settled in the United States.

Port Arthur was an isolated prison settlement where convicts from other parts of Van Diemen's Land were sent for breaking the rules or trying to escape. Several Canadian exiles were sentenced to hard labour here.

Fast Forward

Mackenzie House Museum

Eventually, the British government accepted Mackenzie's request for a pardon. Twelve years after the rebellion, Mackenzie was officially pardoned and returned with his family to settle in Toronto. Mackenzie was the last of all the rebels to receive his pardon. A group of friends purchased a house for him on Bond Street. He lived in that house until his death in 1861. Today, the house is a museum.

William Lyon Mackenzie's daughter Isabel, the youngest of his 13 children, married John King in 1872. They became parents of a son whom they named William Lyon Mackenzie King. In 1921, Mackenzie King became Canada's 11th prime minister.

Skill Building: Resolving Conflict

At the beginning of this chapter, you read a description of change and how it can lead to conflict. Think about the Rebellion of 1837 in Upper Canada. What evidence in that event shows that:

- change involves making or becoming something different?
- change can just happen or it can be made to happen?
- change can involve conflict or struggle?

In a three-column chart, list as many conflicts as you can think of. Use the headings "In History," "In Today's News," and "In My Community." Compare your chart with a classmate's chart. Together, come up with a combined list of conflicts. Talk about the causes of these kinds of conflicts, what changes the conflicts involved, and how the conflicts were resolved. You might also think about conflicts in your own life.

Conflicts often involve groups or individuals with unequal amounts of power. To solve an issue, one party uses its power over the other to force the other party to comply. This power can take different forms, such as threats, withholding money, cutting off resources, confiscating land or property, or violent acts. Using power to win a struggle may lead to a solution, but it may not necessarily be the best one. When one party wins and the other loses, the solution can be called Win-Lose. When both parties feel they have solved the problem but lost on significant issues, the solution is seen as Lose-Lose. When both parties feel the result is satisfactory, the solution is called Win-Win. This is the best kind of solution to aim for and the hardest to achieve.

Think back to the Rebellion of 1837. What kind of solution was achieved for the parties involved? Was it the best way to solve the problem? Was the solution a satisfactory one? Explain. Take another look at your list of conflicts. For each of those that have been resolved, what kind of solution was found—Win-Win, Lose-Lose, or Win-Lose—and why do you think so?

Although many differences of opinion are solved with violence, there are other ways to deal with conflict. For example, a union group and an employer are discussing a new contract. There are some items they agree on and some items that are in dispute. They can use three main strategies to come to agreement.

Negotiation

In **negotiation**, the parties talk over an issue and try to arrange a solution that is acceptable to all. The final agreement is often a compromise that all parties feel comfortable with. In our example, the union and the employer meet many times at the negotiating table to discuss the items that they do not agree on. Over time, with give and take, they come to a solution. Everyone agrees to give up some things in order to gain others. Neither party gets all that it wants, but both parties are satisfied in the end.

Mediation

When negotiation is not successful, the parties in conflict might ask for **mediation**. The mediator helps them reach a solution. The mediator is not directly involved with either side in the conflict. He or she acts as a friendly "intervener" or neutral third party. Mediators often have special training to help them perform their role successfully. The union and the employer in our example can ask a mediator to meet with them to help them sort out an agreement.

Arbitration

Sometimes, parties in conflict may decide on **arbitration** to settle the dispute. An arbitrator listens carefully to all the issues in the conflict and then, acting as a judge, makes a final decision. The parties involved must accept the arbitrator's solution even if they do not agree with it. In our example, the union and the employer will explain all the items they cannot agree on to the arbitrator. Once the final judgement is made, everyone must follow it. The parties can try to alter the decision when they negotiate the next contract.

Try It!

In a small group, try to apply these three conflict resolution approaches. Imagine that it is 1837, and the government and the Reformers have agreed to sit down to negotiations.

1. Organize yourselves into three groups. One group will role-play negotiation, acting out how the conflict might have been solved using this method. Another group will role-play mediation. The last group will role-play arbitration.

2. Within your group, assign roles to each person. Make sure everyone understands all the issues.
   • What were the Reformers trying to achieve?
   • Why was the government reluctant to give them what they wanted?

3. Act out how the conflict might have been solved using your group's strategy. Which approach did you prefer? Why? Do you think that the violent events of 1837 could have been avoided if the leaders had tried to solve their differences this way, or do you think that the rebellion was inevitable?

Activities

Understanding Concepts

1. Define each of the following terms and add it to your personal dictionary.

hustings	chief justice	bill
rebellion	Family Compact	Tory
Moderate Reformer	Radical Reformer	suffrage
responsible government	secret ballot	mediation
arbitration	negotiation	Conservative

2. a) What rights and privileges did the members of the Family Compact hold?
   b) Why did the governor rely so heavily on the Family Compact for advice?
   c) Why did the elected Assembly in the colonies have little real power?

3. How did transportation problems make life difficult for settlers in Upper Canada? What changes would have improved the situation for them?

4. Using an organizer, indicate what a Radical Reformer, a Moderate Reformer, and a Tory would say about
   a) their feelings about Britain
   b) who should run the government
   c) change

5. Decide whether each of the following men is a Radical, Moderate Reformer, or Conservative. Explain your answer.
   a) Samuel Lount
   b) Francis Bond Head
   c) Robert Baldwin
   d) Robert Gourlay

6. How did Robert Baldwin propose to alter the system of government in Upper Canada? Why would Britain find Baldwin's approach more acceptable than Mackenzie's approach?

Digging Deeper

7. **COMPARE** Compare the Rebel and Loyalist forces in the Battle of Toronto using an organizer. Use the following criteria: size of army, weapons available, experience of military leaders, and experience of troops.

8. **PREDICT** How important was the part played in the rebellion by each of the following people? Try to predict how the events of the rebellion might have been different if each person had not been there. Organize your ideas under the headings "Major Characters" and "Minor Characters."
   - Anthony Anderson
   - Van Egmond
   - Sheriff Jarvis
   - William Lyon Mackenzie
   - Colonel Moodie
   - Robert Baldwin
   - Sir Francis Bond Head
   - Samuel Lount
   - Montgomery (innkeeper)

9. **ROLE-PLAY/WRITE** You are the mother or wife of a man who has just left home to join forces with Sir Francis Bond Head or William Lyon Mackenzie. Write a diary entry. Tell
   - why your son or husband decided to go
   - how he would get to Toronto
   - what he took with him
   - how you felt as you said good-bye

Making New Connections

10. **CREATE/WRITE** Write an eyewitness account of the Battle of Toronto. An eyewitness account means you try to write as though you were actually present at the event. Refer to the text and illustrations for specific information. Write from the point of view of one of the following:
    a) Mrs. Sharpe, watching events taking place at the bottom of her garden
    b) John Montgomery, tavern owner, describing the rebels and their leaders
    c) John Powell, relating his exciting news to the citizens of Toronto
    d) a member of the Loyalist forces describing the burning of Montgomery's Tavern

11. **CREATE** Imagine that the rebels put up WANTED posters for the governor. Design one of these posters.

12. **DISCUSS** Discuss Elizabeth Lount's comments about the rebels: "Canadians cannot remain in bondage. They will be free."

13. **ROLE-PLAY** Imagine you are Elizabeth Lount appearing before Sir Francis Bond Head to plead for the life of your husband. Write out the arguments you will present to persuade the governor to spare Samuel's life.

14. **MEDIA/CREATE** The Reformers often used pamphlets and newspaper articles to win people over to their point of view. Work in groups. Design and write a pamphlet to gain support for a change you would like to see in Canada. Try to follow the style of Mackenzie's pamphlet.

Rally at St.-Charles

24 October 1837
St.-Charles, Lower Canada

Dearest Mother and Father,

Each day, the unrest grows more serious. Last night in St.-Charles, more than 5000 habitants gathered to listen to the Patriotes (Reformers). How thrilling it was to hear them! And how frightening too! Wolfred Nelson talked openly of rebellion. He said, "It is time to melt spoons into bullets. It is time to drive the British out."

Four-fifths of the people of Lower Canada are French Canadians like us. For six generations, we have lived quietly and farmed this land. We do not see the need to change. Why can't the English just leave us in peace? All we ask is to be left alone with "notre langue, nos lois, et notre foi."

My husband, Pierre, and all our neighbours complain bitterly about the way the English rule over us. Pierre says that French voices will never be heard in the Assembly. The English governor and his English councils will always reject our laws. How it angers us to spend our hard-earned money to build roads and canals. Everybody knows they are no use to any of us. They are only for the English merchants to use so they can grow richer.

Our son Jean-Luc worries me. He wishes to join the Sons of Liberty. He is going to follow the Patriotes. Jean-Luc says, "The British may kill me, but I will not run away!" Oh, how I fear what might happen to Jean-Luc! Trouble is coming.

May the Lord have mercy on us all.

Your loving daughter,
Marie-Josée

Reflecting/Predicting

1. What issues do you think the people of Lower Canada have?
2. Why do you think the British refuse to listen to the people?
3. How do you think the people of Lower Canada will try to deal with this problem?
4. What similarities do you see between these events and the events in Upper Canada?

Louis-Joseph Papineau, Wolfred Nelson, and other Patriote leaders attend the huge rally at St.-Charles in October 1837.

Changes in Lower Canada from 1800 to 1837

Major changes took place in Lower Canada from 1800 to 1837.

1. Many immigrants came from Britain to work in the timber industry or to build the canals. Although the majority settled in Upper Canada, large numbers located in Lower Canada. French Canadians saw the immigrants as a threat. In their view, the immigrants competed for jobs and added to the English-speaking population in the province.

Many immigrants were poor and they often contracted diseases, such as cholera, on board the ship. In 1832 and 1834, a cholera epidemic killed thousands of people in Lower Canada.

2. Traditional habitant occupations changed. Agriculture declined in Lower Canada because of poor harvests, outdated methods, and soil depletion. Overcrowded seigneuries added to the problems. The fur trade also declined.

3. Business improved for the British business-men. Britain needed more and more wood in order to build warships. Canals were built to improve transport and trade between Upper and Lower Canada.

4. The first railway was completed in 1836 in Quebec. It joined La Prairie to St.-Jean, near present-day Montreal.

5. The Bank of Montreal became Canada's first major bank. It was the prime focus of Canadian business and finance and helped Montreal merchants develop the colony.

6. In 1805, the British business class founded *The Quebec Mercury*, a political paper through which its members could voice their ambitions for business and politics. In 1806, the French Canadians started a paper called *Le Canadien* to show their opposition to the English.

Religious Rights in Lower Canada

Both Upper and Lower Canada were predominantly Christian. Roman Catholics were the majority in Lower Canada and Protestants were the majority in Upper Canada. The number of non-Christians was very small.

By 1800, there were fewer than 100 Jews in both the Canadas. Ezekiel Hart was a Jew born in Trois-Rivières in 1770. His father was a merchant. In 1807, Hart won a seat in the Lower Canada Assembly. However, other members of the Assembly saw him as a supporter of the governor. They declared that he was ineligible to serve because of his religion. In the following year, Hart was re-elected and took the required Christian oath. But the Assembly majority ruled that his faith made his oath invalid. As a result, although twice elected to the Assembly, Ezekiel Hart never did take office.

In 1830, the governor offered Hart's son, Samuel, the position of magistrate and justice of the peace. However, after discussions with his advisors, the governor withdrew the offer. Hart was furious and wrote to the king to complain. At the same time, other Jewish men petitioned the Legislative Assembly, demanding that Jews be allowed to hold public office.

In 1832, Louis-Joseph Papineau, the leader of the Assembly, was involved with the passing of a bill to guarantee full rights to all people practising the Jewish faith. England and its other colonies did not grant these rights to Jews for another 25 years. Samuel Hart eventually won a seat in the Assembly and became the first Jew to sit in a British legislature.

A Visitor's View of Lower Canada

Alexis de Tocqueville was a political scientist and historian from France. In 1831, he spent two weeks visiting Lower Canada as part of his tour of North America. He wrote and published notes and letters about his experience. His observations about the province were both optimistic and pessimistic.

He was delighted to find a people with a distinct national identity. The French-speaking people were leading a peaceful and productive existence in Lower Canada. He commended them for their democratic way of life.

De Tocqueville also noted that the fate of these Lower Canadians was still uncertain. He worried about so much power being in the hands of a small elite. He was concerned that trade was controlled by the British. He predicted that the new settlers could soon outnumber the French Canadians. Alexis de Tocqueville's writings fascinated people in Lower Canada and elsewhere. They provided food for thought and discussion for many.

The Causes of Rebellion in Lower Canada

During the 1830s, at the same time the people in Upper Canada were demanding change, there was also a growing reform movement in Lower Canada. In many ways, the situations were similar. In both cases, there were complaints about the way that the colony was governed. The elected Assembly was pulling in one direction and the two appointed Councils were pulling in the other direction. But in Lower Canada, there was an additional problem. The colony had two languages and two cultural groups—the French and the English.

English-Speaking Rulers

Most of the people of Lower Canada were French-speaking and they dominated the elected Assembly. But the governor chose most of his councillors from among the English-speaking merchants and bankers of the colony. This ruling group was known as the **Château Clique** because they often met at the governor's residence at Château St.-Louis.

The English governor would not agree to all the laws French-speaking members of the Assembly wished to pass. That made the French angry. They wanted to preserve their language, their Roman Catholic religion, and their traditional agricultural way of life. The English-speaking councillors were not interested in the concerns of the French-speaking people. Instead, their goal was to build roads and canals using the colony's tax money. With better transportation, the English merchants could improve their businesses.

This situation was a double insult to the French-speaking population. Not only were they being governed by a few powerful men who would not listen to them, they were being governed by the English.

The Problem of Land

There were other problems in Lower Canada. The population of the colony was rapidly increasing. A large number of English-speaking people were moving into Lower Canada. Many of them were settling in the Eastern Townships, near the American border. They were able to settle there because English-speaking merchants from Montreal had obtained a huge land grant. The French-speaking people, who were mainly farmers, were beginning to feel crowded out. They feared that the English settlers would take all the remaining good farmland. Then, their children would have no land to farm. If this happened, their traditional agricultural way of life would slowly disappear.

More English-Speaking Settlers

The French people who lived in the cities also resented the growing number of English-speaking settlers. The English businessmen wanted to change Lower Canada into a busy industrial place. They wanted to build roads, canals, bridges, and banks. They wanted to encourage more English people to move to the cities in Lower Canada, especially Montreal. The English settlers would bring more business. The French were afraid they would soon be swamped by the growing number of English-speaking people.

Growing Discontent

While William Lyon Mackenzie was actively criticizing the Family Compact in Upper Canada, Louis-Joseph Papineau was leading attacks on the governor and the English-speaking Château Clique. In 1834, the angry Assembly of Lower Canada drew up a document of complaints called the **Ninety-Two Resolutions**. The resolutions included demands for an elected legislative assembly and responsible government. The Assembly members threatened to vote against imposing taxes. This meant that government officials would not be able to collect their salaries. It also meant that the building of bridges, roads, and canals would have to stop. The Assembly hoped that these tactics would force the British into listening to their complaints.

In 1836, the Assembly refused to approve the funds necessary to run the colony. Even the governor was unable to collect his salary. The British government refused to listen to the concerns of the Assembly of Lower Canada. More importantly, it allowed the governor to take money from the treasury to pay his officials.

The Patriotes were furious. Papineau ordered French-speaking people not to buy British goods from English merchants. He branded the governor and the Château Clique as "enemies of the country." Papineau was seen as a hero who stood up to the British governor and supported the rights of the people. In the newspaper *The Vindicator*, another Patriote leader wrote, "Henceforth, there must be no peace in the province. Agitate! Agitate! Agitate!"

A Summer of Agitation

Time passed, but nothing changed. During the summer of 1837, Papineau and the Patriotes became angrier. They began to suggest that the American system of government would be better. Like Mackenzie's reform movement in Upper Canada, the Patriotes lost some support when they hinted that violence might be the solution to their problems. Moderate Reformers did not believe that armed rebellion was the way to bring about change. The Roman Catholic Church warned the people not to take part in any violence. The situation became so serious that troops were sent from Upper Canada in case of trouble.

In Montreal, Papineau's followers began to organize **Les Fils de la Liberté**. It was an organization for young Patriotes. The idea and the name were taken from the Sons of Liberty of the American Revolution. Papineau's son, Amédée, was a member of the executive. By October 1837, 1200 members were practising military drills openly, but without weapons.

A few members of the English minority in Lower Canada sympathized with the Patriotes, but most of the Scottish, Irish, and American immigrants, who had arrived in Lower Canada more recently, were against them. These English-speaking farmers became alarmed and fearful at what they saw happening. They felt very insecure about their position in Lower Canada.

Eventually, in the fall of 1837, Papineau's followers took up arms against the government. Fighting broke out in Lower Canada even before Mackenzie and his rebels in Upper Canada marched against Toronto in early December. The timeline that follows illustrates the dramatic events of the rebellion in Lower Canada.

Events of the Rebellion of 1837 in Lower Canada

Street Fight in Montreal 6 November 1837

Street fighting breaks out in Montreal between the French and English. As they come out of their club, some English officers get into a fight with a group of Les Fils de la Liberté. Amédée Papineau is involved, but he gets home safely. Soon, the violence spreads to other parts of Lower Canada. The governor takes no chances. He calls out the troops and orders Upper Canada to send reinforcements. He is determined to crush the riot before it turns into widespread rebellion. Warrants are issued for the arrest of Papineau and the other leaders. Papineau slips out of Montreal and heads to St.-Denis.

British Attack at St.-Denis

A British army led by Colonel Charles Gore attacks Patriote headquarters in the village of St.-Denis. Gore hopes to capture Papineau, but again Papineau slips away. The British meet a strong defence from about 300 armed Patriotes who are stationed behind the thick stone walls of the village houses. Church bells ring out the alarm. Soon, Patriote reinforcements begin to arrive from the surrounding countryside. After seven hours

23 November 1837. The Patriotes are victorious at St.-Denis.

From the Manifesto of Les Fils de la Liberté

"The wicked designs of British authorities have severed all ties of sympathy for an unfeeling mother country. A separation has commenced ... which will go on ominously increasing until ... one of those sudden events ... affords us a fit opportunity for assuming our rank among the Independent Sovereignties of America."

The Patriote flag was a symbol of the rebels in Lower Canada.

of fighting, the government troops are forced to withdraw. It is a Patriote victory!

After the victory at St.-Denis, many people join the Patriote cause. However, there are no more guns or ammunition to give them. The government offers a reward of 1000 pounds for Papineau's capture.

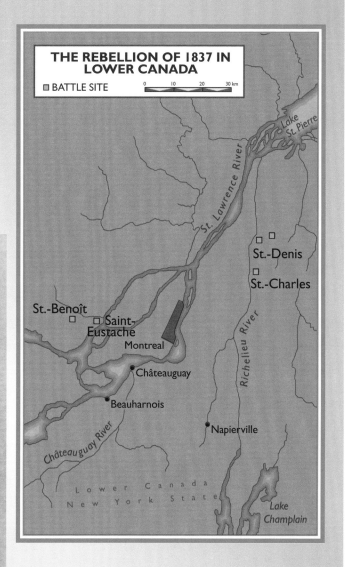

THE REBELLION OF 1837 IN LOWER CANADA

□ BATTLE SITE

A proclamation charging Papineau with high treason was issued on 7 December 1837. A reward of 1000 pounds or $4000 was offered.

Patriotes Defeated at St.-Charles

Two days after their defeat at St.-Denis, a large force of about 400 government troops raids another Patriote stronghold at St.-Charles. The Patriotes destroy a bridge, forcing the advancing enemy to make a detour. But it is no use. The soldiers swarm over the barricade and burn the town. The battle lasts a little over an hour. At least 40 rebels are killed. Patriotes blame their defeat on their worn-out guns and the fact that they were outnumbered two to one. News of the disaster spreads quickly. Papineau, under the name of Mr. Louis, flees to the United States where he tries to raise money for more arms. A few weeks later, Wolfred Nelson is captured in the woods.

The Rebellion Ends

Two thousand troops and Loyalist volunteers advance on the village of Saint-Eustache. There are only about 600 to defend the town. Many flee when they see they are outnumbered. But about 50 Patriotes, led by Jean-Olivier Chénier, fortify themselves inside the village church. The British troops set fire to the church and the Patriotes are trapped inside the burning building. Many are killed or captured as they attempt to escape the flames. Later, the British loot the town. Families are turned out of their homes to freeze in the snow. The next day, St.-Benoît, another Patriote stronghold, is burned to the ground by British troops.

25 November 1837. The British defeat the Patriotes at St.-Charles.

The rebellion in Lower Canada is over. The Patriote resistance is crushed. The rebels are forced to scatter for fear of arrest.

14 December 1837. Greatly outnumbered by the British at Saint-Eustache, the final rebellion is crushed.

Profiles

Louis-Joseph Papineau
1786–1871

A Canada Post stamp commemorates Louis-Joseph Papineau.

Louis-Joseph Papineau was the leader of the French-speaking majority in the Assembly. He was born in Montreal in 1786. Well educated, he became a lawyer and, like his father, was elected to the Assembly. Papineau had natural leadership abilities and could inspire people with his speeches. He became the leader of a reform party in Lower Canada and the champion of the nationalist movement. The Reformers wanted changes that would give French-speaking people a greater share in law-making for the province.

Papineau was not always a Reformer. In his early life, he was an admirer of Britain. But as he grew older, he feared that Britain intended to make his people more like the English. For the rest of his life, he was dedicated to preserving French language, law, and religion. Papineau and his supporters in Lower Canada became known as **Patriotes**.

Wolfred Nelson
1791–1863

Wolfred Nelson was a medical doctor. As a young man, he tried to be part of the English-speaking governing society. He wrote, "In my youth, I was an ardent Tory and came to hate everything Catholic and French Canadian." But his views changed. Nelson became a convert to the cause of the Patriotes and an important Patriote leader. At a public meeting in October 1837, Nelson shouted, "The time has come to melt down our tin spoons and plates into bullets." After the events of 1837, he was exiled from Canada. In 1842, Nelson returned and took up a political career. Later, he became the mayor of Montreal.

---

1. What do you think is meant by "natural leadership abilities"? Why are these important?
2. Have your views about something, for example, an issue in your school or community, ever changed dramatically, like the views of Papineau and Nelson did? Explain.

Skill Building: Comparing Two Persons or Events

When you compare two people or two events, you try to decide in what ways they are similar and different. In the last two chapters, you have studied the Rebellions of Lower and Upper Canada. Suppose you wanted to compare the leaders of the rebellions. How were Mackenzie and Papineau alike? How were they different? How did the personalities of the leaders influence events in Upper and Lower Canada?

A Comparison Organizer

You can record your information in a number of different ways. One way is to use a comparison organizer.

1. Decide which two leaders you want to compare.

2. Choose the criteria for your comparison. Criteria are the characteristics you will compare. Some criteria you might use are family background, speaking ability, and education.

3. Construct an organizer like the one below. List the criteria down the left side. Across the top of the organizer, list who or what is being compared.

4. Think about each of the criteria for comparison. Decide on the important facts. Enter them on the organizer in point form.

5. Review all the facts you recorded. In what ways were Mackenzie and Papineau alike? In what ways were they different? Who was the better leader? Why? Discuss your conclusions with the class.

A Venn Diagram

Another way to record your comparison is to use a Venn diagram.

1. Decide which two leaders you want to compare.

2. Choose the criteria for your comparison and keep them in mind.

Criteria	Mackenzie	Papineau
Family background		
Speaking ability		
Education		

3.   Construct a Venn diagram like the one below. Draw two interlocking circles. Call the circle on the left Mackenzie and the circle on the right Papineau.

4.   Think about each of the criteria for comparison. Decide on the important facts. In the left circle, write words or descriptions about Mackenzie that are different from Papineau according to the criteria you selected. In the circle on the right, list things about Papineau that are different from Mackenzie. In the central space where the circles overlap, list the characteristics that both leaders share.

5.   Review all the facts you recorded. In what ways were Mackenzie and Papineau alike? In what ways were they different? Who was the better leader? Why? Discuss your conclusions with the class.

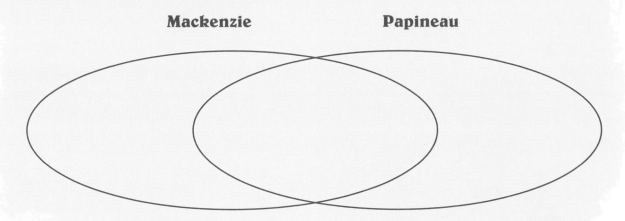

Mackenzie   **Papineau**

Why the Rebellion Failed

The Patriotes in Lower Canada failed for two main reasons—the rebellion was not well planned and it lacked leadership. The politicians could inspire the people with words, but they did not have the skills needed to plan a battle. The former parish priest of St.-Benoît was a committed Patriote. Later, he scolded Papineau, saying, "Alas! If only nature had given you as much courage as eloquence!" Furthermore, only one in ten Patriotes had a gun. Since they were not trained soldiers, they could not fight as well as the British troops.

Another important reason for failure was the fact that the Roman Catholic Church did not approve of armed rebellion. Many of the clergy were also afraid that a Patriote victory would lessen their influence in Lower Canada. The bishop of Montreal, Jean-Jacques Lartigue, publicly condemned the rebellion. He also instructed other clergy to deliver the same message to their parishioners. Many Patriotes were unwilling to go against the wishes of their church. When the Patriotes learned that Papineau, their leader, had fled, many simply gave up and returned home. Therefore, most Lower Canadians did not join the rebellion. In fact, although a large number of habitants supported the Patriotes, the number who actually participated in the rebellion was quite small. The French population of Lower Canada was about 450 000. Only about 5000 to 6000 people were actually involved in the rebellion.

A Second Rebellion

In 1838, radical Patriotes, under Wolfred Nelson's brother Robert, attempted another rebellion. Inspired by Nelson, about 400 Patriotes assembled at Beauharnois and captured some prisoners. Other rebels seized some Loyalist property at Châteauguay.

Meanwhile, with a small army, Robert Nelson attacked from the United States. The rebels had many American sympathizers. They were members of "Hunter's Lodges." These lodges were secret societies organized by Canadian rebels who had fled to the United States after the failure of the 1837 Rebellion.

A soldier of the Royal Dragoons, bundled up against the cutting wind and deep snow, defends Lower Canada at Napierville.

Members were determined to help liberate the British colonies from what they saw as British tyranny. When Robert Nelson attacked Lower Canada from the United States, he was joined by a significant number of Americans.

Nelson's goal was to capture Lower Canada and declare an independent republic. At Napierville, he read a Declaration of Independence. He proclaimed himself president. A Patriote government would replace British rule. Troops of the Royal Dragoons were sent south through the snow to put down the invasion. The attack was crushed by government troops after a two-hour battle. Some of the rebels were killed or captured. Others fled. The rebellions in Lower Canada were over.

Aftermath of the Rebellion

The prisons were quickly filled after the rebellions in Lower Canada. Twelve leading rebels were hanged as a result of their activities in 1837 and 1838.

Eight of the leaders from Lower Canada were sent into **exile** in Bermuda. This group included the Patriote leader Dr. Wolfred Nelson. Fifty-eight other rebels from Lower Canada were sent into exile in New South Wales on mainland Australia.

In some ways, the Lower Canadians in New South Wales were better off than the Upper Canadians in Van Diemen's Land. The Lower Canadians were a close-knit group. Among

Fast Forward

Remembering the Exiles

In 1970, Canadian prime minister Pierre Trudeau visited Australia. He unveiled a plaque near the city of Sydney. It commemorated the ordeal of "the Canadian exiles of 1840." In the crowd that day were descendants of the one Canadian from Lower Canada who chose to remain in Australia.

Large crowds came to see the rebels hanged for their participation in the Rebellions of 1837 and 1838.

them were fathers and their sons, brothers, uncles, and nephews. The whole group was kept together in one place. Although there were physical hardships, the prisoners were not treated poorly. They tried hard to show that they were trustworthy and therefore deserved pardon. When they were pardoned in the 1840s, all but one rebel returned to Lower Canada.

As for Louis-Joseph Papineau, after the rebellion failed, warrants were issued for his arrest. After two years in the United States, Papineau sailed for Paris, where he stayed for almost four years. He was eventually pardoned and, in 1845, was allowed to return to Quebec. For a brief time, he returned to politics, but he soon retired to spend the rest of his life on his estate at Montebello.

Papineau and his wife, Julie Bruneau, had nine children, five of whom survived into adulthood. Their youngest daughter, Azélie, married Napoléon Bourassa, a renowned painter and Quebec art historian. They were the parents of Henri Bourassa, a major figure in Quebec and Canadian political history.

Papineau's estate has been preserved and is now a historic site. The manor house, the site, and the outbuildings all reflect life in Papineau's time.

New Leadership

After the uprisings in Lower Canada, moderate leaders like Louis-Hippolyte LaFontaine appeared. The new French-speaking leaders were opposed to radical measures. They believed that it was better to work within the government to try to bring about change.

The Roman Catholic clergy regained a more powerful leadership role in Lower Canada. They blamed the leaders of the rebellion for steering the people astray. The Church wanted the French-speaking people to give up their radical and rebellious behaviour. The Church demanded that the people commit to preserving and defending the Catholic faith, the family, and the French language. This view would be dominant in Quebec for the next hundred years.

Profile

Louis-Hippolyte LaFontaine 1807–1864

After the rebellion, moderate leaders like Louis-Hippolyte LaFontaine led politics in Lower Canada.

Louis-Hippolyte LaFontaine was born in Boucherville, Lower Canada, in 1807. He became a lawyer and later entered politics. LaFontaine supported Louis-Joseph Papineau in his opposition to the British administration, but he did not approve of the rebellion in 1837.

After the rebellion, when Papineau was in exile, LaFontaine became the leader of the reform party in Lower Canada. He worked hard for many years to achieve genuinely responsible government. LaFontaine brought in the Rebellion Losses Bill to compensate people in Lower Canada who had suffered property loss during the rebellion. He was joint prime minister with Robert Baldwin after Upper and Lower Canada were united as the Province of Canada. His efforts and the efforts of others like him eventually resulted in government by the majority in an elected Assembly.

1. After the rebellion, LaFontaine's more moderate political views became accepted. Why do you think this happened?
2. Who do you think was a better leader for Lower Canada, Papineau or LaFontaine? Why?

Fast Forward

Quebec Separatism

The cry of the Patriotes, *notre langue, nos lois, et notre foi* (our language, our laws, and our faith), can be heard again today in Quebec. The dissatisfaction that led to social breakdown in 1830s Lower Canada can be related to events in present-day Canada. The citizens of Quebec still consider their province and its people to be a **distinct society**. They believe their language, culture, traditions, and institutions are unique within Canada and need to be protected. They fear that their culture will disappear unless steps are taken.

As in 1837, there is disagreement amongst the Québécois about what steps to take. Some feel that Canada has not done a very good job of protecting their language and culture and that they will have to do it themselves. This has led to discussions about whether or not the province of Quebec should become independent of the rest of Canada in order to maintain its unique identity. Some Québécois, called **separatists**, believe the only way to protect their culture is to separate and establish a country of their own. Others, called **federalists**, feel that it is important to resolve the issues so that Quebec can remain a part of Canada. So far, both times the people of Quebec have voted on the issue of separation, the majority have rejected independence.

This 1916 drawing by Henri Julien was adopted as a symbol by extreme separatists in Quebec in the 1970s.

People have debated this issue for many years and continue to do so in both English and French Canada. Most Canadians have an opinion one way or the other. Take a look in your local newspaper and watch the evening newscast for the latest details. Very often, you will find the issue under discussion.

The Atlantic Colonies

In the Atlantic colonies, the struggle for reform was not as bitter as in Upper and Lower Canada. Nevertheless, in each colony, the real power controlling the government rested in the hands of a small, influential group who worked closely with the governor. Gradually, Reformers were elected to the Legislative Assemblies. Men like Joseph Howe in Nova Scotia, George Coles in Prince Edward Island, and Lemuel Allan Wilmot in New Brunswick worked to bring changes and pass the laws they felt people wanted. Gradually, their patience and persistence paid off. When responsible government was achieved, it came first to Nova Scotia. By the mid-1850s, New Brunswick, Prince Edward Island, and Newfoundland all enjoyed responsible government. Reform came to the Atlantic colonies without rebellion and without bloodshed.

Culture Link

Arts and Artists in Quebec

The Past

Cornelius Kreighoff 1815–1872

Kreighoff was one of the first painters to recreate on canvas the everyday lives of average French Canadians. He wanted to show the habitants at work and at play. He produced hundreds of portraits of French Canadians involved in their day-to-day activities such as working on the farm, gathering maple syrup, hunting, trapping, dancing, and socializing. Kreighoff was also an accomplished landscape artist who captured the beauty of the Quebec countryside. In addition, he was commissioned to paint the portraits of a number of important individuals in the province.

Emma Albani 1847–1930

Emma Albani was the first French Canadian woman to achieve international fame. She was born in Chambly, Quebec. Albani was a talented soprano. She spent much of her career singing and performing in opera houses around the world. She made her first appearance on stage in Italy in 1869 and went on to star in productions in London, Paris, and New York. Although she worked most of the time in Europe, Albani was well known and extremely popular in her native country. On her Canadian tours, she was treated like a celebrity. She stayed at the prime minister's private residence and the Canadian Pacific Railway reserved a special car for her exclusive use.

Calixa Lavallée 1842–1891

Calixa Lavallée was born at Verchères, Quebec. As a child, he demonstrated remarkable musical talent. When he grew up, he turned his love of music into a career as a composer and performer. Lavallée played a variety of instruments. He wrote music for bands and orchestras and composed several comic operas.

In 1880, he wrote the music to accompany a poem written by Sir Adolphe-Basile Routhier. "O Canada!" was first performed in 1880. It officially became Canada's national anthem in 1980, 100 years after its debut performance.

Emma Albani has been commemorated with a monument at her birthplace in Chambly, a street named after her in Montreal, and a postage stamp.

Félicité Angers
1845–1924

Félicité Angers was Quebec's first female novelist. She started to write historical novels in the 1870s using the name Laure Conan. At that time, it was not common for women to write and be published. She published nine works.

Anne Hébert
1916–2000

Anne Hébert was a poet, playwright, and novelist. She became one of Canada's best-known writers. Her most celebrated novel, *Kamouraska* (1970), won the prestigious French literary award, the Prix de Libraires, and was later made into a motion picture. Hébert was made a member of the Royal Society of Canada in 1960, was awarded three Governor General's awards for literature, and was a finalist for the Giller Prize for her last novel, *Am I Disturbing You?*

The Present

Artists and the arts have always been an integral part of Quebec culture. Musically, the province is home to a number of successful recording artists. Some Francophone artists, like Céline Dion, have successfully crossed over into the English language market. In the world of classical music, the Montreal Symphony Orchestra has toured extensively throughout the world. The Montreal Opera mounts several productions each season.

Quebec has a lively theatre scene. Its playwrights are known for their originality and bold experimentation. One of the best known playwrights is Michel Tremblay. He is known for his innovative approaches, his portrayal of characters somewhat out of step with the rest of society, and his use of Québécois street language (*joual*).

Quebec is also the home base of the Cirque du Soleil, a circus troupe that combines elements of music, dance, theatre, and acrobatic stunts in its spectacular performances.

In recent years, Quebec films and filmmakers have begun to receive a great deal of attention within Canada and abroad. In the 1980s, Denis Arcand produced two popular and award-winning films. The arts in Quebec support the continuation of the province's distinct culture and provide a vehicle for communicating with the English-speaking world.

The Cirque du Soleil is world renowned for its unique acrobatics.

1. In what ways do you think Quebec art and Québécois artists are similar to art and artists in the rest of the country? In what ways are they unique?

2. In your opinion, why do the arts of Quebec and the Québécois have an important place in the Canadian identity?

Activities

Understanding Concepts

1. Add the following words to your personal dictionary.

Patriote	Château Clique	Ninety-Two Resolutions
exile	distinct society	Les Fils de la Liberté
separatist	federalist	

2. What were the causes of discontent in Lower Canada that led to the outbreak of rebellion in 1837? Were the reasons for discontent similar to those in Upper Canada? How were they different? Using an organizer, compare the rebellions in Upper and Lower Canada. Consider items such as the causes, key participants, main issues, conflicts, and outcomes.

3. What part did the British government and the Château Clique play in causing the rebellion in Lower Canada? Explain your answer.

4. Why did many Patriotes refuse to take up arms against the government?

Digging Deeper

5. **DISCUSS/CREATE** If you had lived in Lower Canada in 1837, on which side would you have fought in the rebellion? Why? Create a poster expressing your position. Imagine that the poster will be seen and read throughout the colony.

Making New Connections

6. **PREDICT** An interesting historical exercise is to play the "What if" game. "What if" Mackenzie and his supporters had moved against Toronto at the exact same time as the outbreak of rebellion in Lower Canada?
   - Would the British have diverted a large portion of their troops back to Upper Canada?
   - If the British had done so, would the French Canadian revolutionaries have had a greater chance of victory?
   - Would the history of the rebellion have turned out differently?
   - Would the history of Canada have been different?

   In groups, discuss the possibilities and present your ideas on what might have happened.

7. **INVESTIGATE** Discuss which causes of discontent in Lower Canada in 1837 are still creating unrest in Quebec today. Start a collection of newspaper or magazine articles about modern Quebec that shows why some people in that province are unhappy today.

8. **RESEARCH** During the fighting at Saint-Eustache, Dr. Jean-Olivier Chénier, a Patriote leader, leaped from a church window and died fighting the government troops. After the battle, the government troops cut out Chénier's heart and displayed it in a tavern for several days. In the October Crisis of 1970 in Quebec, the FLQ (Front de Libération du Québec) members who kidnapped and killed Pierre Laporte called themselves the "Chénier cell" after Dr. Chénier.

    Do some further research on the FLQ crisis. Suggest reasons why the FLQ members might name themselves after Dr. Jean-Olivier Chénier.

9. **DISCUSS** In what ways did the rebellions in Upper and Lower Canada resemble the American Revolution? In what ways did they differ?

At Last, Britain Will Act

LORD DURHAM TO CANADA

London, England, 1838

At last, the British government is going to do something about the colonies in North America.

For years, the colonists in Upper and Lower Canada have been complaining about the way they are governed. Until now, Britain has chosen to ignore their complaints, but it can no longer sit back and do nothing. Recent armed rebellions in both colonies have shown that it is time to act.

Why would the people of Upper and Lower Canada take up arms against the colonial government? It must be that they are desperate. Britain must do something about this situation.

Today, the British government has asked Lord Durham to go to Canada and report on the troubles. He is also to suggest needed reforms. Durham will hold the rank of governor general and high commissioner of British North America.

The appointment of Lord Durham is welcome news. Durham is well known in Britain as a reformer. Although he belongs to the wealthy class, he has supported reforms that would improve conditions for working people. Because of his political views, he has been nicknamed "Radical Jack."

Let him get on with the job of making his report!

After the rebellions, the Tories and the Reformers were more divided than ever, and the two parties became increasingly suspicious of each other's motives. This poster, written by an opponent of Reform, portrays the Reformers as dangerous revolutionaries who resent British authority in the colonies.

ELECTORS
BEWARE!!

THE late "Reform Alliance Society" now sailing under new Colours, with the title of the "Constitutional Reform Society." lately put forth a Document in the Columns of the Correspondent & Advocate, addressed to "their brother Reformers in Upper Canada. This Document was afterwards sent forth in PAMPHLET shape, to distant parts of the Province. Now mark the base conduct pursued on this occasion !! The PAMPHLET contains a most ATROCIOUS PARAGRAPH in allusion to the Lieutenant Governor, which DID NOT make its appearance in the Correspondent & Advocate. The PAMPHLET was sent by thousands ABROAD, where it was no doubt hoped it would escape detection, and at the same time work upon the passions and prejudices of the unwary, into whose hands it might fall.

ELECTORS Beware! be on your guard against REVOLUTIONISTS in the garb of REFORMERS.

The atrocious Paragraph in the Pamphlet is this—speaking of the Lieutenant Governor it says :—

" He betrays the chilling belief, that as the U.
" E. Loyalists shed the blood of their friends &
" kindred to prevent the United States from ac-
" quiring their Independence, they will now e-
" ven in their old age stain our country with our
" blood, to prevent our retaining what Governor
" Simcoe announced to them as the reward of
" their suffering Loyalty !!"

Signed by— T. D. MORRISON M. P. P. Mayor, PRESIDENT,
JOHN McINTOSH M. P. P. VICE-PRESIDENT,
J. E. TIMS, M. D } SECRETARIES.
T. PARSONS }

ELECTORS! Will any honest, candid, reasonable man among you, justify, or in any way uphold such diabolical language being applied to the King's Representative ? Can you conceive any thing more atrocious !!! Or can you believe that a greater prostitution was ever made of the official signature of a Member of Parliament—the Mayor of a City—and the President of a Society, calling themselves REFORMERS !!! Does it not rather look like the language of angry, disappointed, discontented men, who would play upon your passions, to goad you on to *Revolution !!!*

Beware of these men, and of all like them! are they worthy of your confidence ! give your answer at the Hustings !!

A CONSTITUTIONALIST.

Profile

John George Lambton, Lord Durham 1792–1840

During Lord Durham's stay in British North America, he studied the situation in the Canadas very closely. His task was to suggest the best solutions to the problems he identified.

John George Lambton, Lord Durham, was born on 12 April 1792 in England. At the age of 21, he was elected to the House of Commons. In 1835, he was appointed British ambassador to Russia, a post that he held for two years. Following the rebellions in Upper and Lower Canada, the British government asked Lord Durham to go to Canada. His assignment was to find out what was troubling the Canadians and to make a report to the British government. Durham was given considerable powers. He was named governor general and high commissioner of British North America.

Lord Durham brought with him six secretaries and eight aides as well as silver and china for elaborate dinners, a grand piano, horses, and the people needed to take care of them. Two days after arriving in Quebec, Lord Durham paraded through the streets mounted on a white horse.

One of the first decisions Lord Durham made was what to do with the political prisoners from the rebellion in Lower Canada. Most were pardoned. However, Papineau and 15 other Patriotes who had fled to the United States were forbidden to return to Canada under penalty of death. Eight other Patriotes were banished to Bermuda. When news of the banishment reached England, Durham's action was disallowed. This angered Lord Durham. He resigned as governor general later in 1838 because he felt the British government was not supporting him.

Although Durham was in Canada for less than six months, he worked very hard. He set up commissions of inquiry and submitted his famous report in February 1839. He did not take part in the debate about his ideas for Canada that followed the arrival of his report. Lord Durham died of tuberculosis in July 1840.

1. Do you agree with Durham's decision to banish some of the rebels? Explain.
2. If you were a Reformer, how optimistic would you be about the prospect for change under Durham's leadership?
3. Knowing what you do about Lord Durham and the situation he faced, what recommendations do you think he might make in his report?

Lord Durham's Report

After the rebellions in Upper and Lower Canada, the British government realized that something had to be done. As the government's representative, Lord Durham set to work to find out as much about British North America as he could. He spent most of his time at the governor's residence in Quebec, studying the causes of the rebellions. He wanted to listen to both sides. He sent officials throughout both colonies to talk with ordinary people in the towns and with settlers in the backwoods. Durham also talked to delegates from the Atlantic colonies about his idea for a union of all the British North American colonies, but they showed little interest.

Durham spent less than two weeks in Upper Canada, much of it at Niagara Falls. However, he went to Toronto in person to talk to the Baldwins and other Reformers who had been struggling for better government in the colony. William and Robert Baldwin believed that responsible government was the only solution to the problems in Upper Canada. They thought the governor should be required to choose his advisors for the Executive Council from the party that held the most seats in the elected Assembly. The Baldwins argued that since this was the way things were already done in Britain, the colonies should also have the same kind of responsible government.

Durham's Recommendations

After only five months in British North America, Lord Durham thought he understood the troubles of the colonies. When he returned to England, he wrote the famous **Durham Report** for the British government. In the report, Lord Durham made two main recommendations. The first was that the two colonies of Upper and Lower Canada should be joined to create the province of Canada. The second recommendation was that responsible government should be granted to British North America. Lord Durham suggested that the advisors to the governor should be chosen from the largest party in the Assembly elected by the citizens of the colony. Thus, the governor would have to be ready to sign all the bills passed in the Assembly.

Lord Durham made other suggestions, some of which were carried out. He recommended

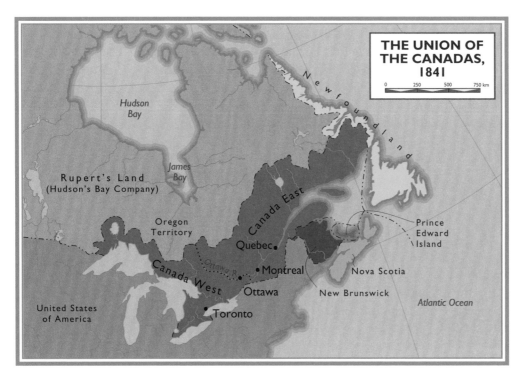

THE UNION OF THE CANADAS, 1841

that the Anglican Church should have no more privileges than any other Protestant church. He suggested that the colonies should be allowed to manage their own affairs. The British government should only be responsible for certain things, such as the defence of the colonies. He also suggested that, some day, all of the British North American colonies might be joined together.

Reactions to the Report

The Reformers in Upper Canada welcomed many of Lord Durham's ideas. However, his comments about French Canada antagonized the French Canadians. Durham had decided that the trouble in Lower Canada had been caused by conflict between the French and English because each group wanted a different way of life. "Two nations warring in the bosom of a single state" is the now-famous phrase he used to describe what he observed. He believed that the situation would continue until the French Canadians were made to speak English and live like the English. But Durham seriously underestimated how much the French Canadians treasured their language and way of life. He failed to understand how deeply they cared about their customs and traditions.

The British government did not accept much of Lord Durham's report. However, it did accept his first recommendation. The government decided to unite Upper and Lower Canada by the **Act of Union** in 1841. Upper Canada became known as Canada West. Lower Canada was renamed Canada East. The new government first met at Kingston and then the capital was moved to Montreal.

Lord Durham's recommendation for responsible government was not granted until 1848. By that time, British trade policy was changing. The colonies were no longer as important for trade. Britain was pursuing trade with many different countries, not just with its colonies. As a result, Britain began to loosen its connections with its colonies and the British

government was more open to the idea of allowing the colonies to govern themselves.

Opposition to the Act of Union

Most people in Canada West were happy about the Act of Union. Among other things, it meant that the debts Canada West owed would now be shared with Canada East. Also, the United Canadas could raise tariffs, bringing in more revenue. However, French Canadians were angry. They felt that the Act favoured the English. Even though Canada East had a larger population, Canada East and Canada West would have the same number of elected representatives. The Act also decreed that English was to be the only official language of the country. French Canadians feared that this policy would encourage more English immigration to Canada East. If this happened, French Canadians would soon be reduced to a minority.

In Canada East, the people demanded the abolition of the Act. French-Canadian politicians like Louis-Hippolyte LaFontaine

Robert Baldwin and Louis-Hippolyte LaFontaine

In 1841, after the Union was proclaimed, Louis-Hippolyte LaFontaine ran for election in Canada East. On election day, his supporters were prevented from voting by a gang who opposed him. LaFontaine lost the election. In the meantime, Robert Baldwin was elected in two ridings in Canada West. He invited LaFontaine to run in a by-election in one of the ridings. LaFontaine campaigned in Toronto and won with a majority. The gesture by Baldwin won the Reformers much goodwill in Lower Canada. Baldwin and LaFontaine demonstrated that French and English Canadians could work together to resolve their common problems.

stressed the importance of keeping the French language vital in Canada East, even under the Act, but French was not given status as an official language until 1867.

The Arrival of Lord Elgin

In 1846, a new governor general was appointed for Canada. He was Lord Elgin, the son-in-law of Lord Durham. Elgin agreed with Lord Durham's idea that the colonies should be allowed to govern themselves. He believed in responsible government.

In the election of 1848, more Reformers than Tories were elected to the Assembly. Therefore, Lord Elgin asked the Reform leaders, Robert Baldwin (Canada West) and Louis-Hippolyte LaFontaine (Canada East), to recommend which elected officials should advise him. Of course, they chose members of their Reform party to sit on the Council. Lord Elgin promised that he would take their advice as long as the Reform party had the most members elected in the Assembly. Responsible government had arrived!

Lord Elgin proved himself an honourable statesman in his years as governor general of Canada.

Montreal, mid-1800s. Lord Elgin arrived in Montreal on 30 January 1847.

The Rebellion Losses Bill

A showdown came in 1849 with the **Rebellion Losses Bill**. This bill proposed that a large amount of money should be paid to the people in the former Lower Canada whose property had been damaged during the rebellion. They would be reimbursed for damage to their homes, barns, fences, livestock, wagons, and other personal property. The Tories voted against the bill. They feared that rebels, as well as Loyalists, would be paid for the losses they suffered during the rebellion. The Tories called it "a reward for those who rebelled." Since the Reform party had the largest number of supporters in the Assembly, the Tories were outvoted. The bill was passed. It was then sent to Lord Elgin to be signed into law.

Lord Elgin's Dilemma

In his carriage on the way to the Assembly, Lord Elgin considered an important decision he would have to make. He knew he would be asked to approve the Rebellion Losses Bill and make it law. He did not think the bill was wise, but the government of Baldwin and LaFontaine favoured it. The elected representatives of the people had passed it in the Assembly. Should the governor general make it a law by signing his name to it?

The Tories were violently opposed to the bill. Their leader had pointed out very strongly to Lord Elgin that there should be "no reward for rebels." Furthermore, the Tory leader warned that if Lord Elgin did sign the bill, more violence could break out.

What should the governor general do? He was following the advice of the leaders who had a majority of supporters in the Assembly. But the thought of violence was disturbing. Lord Elgin's wife, Mary, was about to give birth. According to her doctor, she and the baby were in some danger. Complete quiet was essential. Suppose a mob were to attack the governor's mansion? On the other hand, Mary was the daughter of Lord Durham, who had originally suggested self-government for the colonies. Lady Mary supported the ideas of her father and urged her husband to sign the bill. What should Lord Elgin do?

Lord Elgin (centre) was married to Lord Durham's daughter, Mary (right). Mary supported her father's ideas about self-government in the colonies and urged her husband to sign the Rebellion Losses Bill despite the potential danger her family might face.

Skill Building: Making Decisions

Your school has been vandalized. The computer lab was torn apart and expensive equipment was destroyed. The principal has asked that anyone with information should report it to the office. You and some of your friends know a person who was involved. What are you going to do? On the one hand, you are upset about the damage because you enjoy spending time in the computer lab and you are proud of your school. On the other hand, you really do not want to get another person into a lot of trouble. You will have to make a decision.

Decision making is the process of choosing the best alternative to solve a problem or answer a question. Here are some basic steps you can follow to help you make a sound decision.

Key Steps

1. Clarify the decision to be made.
State the problem as a question.
Should we report the information to the principal?

2. Examine the alternatives.
Brainstorm as many alternatives as possible.
• report directly to the principal
• send an anonymous note
• phone Crimestoppers
• don't "squeal" on your friend
• phone the police

3. Gather information about alternatives and eliminate some.
Which alternatives are not feasible or possible?

4. Evaluate remaining alternatives.
• What are the advantages and disadvantages of each?
• What is important to you?
• What do you believe to be true? (**beliefs**)
• What are your important personal standards? (**values**)
• What are the possible consequences?
• If we decide to send the anonymous note:
  - Will the principal or the police come looking for us?
  - Will our handwriting be recognized?
  - Will anyone believe what we say?
  - Will we feel like cowards afterwards?
  - Will we be proud of what we have done?
  - How will we feel if the person is charged?
  - What will our parents think of our action if they find out?
  - What will our friends think of our action?

5. Decide which alternative is best.
Which alternative is the best answer to the original question?

6. Make your decision.
• What decision have you arrived at?
• What are you going to do?

7. Evaluate the decision.
• Is this the best decision?
• Should any part be reconsidered?

Try It!
Use this decision-making model to help you decide what you would have done if you were Lord Elgin. Would you have signed the Rebellion Losses Bill? Go through each step. After you hold a class discussion, read on and discover what Lord Elgin decided to do.

Lord Elgin's Decision

When the bill was handed to him, Lord Elgin signed it immediately. The Rebellion Losses Bill became law. What happened next was recorded by an eyewitness named Rufus Seaver in a letter to his wife.

The Montreal parliament. In 1844, Montreal was made capital of the United Province of Canada. The parliament building was burned down in 1849.

Montreal
25 April 1849

My dear wife:

I'll attempt to give you an account of what I am doing and what other people are doing, for great things have been talked of today. I begin by saying that I am glad you and the children are not here, for we are on the eve of another rebellion ... It was rumoured that the Rebellion Losses Bill was to be signed. The report spread through town like wildfire. An immense mob assembled and surrounded Parliament to see what the Governor intended to do. When it was finally announced that he had signed the bill, there was trouble.

As his Excellency the Governor left Parliament, he was struck with stones and eggs thrown by thousands of people. His carriage windows were broken, but by the speed of his horses, he was able to escape with no injury except to his carriage.

I stop here, for the cry is raised that Parliament is on fire ... From my door, I can see the red flames lighting up the heavens–I go–more news after I see what the fuss is about.

26 April 1849
It is too true. Last night, at about eight o'clock, while Parliament was still sitting, a mob assembled and commenced the destruction of the building by breaking windows. (It can be called nothing but a mob, though composed of some of our most worthy Tory citizens.) Soon the doors were broken open and ... fires were lit in a dozen places ... Members barely escaped with their lives.

Your affectionate husband,
Rufus Seaver

After the Fire

As Lord Elgin drove into Montreal five days later, he was once again attacked by Tories. In 1837, it had been just the other way around. Tories had supported Governor Bond Head in putting down the rebels. Now Tories were attacking the British governor!

Lord Elgin twice risked his life by facing angry mobs. He did so to carry out the wishes of the elected representatives of the people and to give them responsible government. His carriage was badly damaged by rocks and bricks but Lord Elgin never had it fixed. He wanted people to see it and remember at what cost responsible government had been won.

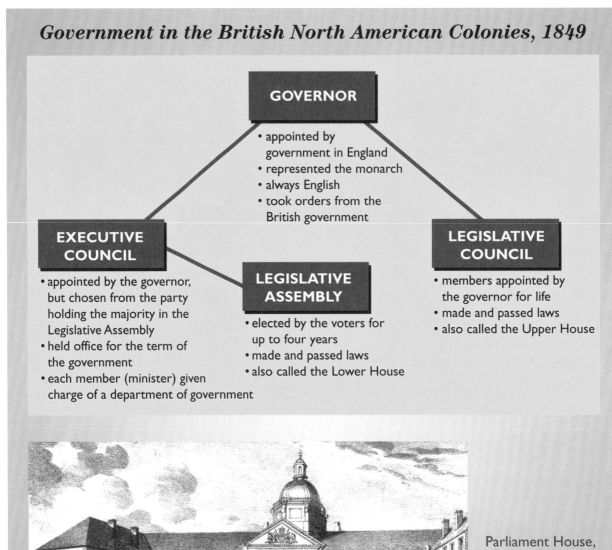

Government in the British North American Colonies, 1849

GOVERNOR
- appointed by government in England
- represented the monarch
- always English
- took orders from the British government

EXECUTIVE COUNCIL
- appointed by the governor, but chosen from the party holding the majority in the Legislative Assembly
- held office for the term of the government
- each member (minister) given charge of a department of government

LEGISLATIVE ASSEMBLY
- elected by the voters for up to four years
- made and passed laws
- also called the Lower House

LEGISLATIVE COUNCIL
- members appointed by the governor for life
- made and passed laws
- also called the Upper House

Parliament House, Quebec City. After the burning of the parliament building in Montreal, the Assembly met in Toronto until 1851 and then in Quebec until 1854.

Fast Forward

Responsible Government Today

Today, the Executive Council is made up of the prime minister and the Cabinet. The **prime minister** is the leader of the political party that wins the most seats in the House of Commons. The prime minister chooses key members of his or her political party to help govern the country. These men and women become Cabinet ministers. They are appointed to the Executive Council by the governor general on the recommendation of the prime minister. The prime minister and the Cabinet ministers are the most powerful people in government. They decide on government policy and make sure that these policies are carried out. If the Cabinet loses the support of the majority of the members of the House of Commons, it must resign. In other words, the government must be responsible to the wishes of the elected members of parliament.

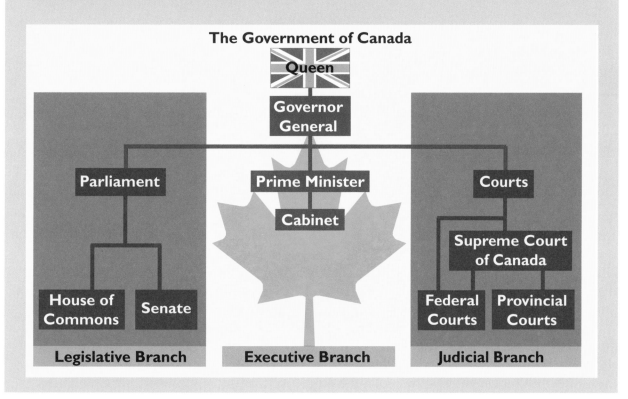

British North America— From Coast to Coast

Other parts of British North America were also undergoing changes during the 1800s. The prairies were finally being settled; the ownership of the Pacific coast was being disputed; Newfoundland fishermen felt increasingly independent from Britain; Prince Edward Island was becoming important for its shipbuilding and farming industries; and the diverse communities in New Brunswick and Nova Scotia were slowly developing their own unique identities. Meanwhile, exploration to the unknown northern reaches of the country was beginning again.

In the West

In the early 1800s, there were no farms west of Upper Canada. Fur trading and exploration

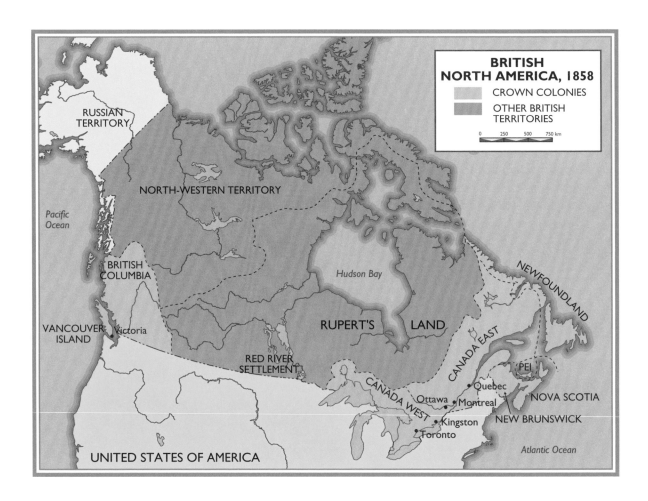

were the only European pursuits in this vast region. Most of the Aboriginal peoples relied on hunting and fishing for food. On the prairies, the buffalo hunt was essential to their livelihood.

In 1812, early European settlement of the West got under way. It had a major impact on the lives of those who were already living there. The first settlement was located in the southern part of present-day Manitoba. Lord Selkirk, who established the settlement, hoped to provide a place for poor Scottish farmers to make a better life for themselves. Unfortunately, the settlers were unprepared for the harsh winters, and they found the prairie soil hard to plow. They faced conflict with the Aboriginal peoples who resented the threat to their traditional buffalo hunting grounds. They knew that if the prairie was used for agriculture, their way of life would disappear.

Eventually, more settlers immigrated to the West from the Canadas. The land was plowed and the farms were improved. Ultimately, the settlers proved that farming on the prairies could be successful. Once the cross-country railroad was built later in the century, the full benefits of this vast western resource started to be tapped.

On the Pacific Coast

Until the 19th century, the central part of the Pacific coast was disputed territory. After the War of 1812, the 49th parallel was established as the boundary between British North America and the United States. However, this boundary applied only to the land east of the Rockies. Both Britain and the United States claimed the coastal region north of California.

• In the 1820s, both countries established settlements in the Pacific Northwest.

St. John's, Newfoundland, mid-1800s. Fishing boats can be seen in the background of this picture of a small, but growing, town.

- In 1827, the Hudson's Bay Company founded Fort Langley on the Fraser River, near present-day Vancouver.
- In 1843–1844, the Hudson's Bay Company built Fort Victoria at the southern tip of Vancouver Island. It was the first regular outpost of British government west of Upper Canada. In 1849, it was proclaimed the capital of a new crown colony named Vancouver Island.
- In 1846, the 49th parallel boundary was extended all the way to the Pacific Ocean. The lines for future settlement were drawn.

In Newfoundland

Until about 1780, Newfoundland's population consisted mostly of seasonal cod fishermen operating from Europe. But conflicts such as the American Revolution and the wars between Britain and France disrupted the cod trade, and the European-run fishery began to collapse.

Many fishermen helped support themselves by cultivating vegetable gardens and keeping some livestock. More women and children were brought over to live in Newfoundland and permanent settlement increased. By 1800, 90% of the summer population consisted of permanent residents. Britain noticed that Newfoundland looked more like a colony than a seasonal fishery. As the fishermen became more self-sufficient and independent, they felt less responsible to their European employers. In 1817, Britain finally gave Newfoundland a full-time governor and, in 1832, a council and assembly.

St. John's became the island's commercial centre. **Outports** (fishing settlements) cropped up along the coast, but all trade went through St. John's. As the century progressed, the outposts became better able to support themselves. As a result, they became more isolated. Newfoundland society was family-based, local, and traditional. The homes were modest and

Newfoundland Enters Confederation

Newfoundland was granted responsible government around the same time as its fellow Atlantic colonies. But unlike them, Newfoundland did not join Confederation in 1867 or in the years immediately following.

Newfoundland remained self-governing until serious economic problems in the 1930s forced the Newfoundland government to seek help from Britain. An appointed commission was set up by the British to govern Newfoundland. Responsible government would not return to Newfoundland until it joined Canada in 1949.

When Newfoundland joined Confederation, many people worried that it would lose its distinctive character. This has not occurred. In 1999, the 50th anniversary of Newfoundland's entry into Confederation was a cause for celebration within the province and throughout Canada.

the lifestyle included few luxuries. When there were rough times for the fishery, poverty was common. There was little incentive for the development of other industries and no demand for roads to inland areas. Farming was not profitable. As a result, the lives of Newfoundlanders remained tied to the fishery.

In Nova Scotia

By the mid-1800s, Nova Scotia was a growing area with a diverse history. The first European settlers in Nova Scotia had been the Acadians. Although they were expelled by the British in 1755, many later returned to Nova Scotia. Since their farms had been given to British settlers, they purchased new land and rebuilt their farms. The Acadians overcame many obstacles to stay in Nova Scotia and have worked hard to preserve their heritage and their culture.

The colony was also home to many families who were descended from Loyalist refugees. These refugees had fled the United States during the American Revolution. Black Loyalists, freed slaves, and Caribbean immigrants had built towns in Nova Scotia. In the early 1800s, people from England, Scotland, Ireland, Germany and Switzerland settled in the colony of Nova Scotia, which means "New Scotland." The growing economy was built around fishing, boat building, logging, farming, and the busy seaport in Halifax.

In New Brunswick

By 1810, Saint John was a commercial town with 3000 inhabitants. But Fredericton, the capital, was little more than a village. All the settlements were surrounded by forest. Although there were a few well-tended farms and dwellings, most were still very rustic. The population of the colony included Acadians who had been the first European settlers, Aboriginal peoples, Loyalists, other American immigrants, and some recent arrivals from the British Isles. The people were heavily concentrated in the Saint John valley.

A small number of wealthy people enjoyed many luxuries, but everyday life for the average settler was challenging. Clearing the dense New Brunswick forests was extremely difficult and time consuming. The settlements were isolated from each other because of the lack of roads. Observers from Britain noted that the customs of the settlers were more American than British. By this, they were implying a lack of refinement and sophistication. Even with these differences, there was a strong sense of community among the settlers, who would gladly help others in need.

In Prince Edward Island

Although Prince Edward Island once had a large French-speaking population, their numbers were greatly reduced by the expulsion of the Acadians in 1755. Most of the settlers in the early 1800s were English, Irish, or Scottish. The island was divided into 67 townships that were given to wealthy landlords in Britain. These landlords were expected to pay rent to the British government and to send settlers to the island. The settlers, in turn, rented land from the landlords. They often had to work for many years before their farms became profitable. Many of the landlords did not pay their rent, so the government did not have enough money to build roads and towns. The settlers had to work hard to create a colony by themselves.

By 1805, the population of Prince Edward Island was 7000. The farmers played an important role in the Atlantic colonies. Their surplus produce was exported to other parts of British North America and to countries overseas. In addition, many skilled carpenters, sailmakers, and blacksmiths found work building ships. By

the 1830s, Prince Edward Island had more than 200 shipyards.

In the North

Ever since the early days of European exploration, a northern commercial route to Asia had been sought. In the 19th century, various explorers were still trying to unlock the secrets of the far north and to find the fabled Northwest Passage. One, Sir John Franklin, surveyed about 1600 km of the northern Arctic coast, starting at the mouth of the Mackenzie River. In 1845, he set out again, this time in search of the Passage. Unfortunately, his ship became trapped in the Arctic ice and he never returned. His efforts and those of the other explorers greatly increased European knowledge of this vast and forbidding region.

The *H.M.S. Investigator*, shown here caught in Arctic waters, was one of several ships that went in search of Sir John Franklin.

British North America, 1849 to the 1860s

In the middle of the century, responsible government arrived in Britain's Atlantic colonies: Nova Scotia in 1848, Prince Edward Island in 1851, New Brunswick in 1854, and Newfoundland in 1844. The granting of responsible government set the stage for new developments in all the provinces.

When Lord Elgin signed the Rebellion Losses Bill, many of the English-speaking people of Canada East thought that the French were being given too much influence over the colony and the government. Some people thought Canada would be better off if it became a part of the United States. In October 1849, English language newspapers in Montreal printed the **Manifesto of the Annexation Association**. This document supported the American annexation of British North America. In 1850, people in Canada West who agreed with this notion formed the Toronto Annexation Association. The annexation movement was most popular in Montreal. But it never really took hold. The lack of support was partly because the economy started to improve and partly because the Americans did not express much interest in expanding north.

Gradually, the Canadas developed a closer relationship with the United States. In 1854, Britain signed a treaty that allowed for **free trade** between British North American colonies and the United States. Free trade meant that tariffs (duties) would no longer have to be paid on natural products such as

Montreal was the largest city in British North America in the mid-1800s. Its increasing population and prosperity as a centre for trade pointed the way to the expansion of commerce and industry as driving forces in Canada's future.

Fast Forward

Free Trade Agreements

The federal government continues to negotiate free trade agreements with other countries. In 1993, the North American Free Trade Agreement (NAFTA) was passed. It eliminated tariffs between Canada, Mexico, and the United States on a variety of goods. In 1997, an agreement with Chile was signed. This agreement removed duties on many Canadian agricultural products, such as wheat, canola oil, and lentils, and various Chilean agricultural products, such as fresh fruits, beef, and wine. In 1997, a trade agreement with Israel was implemented. Tariffs have been eliminated on certain Canadian exports, such as wheat and beef, and Israeli exports, such as cut flowers and some fresh fruit and vegetables.

timber, grain, coal, livestock, and fish. As a result, it would be much easier to transport goods across the border. Also, a growing demand for Canadian products in the United States increased trade between the two countries. The goods were needed to construct American buildings, such as houses and factories, and to feed the large numbers of people living in the cities.

In the 1850s and 1860s, the railway became the major form of transportation. Travel across Canada and to the United States became easier. Four main railways were constructed in the 1850s, linking major cities in Canada and the United States. At the time it was completed, one of the railways, the 1760 km Grand Trunk Railway, was the longest in the world.

Looking Back, Looking Ahead

You have read the story of the foundations of the country known today as "Canada." The earliest settlements were those of Aboriginal peoples. Thousands of years before the arrival of Europeans, Aboriginal peoples had built strong civilizations in every region. Then, the French, and later the British, established their own settlements in this part of North America. These three cultures, Aboriginal, French, and British, were the foundations on which the Canadian nation would be built. Eventually, the founding cultures were joined by people from every corner of the globe. All these cultures were woven into what we proudly call Canada's multicultural heritage.

Although the process of growth was not always smooth, people faced the challenges they encountered with a strong sense of purpose. They used the country's rich natural resources to build thriving communities. By the 1860s, the British North American colonies were ready to join together to form a prosperous, democratic nation.

Our history shows us how the people and events of the past continue to influence the present. Many of the issues we read about in the newspapers have their roots in the early years of the country. Understanding where we come from and how we got here helps us navigate our way into the future.

Activities

Understanding Concepts

1. Add the following new words to your personal dictionary.

Durham Report	Rebellion Losses Bill	Act of Union
decision making	beliefs	values
outport	free trade	prime minister
Manifesto of the Annexation Association		

2. Why was Lord Durham chosen to investigate the problems in the two Canadas?

3. What were the two main recommendations of the Durham Report? How and when did the British government respond to these recommendations? Why do you think they did not act on Durham's other suggestions right away?

4. Why was the signing of the Rebellion Losses Bill a dilemma for Lord Elgin?

5. Describe how the organization of government has changed from 1837 to 1849 to the present. What do you feel is most significant about these differences in how our country is governed? Tell why you think so.

Digging Deeper

6. **DISCUSS** What would be the reaction of the following groups to the recommendations made by Lord Durham?
   - Tories in Upper and Lower Canada
   - French-speaking people in Lower Canada
   - English-speaking people in Lower Canada
   - Reformers in Upper and Lower Canada
   - Protestants other than Anglicans in Upper Canada

7. **THINK/WRITE** Suppose the year is 1850 and you are living in Canada West. Your cousin from the United States is visiting you. She is interested in politics and has heard about the rebellion and the changes it has brought. She asks you and your family how things are different now that there is responsible government. Explain in your own words the changes that have occurred in government since the rebellion. Refer to the charts on pages 302 and 303 to help with your answer.

8. **COMPARE** Develop an organizer to compare the rebellions in Upper and Lower Canada. Use the following criteria in your comparison:
   * causes of discontent
   * leadership
   * support from the people
   * battles fought (won or lost)
   * results in government—for the leaders, for the participants, and for the people of the Canadas

9. **CREATE** Create a mural depicting the mob attack on the Parliament Buildings and the burning of the buildings.

Making New Connections

10. **ANALYZE/WRITE** In what ways were the rebellions of 1837 a military failure but a political success?

11. **DISCUSS** Hold a class discussion on this topic: "Were the rebels justified in taking up arms against the official government?" Here are some questions to guide your discussion.
    * Why do people rebel or riot against a government? Think of recent uprisings you have heard about or seen news reports on.
    * What are the advantages and disadvantages of using violence?
    * What methods could people use instead of violence?
    * Is there any form of government you would feel strongly enough to fight against?
    * Would you be prepared to risk your life to bring about a change in government? Why or why not?

12. **INVESTIGATE** Free trade agreements create a great deal of discussion among people. Conduct a survey of a variety of adults you know to find out their opinions about NAFTA and other free trade agreements. Check the newspaper, books, and the Internet for information about this issue. Then, write a report that summarizes how people feel about free trade and why they think as they do.

13. **THINK/WRITE** Read the following statements carefully. Choose the one that comes closest to describing your point of view about using rebellion to bring about change. Write a short paragraph to explain your viewpoint.
    * Citizens are entitled to rebel against their government if they don't like what that government is doing.
    * Citizens can rebel against the government only as a last resort.
    * Citizens never have the right to take up arms against the government.

Credits

Every effort has been made to trace the original source of text material and photographs contained in this book. Where the attempt has been unsuccessful, the publisher would be pleased to hear from copyright holders to rectify any omissions.

Close-Up Canada Cover credits
front cover, clockwise from top left: Cincinnati Art Museum/Subscription Ford Purchase/Webber/1927.26; NAC/C-073717(S); NAC/C-002774; Artist Claude Picard/originals displayed at Grand Pré National Historic Site;

back cover, (top) C.W. Jefferys/NAC/C-10687/Courtesy of the C.W. Jefferys Estate, Toronto; (centre) Hudson's Bay Company Archives, Provincial Archives of Manitoba; (bottom) National Gallery of Canada, Ottawa

Photo Credits

CMC= Canadian Museum of Civilization
MTL= Metro Toronto Library
NAC= National Archives of Canada
T.R.C.A.= The Toronto Region and Conservation Authority

1 NAC C10521 **5** (top) Richard Harrington/NAC 129589 source: www.canadianheritage.ca (centre) © Canada Post Corporation 1975. Reproduced with permission (bottom) Glenbow Archives, Calgary, Canada ND24-44 **6** courtesy of the artist Arnold Jacobs-Two Turtle Studio **7** (left) CMC S92-4407 (right) Royal British Columbia Museum P242 **8** (top) B.C. Archives F08990 (bottom) Mark Gallant/Canapress **9** (top) CMC S77-1819 (centre) CMC S96-6252 (bottom) CMC S91-6171 **10** The Granger Collection, New York **11** (top) CMC CRP91 (bottom) CMC S90-640 **13** The Telegram, St. John, NFLD **15** David Étienne, d'après Leopold Massard, *Manoir de Jacques Cartier à Limoilou, près de Saint-Malo, 1858,* lithography (Musée du Québec 57.186) **16** Charles Walter Simpson NAC C13938 **18** NAC C12235 **19** (top) NAC C3686 (bottom) NAC C36288 **21** Parks Canada **23** CMC S94-13,215 **24** Nova Scotia Museum, photographer Alex Wilson, Colchester County, N.S. 1979 P113/79.313.2 **25** NAC C09711 **28** Bibliothèque nationale du Québec **29** The Granger Collection, New York **32** Thomas Kitchin/First Light **33** *Canoes in a Fog, Lake Superior, 1869,* Frances Ann Hopkins, Glenbow Collection, Calgary, Canada **34** Tara Prindle-Native Tech **36** MP-0000,1452.134 *Making a bark canoe, Murray Bay, Q.C. ca. 1868* by Alexander Henderson, McCord Museum of Canadian

History, Montreal **37** Hudson's Bay Company Archives/Provincial Archives of Manitoba 1987/363-T-37/14B (N60-97) **38** The Granger Collection, New York **39** Confederation Life Series, courtesy: Rogers Communications Inc. Photography Dick Hemingway **40** NAC C28332 **42** Archives des Ursuline de Québec **43** B. Carriere/Publiphoto **44** Marguerite Bourgeoys Museum **45, 46, 47** courtesy of Sainte-Marie Among the Hurons, Midland, Ontario **48** MTRL T-15468 source: www.canadianheritage.ca **53** The Granger Collection, New York **56** (top) Charles Huot 1929, courtesy The National Assembly at Quebec (bottom) NAC C11925 **57** (left) NAC C4506 (right) Robert J. Marrion, CN 75033, © Canadian War Museum **59** NAC C10688 Reprinted with permission of the C.W. Jefferys Estate Archive, Toronto **60** NAC C1248 **61** Confederation Life Series, courtesy: Rogers Communications Inc. Photography Dick Hemingway **63** (top) Evelyn Kedl/Les Photographes Kedl (bottom) Confederation Life Series, courtesy: Rogers Communications Inc. Photography Dick Hemingway **65** Bibliothèque nationale du Québec **69** The Granger Collection, New York **72** National Gallery of Canada, Ottawa/Purchased, 1954 #6275 **74** Notman Photographic Archive 3235/McCord Museum of Canadian History, Montreal **76** (left) Dulongpré, Louis, *Pierre Casgrain, vers 1805, oil on canvas,* Musée du Québec: 57.446 (right) Dulongpré, Louis, *Madame Pierre Casgrain, née Marie Bonenfant, vers 1805, oil on canvas,* Musée du Québec: 57.447 **78** © 1984, A26578-41 Her Majesty the Queen in Right of Canada, reproduced from the collection of the National Air Photo Library with permission of Natural Resources Canada **79** © 1973, A23616-62 Her

Majesty the Queen in Right of Canada, reproduced from the collection of the National Air Photo Library with permission of Natural Resources Canada **80** NAC C16952 **81** NAC C73589 **83** (top) NAC C73395 (bottom) Cornelius Kreighoff, *Death of a Moose*, Glenbow Collection, Calgary, Canada PN: 13294 **85** NAC C11041 **86** Photo courtesy of the Royal Ontario Museum ©ROM **87** (top) NAC C73399 (bottom) Notman Photographic Archive MP68/75, McCord Museum of Canadian History, Montreal **88** J.-C. Hurni/Publiphoto **90** (top) National Film Board of Canada (bottom) T.R.C.A. **91** Y. Hamel/Publiphoto **92** (top) NAC C4808 (bottom) Magma/Corbis SC005775 **93** Davies, Thomas: *A View of Montreal in Canada, Taken from Isle St. Helena in 1762* (#6272) National Gallery of Canada, Ottawa/Purchased, 1954 **94** (top) NAC C9673 (bottom) PAC C1540 **95** C.T. Krieghoff, Cornelius *The Habitant Farm*, Acc.#2036 National Gallery of Canada, Ottawa/Gift of Gordon C. Edwards, Ottawa, 1923, in memory of Senator and Mrs. W.C. Edwards **96** NAC C85542 **97** (top) Nova Scotia Museum (bottom) Artist Claude Picard: originals displayed at Grand Pré National Historic Site © Parks Canada **99** Nova Scotia Archives/Records Management **102** 14.86 *Radisson & Groseilliers*, F. Remington. Buffalo Bill Hisorical Centre, Cody. W.Y./Gift of Mrs. Karl Frank **103** Hudson's Bay Company Archives, Provincial Archives of Manitoba P-420 **104** Provincial Archives of Manitoba **105** *View from a Warship 1745* with permission of Lewis Parker. Courtesy of Parks Canada National Historic Sites **106** Parks Canada, Fortress of Louisbourg, 5J-3-283 **110** State Historical Society of Washington (X3) 45700 **111** Parks Canada/Dale Wilson/1994 **112** (top) *Deportation of the Acadians from the Isle of St. Jean 1758* with permission of Lewis Parker. Courtesy of Parks Canada National Historic Sites (bottom) Fred Hatfield Photo **113** (top) Fort Ticonderoga Museum (bottom) photograph courtesy of the Royal Ontario Museum, Acc.960.232.19 ©ROM **114** NAC C5907 **115** photograph courtesy of the Royal Ontario Museum, Acc.940 x 54 ©ROM **116** (top) NAC C25662 (centre) NAC C4263 (bottom) National Gallery of Canada, Ottawa/ Transfer from the Canadian War Memorial, 1921 (Gift of the 2nd Duke of Westminster, Eaton Hall, Cheshire, 1918) **117** NAC C21457 **118** M245 *Major General James Wolfe, 1759* Artist: George Townshend, watercolour on paper, McCord

Museum of Canadian History, Montreal **119** NAC C11043 **128, 129** courtesy Rogers Communications Inc. & artist Dennis Rose, photography Dick Hemingway **132** The Metropolitan Museum of Art, Gift of Mrs. Russell Sage, 1909 (10.125.103) **136** The Granger Collection, New York **139** (top) The Granger Collection, New York (bottom) *Invasion of Canada* by Alan Daniel, originally painted for Heritage of Canada, Reader's Digest Association (Canada) Ltd. **140** Peter Johnson/Loyalist Fine Art **141** The Granger Collection, New York **142** Canapress **145** courtesy of the Black Cultural Society of Nova Scotia **147** (top) Glanmore National Historic Site (bottom) G.A. Reid, *Homeseekers, 1910*, Government of Ontario Art Collection, Toronto, Thomas Moore Photography, Toronto **149** The Granger Collection, New York **150** Reg Aitken **152** NAC C121295 source: www.canadianheritage.ca **153** NAC C96361 Reproduced with permission of the C.W. Jefferys Estate Archive, Toronto **157** Loyalist Cultural Centre, Adolphustown **158** NAC C2401 **161** Confederation Life Gallery, courtesy: Rogers Communications Inc. Photography Dick Hemingway **162** MTL 30840 **163** Archives of Ontario F47-11-1-0-231 **164** NAC C73665 **166** (top) Markham Museum and Historic Village (bottom) T.R.C.A. **167** James B. Wandesford *Portrait of Colonel Thomas Talbot* nd.Watercolour on card, 67.3 x 49.5cm. Collection of McIntosh Gallery, The University of Western Ontario. Gift of Judge Talbot MacBeth, 1941 **170** Canadian Illustrated News, Vol. 3, No. 1, 1871, Jan 21, p. 37 National Library of Canada **171** The Granger Collection, New York **174** MTL 18003 **177** NAC C276 **178** NAC C70367 **179** (top) Canadian War Museum AN196 70070-009 (bottom) Royal Ontario Museum ©ROM, Acc.959.270a-c **180** Hulton Getty **182** NAC C10717 **183** The Granger Collection, New York **184** NAC C7763 **185** (top) NAC C9226 (bottom) NAC C3297 **186** courtesy Paul Kelly/The Incorporated Militia of Upper Canada **187** (top) The Granger Collection, New York (bottom) NAC C6243 **189** NAC C7470 **191** (top) courtesy Parks Canada (bottom) NCC/CCN **196** NAC C73435 **198** The Granger Collection, New York **204** Charles T. Webber, *The Underground Railroad*, Cincinnati Art Museum, Subscription Fund Purchase, Acc.1927.26 **205** (top) The Granger Collection, New York (bottom) The North American Black Historical Museum, Inc. **206** Ontario Black History

Society **208** (top) Confederation Life Gallery, courtesy Rogers Communications Inc. Photography by Dick Hemingway (bottom) NAC C5954 **209** NAC C29891 **211** (top) NAC C73702 Reproduced with permission of the C.W. Jefferys Estate Archive, Toronto (bottom) NAC C011805 **212** Canadian Illustrated News, Feb 5, 1870 National Library of Canada **213** (top) NAC C2384 (bottom) MTL JRR Collection 2749 **214** © T.R.C.A **216** © T.R.C.A. **218** ©T.R.C.A. **219** ©T.R.C.A. **220** ©T.R.C.A. **221** NAC C008891 **222** Canapress PA164911 **223** NAC C14363 **226** (top) Reproduced with permission of the C.W. Jefferys Estate Archive, Toronto (bottom) courtesy Her Majesty's Chapel of the Mohawks **227** © T.R.C.A. **228, 229** courtesy of Upper Canada Village, The St. Lawrence Parks Commission **230** © T.R.C.A. **231** © T.R.C.A. **233** NAC C69849 **234** (top) MTL 2488 (bottom) MTL 1434 **235** (top) NAC C1941 (bottom) MTL 16240 **236** (left) The Granger Collection, New York (right) NAC C69350 **237** (left) MTL 16506 (right) NAC C019849 **238** © T.R.C.A. **240** John J. Bigsby, NAC C20885 source: www.canadianheritage.ca **241** NAC C16467 **246, 247** M11588 *The Burning of the Parliament Building in Montreal, Quebec, ca. 1849* Joseph Légaré, oil on wood. McCord Museum of Canadian History, Montreal **249** Jefferys, Charles William, *Rebels of 1837 Drilling in North York 1898*, Art Gallery of Ontario, Toronto: Purchase, 1927, Acc.858 **250** from *The Firebrand* Copyright © 1956 by Clarke, Irwin & Co. Ltd. Reprinted by permission of Irwin Publishing Co. Ltd. **251** (top) NAC C4784 (bottom) MTL 1086 **252** C.W. Jefferys, *The March of the Rebels upon Toronto in December, 1837*, c. 1921 Government of Ontario Art Collection, Toronto. Thomas Moore Photography. Reproduced with permission of the C.W. Jefferys Estate Archive, Toronto **253** MTL **254** Archives of Ontario, Acc.1115-4 source: www.canadianheritage.ca **258** (top) NAC C3305 (bottom) The Law Society of Upper Canada Archives **259** MTL 1248 **260** (top) Rick Radell (bottom) NAC C11095 **261** Culture Division, City of Toronto **262** Culture Division, City of Toronto **264** (top) MTL-Broadside Collection source: www.canadianheritage.ca (bottom left) MTL 1751 (bottom right) NAC C22742 **266** MTL 1749 **267** courtesy of Fort Malden National Historic Site, Parks Canada Agency **269** Ontario Archives, S17839 source: www.canadianheritage.ca **270** (top

left) NAC C1242 (right) ©2000 Dick Hemingway **271** (top) Porcher, Edwin Augustus, *Van Dieman's Land, The Penal Settlement of Port Arthur, 1844* R7515, by permission of the National Library of Australia (bottom) ©2000 Dick Hemingway **276** Bibliothéque nationale du Québec **280** NAC C18294 **281** Archives nationales du Québec/1837/E17,S52,P7 **282** (top) NAC C395 (bottom) NAC C6032 **283** © Canada Post Corporation, 1971. Reproduced with permission **286** Stewart Museum, Montreal **287** (top) NAC C13493 (bottom) NAC 115941 **288** Musée du Château Ramezay **289** NAC C17937 **290** National Library of Canada **291** Russian swing act from the Saltimbanco ® show. © Cirque du Soleil Inc. Photo: Al Seib, Costumes: Dominique Lemieux **294** Ontario Archives, 371 source: www.canadianheritage.ca **295** NAC C5456 **298** (top) Le Musée du Chateau Ramezay (bottom) NAC C21365 **299** Doane, T.C. NAC C88507 **301** Andrew Morris, NAC C21365 source: www.canadianheritage.ca **302** A.J.Russell, NAC C3525 source: www.canadianheritage.ca **305** William Robert Best NAC C5578 **307** Samuel Gurney Cresswell NAC C16105 **308** Raphael, W.: Behind Bonsecours Market, Montreal #6673 National Gallery of Canada, Ottawa.

Index

LEGEND

■ map ● picture ▲ profile ◆ skill